Mar

THE BALKAN CONFERENCES AND THE BALKAN ENTENTE (1930–1935)

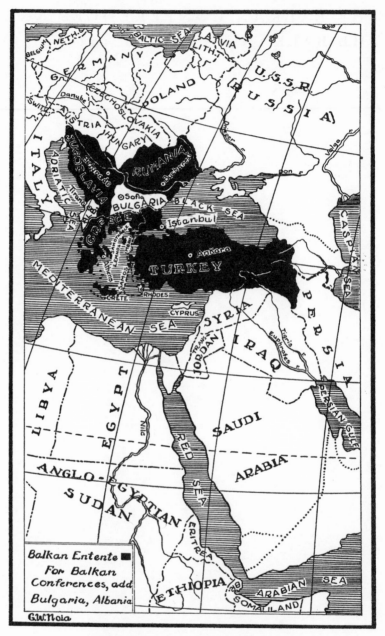

Map 1. The Balkans and the Near East.

The Balkan Conferences and the Balkan Entente

1930-1935

A Study in the Recent History of the Balkan and Near Eastern Peoples

BY

ROBERT JOSEPH KERNER

*Professor of Modern European History
in the University of California*

AND

HARRY NICHOLAS HOWARD

*Assistant Professor of History
in Miami University*

GREENWOOD PRESS, PUBLISHERS
WESTPORT, CONNECTICUT

Originally published in 1936
by University of California Press, Berkeley

First Greenwood Reprinting 1970

Library of Congress Catalogue Card Number 77-110850

SBN 8371-4517-1

Printed in the United States of America

CONTENTS

[v]

PORTRAITS

MAPS

[vii]

PREFACE

IN OFFERING THIS VOLUME, the authors have had in mind the narration of the interesting and hopeful story of the Balkan Conferences in the belief that such an account should not only become a useful and valuable record of history as the future shapes the course of events, but should also help to explain most of the problems which confront statesmen in that part of the world as nothing else can. In this way, much light can be thrown on the existing situation and the road to its betterment.

To achieve this purpose, the authors have had access to the records of the meetings and contacts with the leaders of the undertaking. It has been their objective to follow the ideals and aspirations which guided the forward-looking men and women who participated in the Conferences, to record objectively their successes and their failures, and to fit their endeavors into the course of Balkan and Near Eastern history.

Manifestly, it has not been the task of the authors to treat exhaustively all events in the Balkan and Near Eastern scene or all the moves or countermoves in world politics that have taken place in the period under observation. Such a work is obviously impossible at this time, owing to the inaccessibility of reliable materials. The objective has been much more modest. Only that which directly affected the work of the Balkan Conferences and the particular way in which it fitted into the course of Balkan affairs and European international relations have been brought into the picture.

The men and women who made up the various delegations to the Conferences represented the Balkan countries at their best. Too often have the Balkan peoples been otherwise represented. It is for that reason, if for no other, that a hope has been aroused by their activities—a hope which already is a force to be reckoned with in the public opinion of the Balkans. And once aroused, such a force translates itself ultimately into historic events. In fact, it may be said that it is already beginning to do so.

The writers wish to acknowledge the friendly help and assistance of all who have taken an interest in the production of this volume. M. Alexander Papanastassiou, former Premier and deputy of the Republic of Greece, and other members of the Greek Delegation to the Balkan Conferences, have given invaluable assistance. Appreciation should also be expressed to the other national groups of the Balkan Conferences. In particular, the authors wish to thank M. Hassan Husni Bey, Vice-President of the Grand National Assembly of Turkey and President of the Second Balkan Conference at Istanbul, and M. Rushen Eshref Bey, Secretary of the Turkish Delegation. Dr. Boris Petkov, Secretary of the Bulgarian Delegation to the Balkan Conferences, has facilitated the task in obtaining the necessary Bulgarian data for the study. The Bulgarian, Greek, Jugoslav, Rumanian, and Turkish governments have sent valuable materials bearing on the attitudes of their respective countries. MM. X. Lefcoparidis, editor of *Les Balkans* (Athens), L. Savadjian, director of *La Revue des Balkans* (Paris), and J. Paléologue, editor of *L'Heure Actuelle* (Bucharest), have also very kindly coöperated with the authors. The late Dr. Earle Babcock, *directeur-adjoint* of the Dotation Carnegie at Paris, aided in obtaining certain of the official publications dealing with the Balkan Conferences. Finally, the writers wish to thank Virginia Brubaker Howard for her painstaking work in reading the manuscript throughout the course of its preparation.

R. J. K.
H. N. H.

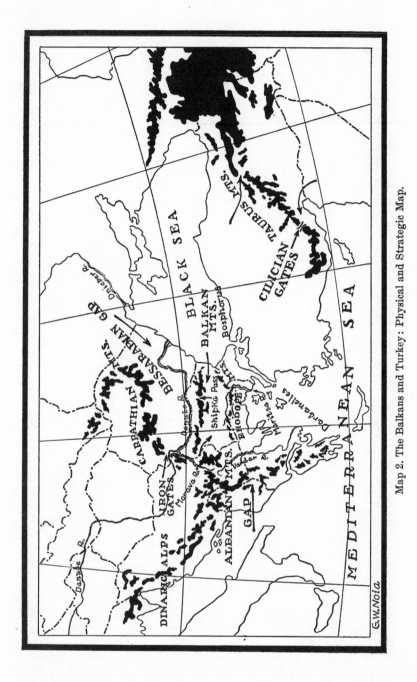

Map 2. The Balkans and Turkey: Physical and Strategic Map.

Chapter I

BEFORE THE BALKAN CONFERENCES:
THE HISTORICAL PERSPECTIVE

THE NEAR EASTERN QUESTION A CHRONIC WORLD PROBLEM

IT HAS OFTEN BEEN SAID that the Near Eastern Question is a chronic world problem. Viewed in this way, it is the oldest, the most continuous, and the most complicated problem known to history. Its origin goes back to the days of ancient Troy or even beyond. It is with us today. Will it be with us tomorrow?

The Near East is the meeting place of three continents, Europe, Asia, and Africa, and three seas, the Mediterranean, the Black, and the Red. It is the crossroads of the most important land, sea, and air highways of the world. In this region, or near it, man first emerged from barbarism into civilization. Later, the Western Mediterranean and Europe, India and far-off China borrowed from the pioneers of the Near East. Here originated three of the five important religions man has evolved to solve the riddle of the universe. Here are to be found the holy places which hundreds of millions of devout believers all over the world hold in reverence. Here, from time immemorial, peoples of widely different civilizations mingled, and trafficked not only in wares and commodities, but, what is more important, in ideas and institutions as well, and then spread them far and wide over land and sea.

Whatever the cause or causes, the Near East did not become the homeland of a single numerous race or nation, even though history records the vast and unwieldy empires of Egyptian, Assyrian, Persian, Greek, Roman, Byzantine, and Turk, each of which had its day of glory and then vanished. On the contrary, this region has been and remains the home of numerous small nations and races or parts of them, not one of which has been able, under the circumstances which it faced, to assimilate the others and establish throughout this area a uniform basis of national, as contrasted with imperial, power.

[1]

With the decline of the last of the great empires—that of the Ottoman Turks—the small nations struggled to be free amidst the desperate rivalry of Great Powers in pursuit of world-wide commercial, political, and strategic interests. There followed, from the middle of the seventeenth century, a long-drawn-out conflict vital to the existence of the small nations that lived in this region and to huge empires from beyond it, not one of which could allow the others the possession of territory or trade route, or fertile field or mine, or of pass or fortress, which played a rôle in the strategy of life in the Near East or the world at large. Thus originated the modern conception of the Near Eastern Question—an intricate and tangled skein of political, racial, strategic, economic, religious, and cultural factors—a chronic world problem.

FUNDAMENTAL FACTORS IN THE NEAR EASTERN QUESTION

Geographical.—There are few, if any, regions on earth where nature and man have become so closely interwoven in such complex disparity as in the Near East. If one views the situation geographically as a whole, one must note that the Near East is essentially a region of passage—a junction of three great continents and three seas—wherein the migration of man in passing from one continent to another or from one sea into another becomes a phenomenon of first-rate importance. It is, therefore, a "position" of movement in which government and institutions must at once be strong and flexible, intelligent and quick. Lacking strength, they invite others from without to interfere. Lacking flexibility, they become unable to adjust themselves to changes in either of the three continents and three seas. Lacking intelligence, for whatever reason it may be, they are unable to keep foreign intervention or invasion from their soil. That the region is very diverse geographically and that this factor sets up centrifugal, instead of centripetal, forces can also be readily seen. Again, this acts against strong centralized political power only too obviously. Such unity as appears is supplied by the famous Straits of the Dardanelles and Bosphorus, which, instead of separating, unite the European and Asiatic portions of the Near East. Around these waters, historically, the power which controlled the Near East was nearly always ultimately stabilized.

North of the Straits, in the European or Balkan part of the region of the Near East, we note, on closer inspection, the rim of the Carpathian Mountains (running east and west) on the north and east and the Dinaric and Albanian Alps (extending north and south) on the west; the Balkan Mountains in the middle spread east and west, creating gateways into the Near East, on the one hand, and into Eastern and Central Europe, on the other. Thus we find the Bessarabian Gap on the east, the Iron Gates on the Danube in the center, and the valley of the Morava and the Vardar to the west. Through these gates there pass highways which converge on Constantinople. When we add the old road—Via Egnatia—from what is now Albania, we can visualize the streams of humanity which poured overland into this region from Europe and from this region into Europe. Balkan Europe, because of its peculiarly arranged mountainous nature, is cut up into valleys; through some of them travel is almost impossible; through others the main highways pass. It will readily be seen that the geography of the region presented obstacles to political unification or racial and cultural amalgamation. Jugoslavia and Rumania now stand guard at the gateways at the north. Albania opens a highway into the heart of the Peninsula. Through Bulgaria to Constantinople run the arteries of commerce and power. Greece is not only exposed to danger by land from the north, but even more so from the sea, as she must seek her food and livelihood chiefly from the sea.

And, if we glance beyond the Straits to the east and south, we see two rather distinctly marked areas: the plateau of Anatolia and the vast desert of Arabia, each inhabited predominantly by a single people, Turk in the one and Arab in the other. Between them the Caucasus Mountains, the Armenian plateau, and the Taurus Mountains yield a key to division and diversity. The Cilician Gates guard Anatolia from the south, and numerous peoples live in the mountainous and diversified belt which divides the Turks and the Arabs—a belt which swings around to the south through Syria, almost touching Egypt. In the course of history, Anatolia and Arabia became the cradles of two of the dominant peoples of the Near East, and the mountainous belt, just described, a *mélange* of many. If we add Egypt, in itself *apart* from and yet *a part* of the Near East, we are able to visualize the fact that, in respect to geography, this is the most diversified region on earth.

Racial.—Great civilizations have been built up not only by contact of cultures, but also by fusion of races and peoples. Of these very fundamental and vital factors we really know very little except that we are still searching in history for the "pure" race and the "pure" civilization. In fact, sound historical analysis appears always to lead us to diversified origins. Viewed from this standpoint, the Near East had a most magnificent opportunity and utilized it in creating and influencing great civilizations.

Without trespassing too much upon differences among anthropologists and ethnologists, we may find at least partial agreement in the position that racially the modern nations that have emerged in the Near East are, in origin, chiefly Armenoid, Alpine, Mediterranean, and Nordic mixtures, with a very slight admixture of the Negro, principally in Egypt, and a much slighter one in Arabia and Asia Minor. It is now believed by many that the population of ancient Egypt was a fusion of basic Mediterranean stock (tinged with the Negro) and of Armenoid and possibly Nordic elements. The ancient Greeks may have been Mediterraneans mixed with Nordics, Armenoids, and possibly Alpines. The Arabs were Semitic, a subwhite race. The Turks were probably a mixed Armenoid type. The Southern Slavs (Serbs, Croats, Macedonians, and original Slavs of Bulgaria) were generally Alpine with local admixtures, Dinaric, Mediterranean, and Bulgar (which was originally probably Central Asian Alpine). The Dinaric probably was a mixture of Armenoid with Alpine and Nordic types from which came the Albanians. The last to emerge, the Rumanians, were probably a mixture of Roman, native Dacian, and Alpine Slav elements.

And today we see among the nations in the Near East, in round numbers,[1*] some ten to eleven million Jugoslavs (six million Serbs, two and one-half to three million Croats), some eight hundred thousand Albanians, about six million Greeks, and some six million Bulgarians in Europe. In Asia there are about twelve to thirteen million Turks and an equal number of Arabs, one and one-half million Kurds, about whom we appear to agree only that they are

* Superior figures refer to notes which will be found at the end of this chapter.

"Indo-European," about one to one and one-half million Greeks, a half-million Jews, and maybe a million or two of other peoples. Egypt adds some fourteen or fifteen millions. Thus counting all together the peoples which inhabit the Near East, we may say that we are dealing with more than eighty-five millions of people.

Are we not justified in concluding that no contemporary nations in the Near East are "pure" racially, but that they are fusions of nearly all the chief early races which lived on the three continents, with the exception of the Mongoloid? So mixed, indeed, do they appear to be that the word "race" may be said to have lost its significance as a factor of homogeneity or of diversity when the racial composition of each contemporary nation is brought into relief against that of its neighbors. Apparently, it is not at bottom *race* which divides the peoples of the Near East. And history has left on the doorstep of the Near East relatively small nations—not one of which by virtue of numbers or other preëminence may claim today the right to rule all or any of the others.

Cultural and religious.—Whatever the source of the earliest urban civilizations of Central Asia, Persia, and Northwestern India, which archaeologists are now exposing to our view as having existed some eight thousand years ago, Egypt and the Mesopotamian valley became the center from which *historical* civilizations originated about six thousand years ago. In other words, the Near East, or regions near it, saw the birth of civilization. From here China, India, Europe, and Africa borrowed their cultural beginnings.

We note also that, in spite of conquests by peoples from outside of the Near East, the original cultural base, Egypt-Mesopotamia, after submergence and absorption of certain accretions from the conquerors, usually emerged triumphant. Persian, Greek, Roman, and European fell seduced before the lure of the Oriental Near East. Egyptian bureaucracy, Persian imperialism, and Near Eastern religious systems, in addition to the many other ingredients of Near Eastern cultures, streamed out to make their triumphs. Breasted most aptly caught this process when, in describing the Later Roman Empire, he wrote that it was in the position in which Egypt was two thousand years before, "where the peasant on the

Nile had been for thousands of years. The Emperor had become a Pharaoh and the Roman Empire a colossal Egypt of ancient days." Soon Rome was abandoned and Byzantium (Constantinople) was made the capital. This was done not only because of the necessities of imperial strategy, but also by reason of cultural attraction.

Although the earliest religions of this region made converts beyond its frontiers, the Hebrew, the Christian, and the Moslem religions made world-wide conquests from their base in the Near East and today count hundreds of millions of believers the world over. Followers of these religions revere the holy places—the physical origins of their faiths—and in turn exert a significant influence in world politics or world economics if they are disturbed in one way or another. The Crusades and the Crimean War found at least partial causes or excuses in religious conflicts, and the recent happenings in the Mandate of Palestine offer further illustrations. Thus we note the ancient Oriental base emerging like a gigantic tree with three great cultural branches, Hebrew, Christian, and Moslem—unity in divergence, divergence in unity.

Many may see in the babel of languages and religions of Near Eastern nations the greatest possible differences. This is certainly true on the surface. On closer examination we may also perceive a basic cultural homogeneity which, with toleration and justice in a new age, may be once more triumphant in the peaceful coexistence of the new nations. The successive empires which ruled the Near East have left to the new nations heirlooms of common institutions, legal, political, social, and economic. For centuries at a time the ancestors of the present inhabitants had a common history, a common mentality, and a community of interests. And in spite of the divisive force of political, linguistic, and economic nationalism, it may be that wise and intelligent statesmanship, while preserving the national institutions intact, will triumph in bringing out the basic forces of an essentially common culture and common traditions of living together.[2] May we not, then, conclude that in this sphere also there is a possibility of a federation of nations? At least, it is more difficult to conclude that there is not such a possibility. These peoples have lived together before—they may find a way to live together again.

Economic.—Two basic economic factors have influenced the Near East in the past. In the first place, there was world trade. For long periods of time, the most important trade routes by land and sea ran through this region. In the second place, there were local resources, rich agricultural products and minerals.

Though favored in its own right, the Near East was richer or poorer according as the world trade routes ran through it at a given period. If they did, the Near East was the crossroads bazaar of the world. It was after the Portuguese, at the end of the fifteenth century, discovered a way around Africa to transport the commodities of India and the Far East cheaper and in larger quantities than could be done by sea and land transit through the Near East, that the Near East suffered an eclipse and was thrown in large part upon its native resources and the lesser trade by land.[3] This eclipse lasted until the digging of the Suez Canal (1869) and the building of the Berlin-Bagdad railway network.

Although the Near East was at times the seat of manufactures, in the true and ancient sense of the word, agriculture and mining were probably its steadiest local sources of wealth. Far back in ancient times the Near East was a center of industry and supplied many parts of the world with its products. With the development of maritime navigation and the coming of the Industrial Revolution, agriculture and mining, always important, became relatively more prominent. Today, we find them supreme in the economic life of the Near East.

Now that the Near East is again the crossroads of world trade, by sea, by land, and by air, a revival has been taking place during the past few decades and both factors indicated above are influencing economic conditions in this region. The nations of the Near East necessarily must give heed to them both. The first factor, world trade, with its attendant danger to the little Near Eastern states, leads to mighty commercial conflicts in which the Great Powers engage along the trade routes, and the second factor, local resources, points to inter-Balkan competition for extra-Balkan markets or to coöperation. In such a situation, manifestly there is need for the unity of action and strength which a federation would bring and which would at the same time leave diversity of economic activity room for play. Alone, the Balkan and Near Eastern states may become the victims of the commercial rivalries of the Great Powers or of cutthroat competition among themselves for other markets. United, they may be able to play their legitimate rôle in the economic life of the world.

Social and political.—Of particular significance is the similar social and political heritage of the Balkan and Near Eastern peoples. About seventy-five to eighty per cent of the Balkan people gain their daily bread through tilling the soil. In this region, for a long period of time, small peasant farms have prevailed. In the old Serbia (and it is in large measure true of the new Jugoslavia) and in Bulgaria there is no landed aristocracy. An essential social democracy on an agricultural and peasant foundation subsists. Social life is similar throughout the peninsula. Folk tales and epics, folk songs and dances, from one end of the Balkans to the other, go back to common origins. One may say that through the entire Balkan region, in Turkey, and even in Egypt and Arabia, there are today significant indications of the rise of the "common man." Moreover, the legal, political, and constitutional institutions of the new states which emerged in the nineteenth century all reflect their Romano-Byzantine, Ottoman, and even French origins. As one writer has said, there is a "community of ideas imposed on the Balkan peoples, at least along general lines, by their common descent, their common history, their common mentality, and finally by the community of their interests."[4]

ITS HISTORICAL EVOLUTION

We of the present day know altogether too little about the cities of Accad (Babylonia), Memphis (Egypt), and Troy of some four or five thousand years ago. The little we are beginning to comprehend is giving us the dim perspective of struggles not unlike those of days with which we are better acquainted. Sargon of Accad extended his empire to the Mediterranean and brought the civilization of the Euphrates there. Egypt spread over Syria, to be checked only by the Hittites at the north, while Troy evidently guarded the entry into the Straits and the Black Sea.[5] It was only when the Persians and the Greeks engaged in conflict, which did not end until Alexander the Great conquered the whole of the Near East, that the Near Eastern Question was exposed as strategically the control of the Straits and the Suez Peninsula by one power. It has remained so from that day to the present time.

Neither the Greek city states, which were unable to federate among themselves, nor the vast Alexandrian Empire, with its feeble decentralization, or its successors were able to solve the riddle of the Near East. The Greeks were too few in numbers physically to amalgamate the diversified peoples of the region, even though for centuries they gave their mentality and their language to the upper classes. Even less might be said of the Romans, who came as conquerors in the second century B. C., though they did learn to value the possession of the Straits and the Suez Peninsula as controls strategic to their domination of the Near East. When, finally, Constantine built his capital on the Straits, he merely recognized the basic factors of power in military and naval strategy, in commerce, in religion, and in the intellect. The Byzantine Empire carried on even after it lost the hinterland of Asia Minor and the Suez Peninsula to the Arabs. But the Arabs, though they built an empire extending through Africa to Spain, were unable to dislodge the Byzantines, in spite of the fact that the latter were simultaneously attacked through the Balkan Peninsula by others. It was not until the Turkish newcomers in Asia Minor became almost as Byzantine as the inhabitants of Constantinople that the great city fell, and, some sixty years later, the Suez Peninsula and Egypt also. As we look back from this point to the days of Accad, Memphis, and Troy, we note that empires succeeded empires, but the Near East remained, as before, the home of many small peoples. Imperial power had not crushed them, nor did it seem to be the instrument to weld them together.

THE RISE AND FALL OF THE LAST OF THE EMPIRES—THE OTTOMAN EMPIRE

Like the Greeks and the Romans, and for a time, the Byzantines, the Ottoman Turks seized and held both the Straits and the Suez Peninsula. They came to dominate the Near Eastern complex at a time, as we have pointed out, when the world trade routes shifted

from the Near East to the open seas around Africa. They brought
to the scene fresh martial vigor and shrewd political and diplomatic ability. They pushed their empire past the gates of the Balkans up to the very walls of Vienna and around the Black Sea. By
the middle of the seventeenth century, however, the Turkish Empire had received several checks from without and was already
showing signs of decay from within. The last half of the seventeenth century saw the beginning of a decline, which in the eighteenth century was accelerated by partitioning at the hands of the
Great Powers, Austria and Russia, and, in the nineteenth, of
England as well. After the Treaty of Kuchuk-Kainardji in 1774,
which celebrated the triumph of Catherine the Great of Russia
and first legally gave Russia full entry, commercial and naval, on
the Black Sea, the Turkish Empire was doomed.

Whatever the specific causes, they may perhaps be generalized
into the statement that, given the circumstances, the Turkish Empire failed because it could not solve the problems which confronted it. It had not made Turks out of its numerous peoples. It
could not, because of its inherent internal weakness in a position
of commanding world importance, prevent the new Great Powers
of Europe from interfering in its internal affairs and, through
their rivalry, from beginning the process of nibbling which was to
end in its total disappearance in 1923. The waning power of the
Turkish Empire led simultaneously to two processes: the emer-
gence of the Near Eastern nations, and the rivalry among Great
Powers for the control of trade routes and territories.

The first of the nations to begin the thorny road to national independence was the Serb. It was followed by the Greek, then the
Rumanian, then the Bulgarian and the Albanian peoples. Next the
Turks, as a nation, themselves caught the spirit, to be followed by
the Arabs and the Egyptians, not to mention others. One by one
the nations of the Near East rose up against the ancient Ottoman
Empire, which, in 1923, at the Conference of Lausanne, was un-
mourned even by the vast majority of the Turks.

Simultaneously encouraging or blocking the process of the national devolution or decentralization of the Ottoman Empire, the
rivalry of the Great Powers continued apace.[6] Not one of them

could permit to another a greater share in the commerce or the territories of the dying empire. In spite of the great burden of ruling the Germanies and Central Europe, the Habsburgs could not permit the Russians to advance into the Balkans and block their way to the Black Sea or the Aegean, or to inspire the Slavs of Austria-Hungary from the Balkans to revolt and dissolve the Dual Monarchy. In spite of the vast, but landlocked, expanse of the Russian Empire, the Russian tsars from Peter the Great to Nicholas II could not permit Austria or England to block their route into the Mediterranean—the route which might develop and did develop into Russia's chief commercial highway. In spite of their far-flung empire, involving serious responsibilities in all seas and on all continents, the English, after the acquisition of India in 1763, and the coming of the Industrial Revolution, could not permit Russia, or any other power, to control the highways that lead to India and Australia; in other words, to control the Straits and the Suez Peninsula. Nor could the French, with the newly added burdens across the western Mediterranean in Africa, permit any one power to dominate the eastern Mediterranean, commercially or strategically. For the Italians, this was a matter of life or death in the sea that once was Roman. And, finally, to the Germans, after William II came to the throne and encouraged the building of the railroads, the Near East was the springboard into world power. The Germans now traded places with the British in "maintaining" the Ottoman Empire, while the British gradually adopted the policy of "decentralizing" it to their obvious advantage.

The result of these policies and these rivalries led to Russia's advance to the Black Sea and the Caucasus Mountains, to England's acquisition of Cyprus, Egypt, and the Suez Peninsula, with the canal, and various holds on the shore line of Arabia and the Persian Gulf, to Austria's advance into Dalmatia and Bosnia-Herzegovina, to France's claims on Syria, to Italy's seizure of Tripoli and the Dodecanese, and to Germany's hopes of dominating the entire Ottoman Empire or at least of obtaining possession of the territories drained by the Berlin-Bagdad route. Just before the World War, and increasingly in the course of it, the Great

Powers converged upon the last and greatest prize, the Straits. The opening gun in that conflict was the sending of the Liman von Sanders Mission to Turkey by Germany in 1913,[7] and the last was the Peace of Lausanne (1923), whereby, though England did not get all that she desired, matters were so arranged that the strongest naval power might, in an emergency, control the Straits. Has history once more verified the ancient truth that he who controls one of these points must control the other or lose out in the end? The Mandate of Palestine, as well as the conditions laid down by England to Egypt, together with the retention of Cyprus, and the balance held between France and Italy in the Mediterranean and the Red Sea, define the axis of British policy on the south. The relations with Iraq and Persia, as well as the new status of the Straits, define the axis of British policy on the north. Both indicate that to the British the Near Eastern Question is not a riddle. The Straits and the Suez Peninsula still yield the keys to it.

It may, then, be concluded that the historical evolution of the Near Eastern Question has resulted in the disappearance of the Ottoman Empire and in the independence of most of the Near Eastern peoples. It has perpetuated in the southern portion, in Arabia and Egypt, the control of the British, and in Syria that of the French; and in the northern part, the domination of Italy in Albania. If the remaining nations develop in the pattern shown by the forces at work in the past, the future is likely to see all of them take the course already marked out by the Balkan nations and by the Republic of Turkey.

THE FAILURE OF IMPERIALISM TO SOLVE THE QUESTION

It is not difficult to conclude that imperialism, as it has been practiced by the nations within the Near East, has failed to solve the Near Eastern Question. Not one of them has had the resources or the vitality for that or is likely to have in the future. Control of a similar kind from outside the region, though it may supply for a time the needed qualifications, is likely to be both precarious and ephemeral, dependent not only on what happens within this area, but also on what might happen elsewhere. No nation in the Near East is willing to submit to the overlordship of a neighbor, and the region as a whole is becoming less and less patient with interference from the Great Powers. It is from a realization of these facts that the cries of "The Balkans for the Balkan peoples" and "The Near East for the Near Eastern peoples" are not mere slogans, but are beginning to represent the force of matured public opinion. In fact, these ideas are already taking shape in the form of action. How may they be translated into realities, into actualities in which the nations in free union not only guard their individualities but also preserve the legitimate rights of World Powers free from abuse by any one or a group of them and exercised for the benefit of all? For, apparently, we are dealing here with a twofold problem, the preservation of the nations and the interests of the Great Powers in what is, strategically, the most important region of the world. If, indeed, there is to be a solution, it must satisfy this twofold aspect of the problem.

THE CONFEDERATIVE IDEA

That it is easy to jump to the conclusion that the confederation of these nations would solve the problem is only too evident. It is, in fact, easier to imagine it than to see how it can be realized. It is not difficult to point out that these nations cannot stand alone or that they will not willingly submit to one another. But can they come together in peace, iron out their difficulties, keep others from interfering, and create a workable framework—some sort of federal relationship—that will give them what they have lacked for so many centuries, even though the fundamental factors point to decided possibilities in this direction?

Whatever may be the future evolution of the set of factors here analyzed, it may be said that in history, at least, the confederative idea has never had a test in this region on any scale worthy of the name for a time long enough to be of significance.

In ancient and medieval times there was no conception of nationality comparable to that in modern times. Greece, indeed, has been called the "classic land of federations." Of these, the religious federations, built around some temple, appeared to be the chief instruments of implanting the idea. Political federations played a minor rôle in an age dominated by municipal imperialism. The Greeks might unite before some danger from without or within, but they would separate soon after the danger had passed. This and the spirit of municipal imperialism are well illustrated in the history of Athens and the Confederacy of Delos. The disunited and weakened cities of Greece fell before Philip and Alexander of Macedonia. Even though the domination of Macedonia had taught them the value of union, they formed *two* leagues, the Achaean and Aetolian, rivals politically and economically, an act which led them into the hands of the Romans.[8]

The Byzantine Empire did not develop the idea of confederation, even though it became feudal in form. It stressed Roman centralization, though it often lacked the power to impose it. Among the Slavs in the Balkans, however, the federal idea may be seen in the empire of Siméon of Bulgaria (893–927) and that of Stephen Dushan Nemanja (1334–55). We note here a certain provincial federalism which appeared to preserve national or tribal and municipal and religious entities with general assemblies under the tsars. Too much, however, may be made of this, especially if it is sought to use this as a model for the present day under the guise of seeking to preserve entities which, so far as modern nationalism is concerned, have lost all or most of their significance in the stern rivalry of larger units.[9]

The modern period in the Near East saw the establishment of the Ottoman Empire. The fall of Constantinople was the occasion for frantic appeals by popes and patriarchs for crusades against the infidel Turks in order to rescue the Christian populations and the Church of St. Sophia. And in the period from the fall of Constantinople in 1453 to the end of the seventeenth century, pope and patriarch and emperor besought Russia to "take up the cross"— in fact, outlined in great detail "Russia's historic mission."[10] But Russia in those days had need of Turkey's friendship, surrounded as she was by Poles, Lithuanians, Swedes, and Tatars; and when, at last, under Peter the Great, she was ready to advance "the historic mission" which others had so aptly pointed out as her duty to civilization, they were no longer interested; in fact, from that time they feared her. By that time, also, Russia had shown to the Near Eastern nations, by her treatment of the Ukraine, that imperialism, not federation, would be her policy. Jurii Krizhanich, the South Slav, had urged reform in Russia and a federal outlook beyond her frontiers. The Slavic and Orthodox nations looked to Russia for delivery, but not without fear; for, since the trampling upon Ukrainian liberties in the middle of the seventeenth century, there were Russophobes as well as Russophils in the Near East.[11] Later, in the eighteenth, nineteenth, and twentieth centuries, when the idea of Pan-Slavism was developed further, it was always seen that the Pan-Slavism of Austrian and Balkan Slavs was essentially federal, while that of the Russian Slavs was tinged at least with imperialism of one sort or another; since, after all, Russia as a state, pursued, in the haze of Pan-Slavism, as Germany and Austria in Pan-Germanism, a realistic policy of definite aims. For the state of Russia, the control or possession of the Straits was a goal to be attained with or even against Pan-Slavism.

When, at the time of the French Revolution and in the years following, the various Balkan nations began to awaken from their lethargy, it was through the spirit of modern nationalism. Each patriot called for the liberation of his nation—in a vaguer and more mystical fashion the other nations were also called upon to liberate themselves—and, now and then, a federation was suggested, even though the awakening nations did not hesitate to look longingly on lands properly belonging to less awakened peoples. It is in this light that we may envision the activities of the Greek, Rigas de Féréo; the Serbs, Obradovich and Karadzhich; and the Croat, Gaj, to mention only a few in the first wave of modern nationalism to reach the Balkans. Other waves followed until they engulfed all Asia Minor and Egypt, as can be seen from the present unrest in those regions.

Napoleon's creation of the Illyrian Provinces in 1809, like the exploits and negotiations of Peter the Great and his agents a century before, sent a thrill through the peninsula. Dreams and plans, native and foreign, succeeded one another.[12] For a time it was thought that the Illyrian Provinces and the Illyrian movement (chiefly Croatian) would become the center of an advance toward confederation. But Karageorge of Serbia (with a Greater Serbia plan) and Napoleon could not agree.[13] In 1844, Ilija Garashanin, at first Minister of Interior and later Minister of Foreign Affairs of Serbia, conceived a plan, since called his *Nachertanija,* which demanded a policy of Serbian activity free from both Austria and Russia, in expectation of the dissolution of the Ottoman Empire, and calculated to draw not only Croats and Serbs together under a newly reconstructed Serbia, but the Bulgarians as well. In 1853, Garashanin was forced out of office by Russia. In 1860, under Michael Obrenovich, Garashanin was entrusted with the mission of accomplishing his projected federation. There followed in 1867–68 a series of treaties and agreements: between Serbia and Montenegro, Serbia and Greece, and Serbia and Rumania, as well as an agreement with the delegates of the Bulgarian people, known as the "Programme of Political Relations of the Serbo-Bulgars or Bulgar-Serbs or their Entente Cordiale," whereby a reconstructed Serbo-Bulgarian state was envisaged under the title of the Jugoslav Empire. From this, a Jugoslav Empire in alliance with Greece and Rumania was to emerge, but not yet a confederation, for it appears that Prince Michael thought that both the Kossuth plan for a Danubian Federation headed by Hungary, Rumania, and Serbia, as well as Garashanin's Balkan Federation headed by Rumania and Serbia, were as yet unrealizable. In the summer of 1867, he had a conference with Count Andrássy, Minister of Foreign Affairs of Austria-Hungary, which country now adopted an aggressive policy in the Balkans. A few months later, he dismissed Garashanin from his post and let it be known that Serbia would not follow her recent policy. Although, in the next year, he appeared once more to return to the previous plans, his assassination followed on June 10, 1868. The hesitation of Prince Michael and his probable adhesion to Austrian schemes in regard to Bosnia-Herzegovina was a death-blow to the reshaping of the Balkans under the Balkan peoples.[14] Russia, soon thereafter, pressed forward to create a new Slavic state in the Balkans, a Greater Bulgaria, the first concrete step being to secure the Exarchate for the Bulgarians in 1870. Plans and dreams rapidly receded into the background in the events which culminated in the Russo-Turkish War of 1877–78 and the Congress of Berlin. The reshaping of the Balkans by the Balkan peoples themselves gave place to the rivalry of Great

Powers, each of which used the Balkan states like pawns on the chessboard.

From that time until 1911, few, if any, practical steps were taken toward the realization of a federation. Plans there were legion, some honestly meant, others barely concealing the national interests of the various powers. The Russians, Komarovskii and Danilevskii; the Italian, Garibaldi, and the Croat, Pavichich; the League of International Peace and Liberty; the Frenchmen, Robert and Blanqui; and the Balkan publicists, Dobrovsky, Karavelov, Markovich, Botev, Rakovsky, Levsky, Rattos, and Jonescu; as well as the League for the Balkan Confederation and the Balkan Committee of London (with James Bryce, Noel Buxton, and other Englishmen as members)—all these evolved and advocated plans of confederation of one kind or another.[15] The Macedonian Revolutionary Organization, founded in 1893, had its plan, to which it has clung tenaciously through thick and thin to the present. It was the internal weakness shown by Turkey in the Turco-Italian War (1911–12) which ended the period of plans and led to action. The Young Turks had failed, in large part as a result of German advice, to solve the problems which confronted Turkey, and their connivance with or relations to the Armenian massacres and the Albanian raids discredited them and made coöperation possible among the Balkan states.

The series of alliances, political and military, which were signed among the Balkan states and which constituted the Balkan League, were meant to end Turkish rule in Europe. When the Serbo-Bulgarian Alliance of February 29–March 13, 1912, was signed through Russia's mediation, Russia hoped that the Balkan alliances would serve as a bulwark against the Austrian advance into the Balkans, as indicated by the annexation of Bosnia-Herzegovina in 1908, until Russia had recovered completely from the revolution and was prepared to take up an active policy. The successful First Balkan War and the disastrous disagreement over Macedonia which brought on the Second Balkan War, led not only to the Peace of Bucharest,[16] but also to Bulgaria's entry into the World War in 1915 on the side of the Central Powers and to the Treaty of Neuilly in 1920 and that of Lausanne in 1923.

Bulgaria has smarted under the loss of the Dobrudja, of Macedonia, and of territorial access to the Aegean Sea. Many Bulgarians, and especially Macedonians, have not ceased to complain against the nonfulfillment of the minority clauses of the various treaties and to insist that no peace, not to speak of a confederation, is possible until Bulgaria is given justice and satisfaction on these points.

The relations of Italy and Albania, especially since the advent of Mussolini to power, have further complicated an already chaotic situation. Italy had been freed by the World War of the fear of a Great Power resting heavily on the Alps and the Adriatic. To the Italians came a new vision of opportunity for predominance in the valley of the Danube, in the Balkan Peninsula, and in the Near East as a whole. Dissatisfied with their treatment at the Peace Conference and solicitous for the protection of routes bringing food and natural resources from Russia and the Black Sea, the Italians, in the face of French predominance in the western Mediterranean, are determined to play a decisive rôle in the destinies of the entire Near East and beyond.

We may now leave it to the Balkan peoples to tell their own story of hope for the dawn of a better day—a day when they will settle their own troubles in peace, free from the interference of others.

NOTES TO CHAPTER I

[1] These rough estimates do not include the minorities in Jugoslavia, Rumania, and Turkey.

[2] Nicolae Iorga, *Le caractère commun des institutions dans le sud-est de l'Europe* (Paris, 1929).

[3] A. H. Lybyer, "The Ottoman Turks and the Routes of Oriental Trade," *English Historical Review*, CXX (October, 1915), 577–88.

[4] C. Evelpidi, *Les États balkaniques: Étude comparée politique, sociale, économique et financière* (Paris, 1930), 291.

[5] Walter Leaf, *Troy: A Study in Homeric Geography* (London, 1912) and "The Dardanelles," *Quarterly Review*, CCXXIV, No. 444 (July, 1915), 108–23; and Félix Sartiaux, *Troie: La guerre de Troie et les origines préhistoriques de la question d'Orient* (Paris, 1915).

[6] As an illustration see Vernon J. Puryear, *England, Russia and the Straits Question, 1844–56* (Berkeley, University of California Press, 1931); *idem, International Economics and Diplomacy in the Near East, 1834–1853* (Stanford University Press, 1935); and Konstantin D. Kozhukarov, *Istochniiat V"pros i B"lgariia*, 1875–90 (Sofia, 1929), 1–254.

[7] Robert J. Kerner, "The Mission of Liman von Sanders," *Slavonic Review*, VI, Nos. 16–18 (June, December, 1927; March, 1928), 12–27, 344–63, 543–60; VII, No. 19 (June, 1928), 90–112, and "Russia, the Straits and Constantinople," *Journal of Modern History*, I, No. 3 (September, 1929), 400–15; Carl Mühlmann, *Deutschland und die Türkei, 1913–14* (Berlin, 1929); and Harry N. Howard, *The Partition of Turkey: A Diplomatic History, 1913–23* (Norman, University of Oklahoma Press, 1931), 39 ff.

[8] Louis LeFur and Paul Posener, *Bundesstaat und Staatenbund* (Breslau, 1902), 15–33, and Marcel Dubois, *Les ligues achéenne et étolienne* (Paris, 1885), 22–46, 113–212, 213–16.

[9] Constantin H. Rindov, *Les états-unis des Balkans* (Paris, 1930), 160 ff.

[10] See especially Sergius Zhigarev, *Russkaia Politika v Vostochnom Voprosie* (Moscow, 1896), 2 vols.; N. S. Derzhavin, "Russkii absoliutizm i iuzhnoe slavianstvo," *Izvestiia Leningradskogo Gosudarstvennogo Universiteta* (Leningrad, 1928), 43–82; and *Proslava na osvoboditelnata voĭna, 1877–78 g., Rusko-B"lgarski Sbornik* (Sofia, 1929), 1–94, 144–55.

[11] Mikhail Hrushevskii, "Sjednocení východního Slovanstva a expansivní plany na Balkaně v letech 1654–55," *Sborník věnovaný Jaroslavu Bidlovi* (Prague, 1928), 340–45.

[12] Here we can note only a few of them, for their listing alone would take up several pages. For the Illyrian project in general see Melitta Pivec-Stelè, *La vie économique des provinces illyriennes, 1809–1813* (Paris, 1930), and F. Zwitter, "Illyrisme et sentiment yougoslave," *Le Monde Slave* (April, May, June, 1933), 39–71, 124–26, 161–85, 232–45.

¹³ Robert J. Kerner, "The Jugoslav Movement," in *The Russian Revolution. The Jugoslav Movement* (Cambridge, 1918), 81 ff.; Rindov, 164.

¹⁴ V. Vrzalová, "Jihoslovanský státní a národní program Iliji Garašanina," *Slovanský Přehled* (Prague, 1932), XXIV, No. 3, pp. 134–43; George Y. Devas (pseud.), *La nouvelle Serbie* (Paris, 1918), 152–57, 174, 203–11; Rindov, 167–72. See also David Mitrany, "The Possibility of a Balkan Locarno," *International Conciliation*, No. 229 (April, 1927).

¹⁵ Sister St. Francis Sheerin, *Plans Proposed for a Solution of the Question of the Straits, 1833–1924* (University of California, M.A. dissertation, 1931. Unpublished), 239 pp.; Rindov, 175–84.

¹⁶ Howard, 31 ff.

Chapter II

THE FOUNDATIONS OF
BALKAN UNITY

THE FIRST BALKAN CONFERENCE (ATHENS, 1930)

THE DANGER OF THE RETURN of the Habsburgs brought to a head a series of developments which led to the making of the Little Entente between Jugoslavia, Rumania, and Czechoslovakia in 1920–21. Greece was included in the early proposals for the creation of this Entente. Even Bulgaria, though embittered by the Treaty of Neuilly and isolated among her former enemies, not only joined the League of Nations, but also advanced the idea of collaboration with the Little Entente.[1*] The government of Stambuliski in Bulgaria was especially determined on collaboration with Jugoslavia. The Greeks and Turks, after their disastrous war of a decade, signed the Treaty of Lausanne in 1923, and these two ancient enemies henceforth entered into peaceful and even friendly relations.

THE BASES OF THE MOVEMENT

The fact that an all-Balkan confederation, or even a regional understanding of any sort, was neither approached nor worked out as a matter of practical politics, did not retard the sentiment for union among the Balkan nations. The conclusion of the Locarno agreements in Western Europe in 1925–26 gave impetus to the movement for a Balkan Locarno of similar import; and the Briand proposals for a United States of Europe (1929–30) made a favorable impression in the Balkans.[2] The conclusion of several bilateral Balkan agreements was an important factor for promoting stability in the region. As members of the Little Entente, Rumania and Jugoslavia signed a general act of conciliation, arbitration, and judicial settlement in 1929; Rumania and Greece negotiated a treaty of nonaggression and arbitration in the spring of

---

* Superior figures refer to notes which will be found at the end of this chapter.

1928; and Rumania and Bulgaria reached a property settlement in January, 1930. Greece and Jugoslavia disposed of their outstanding difficulties with reference to Salonica in March, 1929. Friendship between Greece and Turkey had gone so far by October, 1930, that a treaty of neutrality, conciliation, arbitration, and friendship was concluded. By September, 1933, these two countries were not only guaranteeing their common frontiers, but also providing for common representation at certain international conferences. Jugoslavia and Turkey signed a treaty of friendship as early as 1925, renewed it in 1933, and at the same time signed a commercial convention. Turkey and Bulgaria were bound in a treaty of neutrality, arbitration, and conciliation signed in 1929 and renewed in the fall of 1933. There was, however, no fundamental political agreement between Jugoslavia and Bulgaria, a fact of great importance in any consideration of the problem of Balkan confederation. In the spring of 1934, however, a *détente* appeared to be developing between these two South Slavic states, and commercial and veterinary conventions were finally signed.

As part of this network of treaties, the series of commercial agreements among the Balkan nations should not be neglected, for economic factors are important bases of political relations. In recent years the following commercial treaties have been concluded :[3]

(1) Albania with Bulgaria (1926); Greece (1926); Jugoslavia (1926, 1934).

(2) Bulgaria with Albania (1926); Greece (1927); Turkey (1930); Jugoslavia (1934).

(3) Greece with Albania (1926); Bulgaria (1927); Turkey (1930); Jugoslavia (1927); Turkey (1934).

(4) Turkey with Bulgaria (1930); Greece (1930); Rumania (1930); Jugoslavia (1933); Greece (1934).

(5) Rumania with Turkey (1930); Jugoslavia (1930).

(6) Jugoslavia with Albania (1926, 1934); Greece (1927); Rumania (1930); Turkey (1933); Bulgaria (1934).

The *desideratum* of the Balkan federation is not only to complete the edifice of these treaties, but also to build a multilateral commercial treaty structure.

Apparently, as we have seen, there were insuperable difficulties in the way of the creation of a United States of Europe, but a

Balkan federation appeared to be among the more practical possibilities. The Balkan region constitutes a rather distinct geographical entity in the southeastern corner of Europe and extends into Asia (including Turkey's Asiatic territory). Its area is more than 600,000 square miles, one and one-half times that of France and twice that of Great Britain. Its population of some 60,000,000 exceeds that of France, Italy, or Great Britain. Politically, a federation in the Balkans would be equivalent to a Great Power, and economically such a union would offer large possibilities for Balkan commerce, agriculture, and industry.

The Balkan Peninsula is primarily agricultural, about seventy-five per cent of the entire population being engaged in farming. Nearly one-half the revenue of the states comes from the products of the soil. Three-fourths of the exports are farm products, and manufactured articles constitute almost sixty per cent of the imports. Inter-Balkan commerce forms only a very small part of the total foreign trade of the nations: Greece, 24 per cent; Bulgaria, 12 per cent; Albania, 11 per cent; Jugoslavia, 8 per cent; Rumania, 5 per cent; and Turkey, 5 per cent. A clearer picture of inter-Balkan trade is illustrated by table 1⁴ (p. 24).

An examination of Balkan trade with Central and Western Europe is necessary to a consideration of the problem. Trade with Central Europe represents 67 per cent of the total foreign commerce of Rumania, 56 per cent for Jugoslavia, 45.6 per cent for Bulgaria, 19 per cent for Greece, and 6.7 per cent for Albania. Trade with Western Europe represents 65.7 per cent of the total for Albania (62 per cent with Italy), 37.5 per cent for Greece, 30 per cent for Bulgaria, 26.8 per cent for Jugoslavia, and 25.5 per cent for Rumania. About 30 per cent of Turkish commerce is with Central Europe and about 50 per cent with Western Europe.

That most of the Balkan trade is extra-Balkan is because the Balkan countries are predominantly agricultural, and because customs, railway, and banking facilities are lacking for intra-Balkan commerce. Nevertheless, there are rather large possibilities of increasing this trade, even though limitations are imposed by the general similarities of the products of the region. Greece and Turkey both buy wheat, and both could sell olives, olive oil, raisins, cotton, and various derivatives to other Balkan nations. Rumania, Bulgaria, and Jugoslavia might reach an understanding for the sale of their cereals within the peninsula and abroad; and Turkey, Greece, and Bulgaria might take similar action concerning tobacco, raisins, and olive oil. Rumania, ranking sixth in the world produc-

TABLE 1

INTER-BALKAN TRADE

Yearly averages (1930–1931–1932) in percentages of monetary value

		Albania	Bulgaria	Greece	Jugo-slavia	Ru-mania	Turkey	General Balkan
Albania:	Export.......			13.81	2.24		0.03	19.20
	Import.......		1.52	3.34	8.70	1.66	0.30	15.54
Bulgaria:	Export.......	0.01		2.16	0.28	0.27	1.35	4.09
	Import.......			.96	.68	5.35	2.05	9.71
Greece:	Export.......	0.26	0.40		0.70	1.19	0.22	2.79
	Import.......	.27	.69		5.08	6.10	4.06	16.41
Jugoslavia:	Export.......	0.41	0.18	5.26		1.20	0.14	7.14
	Import.......	.03	.13	.83		2.61	.19	3.79
Rumania:	Export.......	0.01	1.02	3.26	1.76		0.52	8.43
	Import.......	.01	.12	1.01	.37		.89	2.33
Turkey:	Export.......	0.02	0.63	6.80	0.13	0.82		8.41
	Import.......		.57	.28	.21	1.29		2.33

tion of oil, needs an expanding market, even in the Balkans. Acting together in a preferential régime, a confederation might attain a better place on the world market, as well as a better development of the Balkan market.[5]

It must be noted, however, that influence is exerted by the Great Powers through the financial control which they have had on the economic development of the Balkan nations. Foreign capitalists control 28 per cent of the capital of banking establishments in Greece, 33 per cent in Jugoslavia, 34 per cent in Bulgaria, 45 per

cent in Rumania, and almost 100 per cent in Albania. Most of the
capital is in French, English, and Italian hands today.[6]

THE TWENTY-SEVENTH UNIVERSAL CONGRESS OF PEACE[7]

The spadework in preparation for the actual calling of the Balkan
Conferences, which were the first semiofficial approach toward a
possible Balkan federation, was performed at the Twenty-seventh
Universal Congress of Peace, held at Athens, October 6–10, 1929.
The third commission of the Congress, given over to the problem
of the federation of peoples, studied the special subject of Balkan
union. M. Papanastassiou, a former president of the Council of
Ministers of Greece, presided over the deliberations of this commission. He pointed out the difficulties in the formation of either
a world federation or even a United States of Europe. These difficulties involved the weaknesses of the League of Nations because
of the position of the United States and the Soviet Union, the lack
of security, and the failure to achieve a substantial degree of disarmament. But, he stated,[8]

> There would still be occasion to pursue its [the confederation's] realization
> in a yet more limited region: among the peoples of the Balkans, including ...
> Turkey. The destinies of these peoples and their vicissitudes have been similar
> or common; they have lived for centuries within the framework of the same
> political organization; they have similar habits and ideas and sufficiently com-
> mon interests; in a word, they present numerous common elements which
> facilitate their union.

This position met with general and enthusiastic agreement. On
October 9, M. Papanastassiou presented a resolution to the plenary
session, which was, he said, "not simply a declaration," but "a ges-
ture, a beginning of action." It stipulated the necessity for annual
Balkan conferences, which would study all questions of common
interest to the Balkan peoples, and asked the International Bureau
of Peace to take the initiative in calling the first meeting. It also
urged the League of Nations to create an Institute of Balkan Cooperation.[9] The Congress adopted the resolution by acclamation.
The Balkan representatives, including M. Kirov, the Bulgarian
delegate, received it with favor. The question of minorities, in
which Bulgaria was particularly interested, was considered two

days later. In a motion adopted on October 11, M. Léon Maccas, the *rapporteur*, expressed the general principle that all powers possessing minorities should sign minorities treaties under the aegis of the League of Nations, that existing treaties on minorities should be observed, and that both majority and minority populations should be brought into closer and more friendly relations "within the framework of existing treaties."

In accordance with the instructions of the Universal Congress of Peace, the International Bureau of Peace sent to the six Balkan foreign ministers on May 12, 1930, a circular invitation to attend a Balkan Conference at Athens in October. The invitation pointed out that "the Balkans will cease to be the neuralgic point of Europe only when, having understood that their interests will never be better protected than by themselves, they look only to themselves for remedies to the maladies from which they have suffered in the past."[10] The Greek Parliament offered its chambers for the use of the meeting. By the end of June all the Balkan states had signified their approval of the aims of the conference and their willingness to send delegates.[11]

A set of provisional regulations for the First Conference was drawn up. The purpose of the organization was "to contribute to the *rapprochement* of the Balkan peoples ... and ... to create a union of the Balkan states." The first meeting would deal only with the general principles on which the future union was to be constructed. The delegates were to come from every walk of life, and the Conference was to be organized conveniently into a Council and an Assembly, with commissions for the study of specific problems.[12]

In the months preceding the Conference, preparations were made for meeting the complicated issues, and the foundations for the structure were sketched. The delegations prepared a series of memoranda which may be taken as indicative of the developing ideas concerning the nature of the union to be achieved.

The Hellenic group was particularly active in promoting the ideal of confederation. M. Papanastassiou proposed that[13]

the union must have the character of a grouping of independent nationalities, bearing no reflection on the sovereignty of the participating states, having no tendency to stifle the existing ethnic entities, but only consolidating peace among them, and by a free and more direct relationship, a closer *entente*, a more systematic collaboration, multiplying their common elements of civilization and harmonizing their forces for the good of all without discrimination; moreover, it must be within the framework and spirit of the League of Nations.

M. Maccas thought that the future union should endorse conciliatory procedure, periodical meetings of the six foreign ministers, and a Balkan treaty for the outlawry of war. Professor Jean Spiropoulos, of the University of Salonica, also emphasized the conclusion of a Balkan pact based on the outlawry of war, pacific settlement, and mutual assistance modeled on the agreements provided by the League of Nations.[14]

The Greek memoranda did not neglect the important social, economic, and intellectual aspects of Balkan coöperation. They emphasized the impossibility of a Balkan union "if the most complete freedom were not assured to citizens of all the countries to travel without formalities and restrictions in all these countries and to pursue their trade, business, industry, profession or calling in each country of the union." There was outlined a definite plan for economic collaboration among the Balkan nations, to be realized in a common commercial policy, in export and import quotas, and in the formation of Balkan cartels and coöperative organizations. The further development of communications and organization of credit facilities would be necessary. All these ideas were to be embodied in a "pact of economic solidarity or partial customs union." In accord with this proposal was one for the foundation of a Balkan economic institute. Monetary union was advocated.[15] Another set of memoranda dealt with the complicated problems of railway, highway, water, air, postal, telephone, and telegraph communications.[16]

The questions of cultural relations and the rôle of women were also considered. A study of the schools and national instruction stressed the responsibility of the schools in the teaching of nationalism and insisted on an education in which "universal humanism" would be the guiding ideal. History should be broadly cultural, not narrowly political, in its approach. Opportunities for study and travel for both students and teachers were urged. Through education a new spirit would have to be created before confederation would be possible. One memorandum suggested the organization of a Balkan Week for the promotion of contacts and stressed the significance of the unification of Balkan law concerning women and children. A general plea was made for the unification of social legislation, dealing with hours of labor, workmen's compensation, social insurance, and freedom of association.[17]

The Jugoslav contribution to the preparation of the Balkan Conferences was much more limited. It emphasized the economic aspects of the problem. Not one of the official memoranda touched the political issue, perhaps for the reason that the Jugoslavs believed that the economic question was the most important, but also because the delegation did not desire to see such troublesome controversies as that of the minorities raised. Professor Th. Georgevich, of the University of Belgrade, postulated his conception of the union on the creation of a Balkan customs association, and believed that the establishment of such economic institutions as a Balkan bank would facilitate agricultural recovery in the peninsula. He foresaw "a brilliant future" if the union were realized in the form of a customs régime, but he asked only "an economic and cultural understanding," not a political confederation.[18] A customs union would be especially useful for protecting agriculture and developing Balkan industry—only by uniting their resources could the small states of Eastern Europe hope for economic safety and prosperity. It was suggested that Balkan commerce could be increased only in the single domain of agricultural products and those of agricultural industry, a logical deduction from the general character of Balkan economy. Two final studies dealing with economic issues treated of the creation of a Balkan Chamber of Commerce to facilitate trade relations, the internal reorganization of agriculture, and concerted action on the world markets. The creation of coöperative organizations bound together in a Balkan coöperative society was urged.[19]

Other Jugoslav memoranda approached the problem with a view to cultural ends. They recognized the fundamental common elements in the development of Balkan civilization. The promotion of coöperation among the Balkan peoples through education, particularly through a broader interpretation of history, was especially advocated.[20]

The Rumanian group presented but one memorandum, that of Professor G. Cantacuzène, of the University of Bucharest. He proposed the establishment of an Institute of Balkan Coöperation which should be made up of a political, a university, a press, and even a religious section. It would become "a center of the social and intellectual life of the Balkans, a high cultural academy which would disseminate common political and social ideas in all the Balkan states." In the Balkans as elsewhere, "civic and intellectual disarmament must precede political disarmament."[21]

Though the Bulgarian delegation submitted no official statements to the Conference, D. Mishev and Boris P. Petkov, both well-known scholars and later members of the Balkan Conferences, did present, in a brief study, the Bulgarian ideas on the subject of union.[22] They believed that the federation "must become the sole means of guaranteeing peace among the small states," but insisted that the idea must be based on confidence, equity, and mutual respect, "as well as on the profound consciousness of common cultural and economic interests." They emphasized the making of the *entente* "on the basis of absolute respect for and within the framework of existing treaties," including the "faithful application of the minority clauses of the treaties." The Bulgarian authors concluded :

The application of and complete and integral respect for the stipulations regarding the protection of the Bulgarian minorities in the Dobrudja, in the western confines of Thrace, on the Aegean coast and in Macedonia, conforming to the norms of the minority treaties ... , is the condition *sine qua non* for any coöperation, *rapprochement, détente,* and *entente* among the Balkan peoples. Only on this legal and moral basis can we envisage the great and salutary idea of Balkan confederation.

It was felt that the process of fusion would in any event be a long one. First would come preliminary technical and economic agreements, then the formation of a customs agreement, and finally "the federation of the Balkan states."

Such were the bases and the fundamental conceptions of the possibilities of a Balkan confederation when the first Conference met in Athens in the fall of 1930.

On October 5, 1930, the First Balkan Conference assembled in Athens. It was a semiofficial, private gathering of about one hundred and fifty delegates, experts, and observers from the six Balkan states.[24] A new Balkan flag of six golden stars and six stripes of white, blue, green, yellow, red, and white symbolized the hoped-for union, and a military band played a "Balkan Hymn of Peace" composed for this auspicious and triumphant occasion. Balkan Olympic games brought the youth of the peninsula together in peaceful and friendly athletic contests. It seemed that a new epoch in Balkan history was about to begin.

A week before the meeting, the Bulgarian delegation created a sensation by its refusal to attend the sessions because the problem of minorities was not on the agenda. In spite of the explanation that the Conference was to deal only with the general principles of organization, the Bulgarian group, acting on the advice of Premier Liapchev, insisted on expressing its views. The day before the formal opening of the Conference, M. Papanastassiou, the president of the Council, was forced to say that, though the question of minorities might be discussed "in principle," the Conference "must be prudent and await the creation of a friendly spirit" before entering upon such dangerous ground.[25] Neither the Bulgarian nor the Albanian delegation was entirely satisfied with this position; both felt that the issue should be discussed. Finally, the Bulgarians were somewhat mollified by M. Papanastassiou's stand, and became part of the Conference. M. Sakazov, leader of the Bulgarian Socialist Party, admitted that even if the question of the minorities were "the great stumbling block" which had to be "cleared away," it was expedient "to proceed with caution and to defer difficult questions to a later period when feelings have had time to become calm."

The formal and solemn opening of the Conference was held in the hall of the Hellenic Chamber of Deputies on Sunday morning, October 5. M. Papanastassiou delivered the address of welcome to the national delegations, and, after tracing briefly the history of the idea of Balkan confederation, concluded :[26]

The achievement of our ideal will mark a new era of prosperity and progress. It has been the custom to consider [the Balkans] as a center of misunderstandings and conflicts. But this is the first time in our history that we have assembled of our own free will, determined in spite of all obstacles to cement a solid and durable understanding among ourselves. Today, by our attitude in the Conference and by its continuation, we prove that we, the Balkan peoples, are to become the masters of our destinies and are to develop again in this corner of Europe a new and glorious civilization which will illuminate the world.

In the responses which followed, both M. Mehmed Konitza, of Albania, and M. Kirov, of Bulgaria, referred to the minorities. The latter said, "... if we remove the questions which divide us there will be only those which unite us." M. Ciceo Pop, president of the Rumanian delegation and long an advocate of confederation, reminded the Conference that the Balkan union must rest within the framework of existing treaties, including those dealing with minorities. The minority populations, he felt, must give full loyalty to the state in which they lived. The chief of the Turkish group, M. Hassan Husni Bey, vice-president of the Grand National Assembly of Turkey, was warmly enthusiastic about a possible union. M. Jonich, a member of the powerful nationalist society, the Narodna Odbrana, who gave the response for the Jugoslav delegation, expressed the belief that the first step toward union lay in the economic realm. Such a union, he declared, would not only assure peace in the peninsula, but would also give the Balkans an important rôle in world history.

STUDYING THE PROBLEMS OF BALKAN UNION

The essential work of the Conference was performed by the six commissions which had been appointed to study the various problems of confederation.[27]

The Commission on Organization prepared the statutes and rules, which were based on the draft formulated by the Greek delegation. After some modifications they were presented to the plenary session for approval.[28] The function of the Balkan Conference, the name adopted for the permanent organization, was

to contribute to the *rapprochement* and collaboration of the Balkan peoples in their economic, social, intellectual, and political relations in order to direct this *rapprochement* ultimately toward the union of the Balkan states [Albania, Bulgaria, Greece, Jugoslavia, Rumania, and Turkey].

The Conference was to meet in turn in each of the Balkan capitals, and was to coöperate with its constituent elements, the national groups of each country, which composed the delegations of each Conference. The organs of the Conference were to be the General Assembly, the Council, the Presidency, and the Secretariat.

Each delegation in the Conference was entitled to thirty voting members. The membership of each group was to be drawn from the important political, social, economic, and intellectual elements of the country. Strictly speaking, the Conference and its membership were to be unofficial and private in character, since the governments did not officially participate in the deliberations and were not obligated, therefore, by any decisions reached by the Conference. M. Papanastassiou has well described the character of the Conference in the following statement:[29]

> Though based on the national groups, composed of politicians, representatives of peace organizations, universities, and professional organizations, and though its decisions do not obligate the governments, this organization has nevertheless an official character, not only because the governments of the six countries support the activities of the national groups, but also because the delegations of each country to the Conferences are chosen after consultation with the government, and these governments are represented at each Conference by their diplomatic officials (who follow the deliberations in the capacity of observers) in the country in which the Conference meets.

The Council, composed of the chiefs and two members of each delegation, was to serve as the "executive" organ of the Assembly. The entire delegations made up the General Assembly. There were to be six commissions for the purpose of facilitating the work of the Conference: organization, political relations, intellectual coöperation, economics, communications, and social policy. The president was to be the chief of the national delegation in whose state the Conference was meeting, and the prime ministers of the various countries were to be honorary presidents. The Secretariat was to constitute the Bureau of the Presidency and to perform the duties usually devolving on such an organ. The finances were to be provided through quotas assigned to the national groups.

The work of the Commission on Political Relations was of primary significance.[30] It met on Monday morning, October 6, under the presidency of M. Pella, of Rumania. The discussions were long and detailed, involving fundamental differences of view. M. Maccas, of the Greek delegation, urged a cautious, practical, and acceptable program, which would fit into the spirit and within the framework of the League of Nations. In consonance with his memorandum, he suggested a purely Balkan committee of conciliation, composed only of Balkan citizens, for the settlement of Balkan disputes. He also desired a periodic meeting of the Balkan foreign ministers, preferably two or three times a year. Though M. Papanastassiou approved these suggestions, he favored "the adoption of a treaty, which would be concluded simultaneously by the Balkan states, outlawing war and containing the material and moral guarantee of the five other signatories of the treaty against an aggressor." M. Spiropoulos insisted that the question of political *rapprochement* rested on disarmament, obligatory arbitration, security, and the protection of minorities. Locarno offered no solution of the Balkan problem; there were *lacunae* in the *Covenant* of the League of Nations; and the Pact of Paris lacked sanctions. Hence a Balkan pact embodying the principles of nonaggression, obligatory arbitration, and mutual assistance was necessary.

Just after this discussion, M. Kirov, president of the Bulgarian delegation, again injected the question of minorities into the deliberations. He believed that the national minorities, if given equitable treatment, might become "a bridge between the Balkan peoples and civilizations," instead of "a subject of discord and hatred." A solution of the problem was a necessary "first step toward any sincere and profound friendship among the Balkan peoples." M. Kirov offered a resolution that "the governments of all the Balkan countries as well as the minorities fulfill integrally and loyally their mutual engagements in accordance with the minorities treaties." He asked the coöperation of the Bureau of International Peace and the national groups.[31] The Albanian group supported the resolution, but M. Topalovich, of the Jugoslav delegation, strongly opposed it. He reminded his colleagues that "there was a decisive moment in the history of our peoples" when "the Bulgarians were on the other side of Thermopylae. . . . Let us say frankly to Bulgarian public opinion that only through political understanding and collaboration can [the Bulgarians] win the sympathy which will help them out of their present difficulties." For these reasons, he urged his Bulgarian friends "to participate loyally and without reservation in the concert of the Balkan peoples."

The discussions of the commission at its next session dealt more closely with the problem of effecting some kind of organized friendship among the Balkan states. Rushen Eshref Bey, of the Turkish group, approved the suggestions of his Greek colleagues. Turkey was not a member of the League of Nations at the time, and had less than 10,000 square miles of territory in Europe, but could not be left out of a Balkan confederation. The Turkish delegate felt that the treaties concerning minorities ought to be respected, but he did not think the problem ripe for mature discussion. In the end, it was proposed that the problems of a Balkan pact and the minorities should be referred to a special subcommittee for detailed study.

Because fears had been expressed on the subject of the Albanian-Italian alliance, which had created a virtual protectorate giving Italy control over the Adriatic Sea and a key to penetration into the Balkans, M. Stavro Stavri explained that Albania was in no danger of losing her independence, and that "the alliance with Italy would have no *raison d'être* if our country were not threatened." Although this explanation left much to be desired, it was a direct thrust at Jugoslavia, and symbolized one of the difficulties in the achievement of closer relations among the Balkan states.

By the time the third session of the commission was opened on Wednesday morning, a draft resolution had been prepared. The preamble not only spoke of the "sincere desire for mutual security and protection" and the necessity of eliminating those obstacles which stood in the way of friendship, but also stated definitely that it was "indispensable to give to the Balkan nations complementary guarantees of security within the framework of existing treaties and to insure the loyal execution of all the other obligations arising from the said treaties, including those concerning minorities." Specifically, the resolution, which was adopted by the commission, called for: (1) periodic and regular meetings of the Balkan foreign ministers; (2) study of a Balkan pact based on the outlawry of war, pacific settlement, and mutual assistance; and (3) creation of a subcommittee to formulate a draft pact.[32]

M. Hamdula Subhi Bey, of Turkey, presided over the Commission on Intellectual Coöperation.[33] The discussions centered around the promotion of more direct relations among the intellectual institutions of the Balkans through the exchange of university professors, students, and intellectual associations. The creation of chairs of comparative Balkan law in the various universities, instruction in a Balkan language (other than that of the national state) in all national universities, and the establishment of Balkan student centers in the universities were among the propositions suggested for the promotion of intellectual relations. The Albanian group proposed the translation of Balkan folk songs. Use of the cinema and radio in the interest of Balkan friendship was suggested. Other discussions were concerned with the teaching of history as an aid to union, travel facilities for students and teachers, and the establishment of a Balkan Institute of Intellectual Coöperation. The creation of a women's section in the institute was approved.

Preparation was also made for the foundation of a Balkan Press Association, though the organization was not to be perfected until some two months later at Sofia.[34]

The question of economic relations fell within the province of the Economics Commission, under the presidency of M. Jonich, of Jugoslavia.[35] It was generally agreed that the first step toward Balkan union was "economic collaboration." The problem lay essentially in agricultural production, the population being predominantly agrarian. The general aim was "to protect agriculture and industry in the Balkans." A subcommittee on the organization of a Balkan Economic Institute was appointed. The final resolution of the commission recommended, among other things, the foundation of a central Balkan Economic Institute, the development of a concerted commercial policy, encouragement of agricultural coöperation, and study of the monetary problem and agricultural credits. All these principles were to be brought together in a "pact of economic solidarity," which the governments were urged to consider seriously.

The discussions of the Commission on Communications were under the direction of M. Natsi, of Albania.[36] The commission was organized into subcommittees on tourist traffic, routes and railways, postal services, and maritime transportation. Everyone was aware of the necessity of greater development of the means of communication, but experts were lacking. Among the proposals submitted to the plenary session were the improvement and completion of railway trunk lines and highways, telephone and telegraph communications, and air routes. The commission also proposed the formation of a Balkan Postal Union and a Balkan Tourist Federation. Nor did it neglect the more equitable treatment of Balkan maritime traffic.

The Commission on Social Policy studied the personal status of Balkan citizens in the different Balkan countries and the regulation of the movement of labor from one country to another. But these issues were so serious that they could not be discussed in detail.[37]

The second plenary session met on Thursday morning, October 9, and began the examination of the principles of the Balkan union, with M. Papanastassiou as the *rapporteur*. He emphasized that the union could not be formed immediately. It could not be modeled after either the United States of America or Switzerland, but would have to be in the spirit and fabric of the League of Nations. It would be one of equals and would not be "directed against any power whatsoever." The resolution presented merely called for a systematic effort toward the realization of a federation of independent sovereign states which would not stifle existing ethnic groups, and for the preparation of a questionnaire by the Council on the details of the organization.

The Turkish delegation did not feel that nonmembership in the League of Nations was an obstacle to participation in the Balkan union, but objected to the mention of the League in the text of the resolution. The Rumanian delegation wished to insert a statement that "participation in the Balkan union did not infringe on treaties concerning interests outside the Balkans," an obvious reference to such extra-Balkan connections of the Rumanian state as the Little Entente and the alliances with France and Poland. The Jugoslavs were satisfied. And M. Kirov said he was "convinced that we have laid the bases of the Balkan union"; he voted "without hesitation for the resolution." The session adopted the political resolution and adjourned.[38]

The next session, on Friday morning, met under the presidency of M. Sakazov, and dealt with communications and economic cooperation.[39] The resolutions stressed the importance of connecting the Balkan capitals by rail and the need for direct railway communications from north to south (from Central Europe to the Aegean Sea), and for another railway replacing the old Roman Via Egnatia, crossing the peninsula from east to west. Common railway rates and simplification of the regulations for passenger and freight traffic were part of this program. In the matter of sea communications, it was urged that special consideration be given to Balkan ships and merchandise and that traffic from the Adriatic to the Black Sea be further developed. The creation of a well-formulated system of aerial communications constituted an essential feature of this proposal. Provision was made for the establishment of a Balkan Postal Union and for the improvement of telegraph and telephone facilities. The resolutions, which were adopted, also called for the formation of a Balkan Tourist Federation to study and encourage tourist traffic.

The discussion on the economic questions, to which the Conference now turned its attention, touched a vital set of issues. M. Mylonas, the *rapporteur,* dwelt on the world agricultural crisis and the significance of economic war in the Balkans. "Free competition," he insisted, "means offensive economic war among the states . . . ; a protective tariff represents a defensive war." The commission recommended a customs union or economic understanding as a solution of this phase of the Balkan situation. A policy of economic solidarity, which alone could promote economic stability and prosperity, would include a Balkan *Zollverein,* with uniform customs and railway rates and facilities, protection of Balkan products on foreign markets, encouragement of coöperative societies, monetary stabilization and possible unification, and a Balkan Economic Institute. The Conference approved all these proposals.

The question of intellectual collaboration was discussed in the afternoon. The resolutions finally approved stipulated in the main :

(1) the promotion of cultural relations through exchanges among institutions and teachers and through the organization of a Balkan Week; (2) the creation of a Balkan sentiment through courses in comparative Balkan law, reform in the instruction in history, diffusion of classical humanism, and translations of Balkan dramatic and literary works and folklore; and (3) the establishment of an Institute of Balkan Coöperation, which would "prepare the ground for Balkan coöperation in the realm of intellectual and social life."

The major consideration of the problem of political relations came in the session of Saturday morning, October 11.[40] This was probably the most important single issue before the Conference—and certainly the most difficult. The president of the Political Commission, M. Pella, reminded his colleagues that union could be achieved "only step by step." He suggested that the significance of the commission's work lay in the recognition of "the need of increasing the security of the Balkan states and of reaching an agreement with the hope of suppressing the moral frontiers." In addition to the meeting of the foreign ministers, M. Pella advised periodical meetings of the journalists and the progressive unification of law as effective means for creating the background for political solidarity.[41]

M. Spiropoulos then presented the legal side of federation. He argued that a Balkan pact was "a juridical necessity and a political opportunity : a juridical necessity because the existing treaties contain *lacunae;* a political opportunity because of the importance of the Balkan pact." M. Maccas, who spoke more of the political aspects of the problem, pointed out the need for a "more complete, definitive security." The Conference was "directed against no one," and would not infringe on extra-Balkan ties of some of the states. The object was "to prepare union, not to foment disunion."

It was obvious that some kind of association was necessary; but it was just as evident that the obstacles to union had to be removed. Unsatisfied with the treatment of the question of minorities, the Bulgarian group, this time through M. Sakazov, stated clearly that it did not consider itself on an equal footing with the other states in a union which did not solve that issue. Answering this objection,

M. Papanastassiou remarked that other nations also had minorities and that the solution "would not be so difficult if we would create our union immediately"—it was a matter of reducing the moral significance of boundary lines. M. Sakazov appeared satisfied with this statement and declared that it could be taken as "a line of conduct in our relations with our peoples." After the adoption of the political resolutions the session came to a close.

In the afternoon, the proposals on the unification of Balkan law and social policy were adopted. It was agreed that the Council should appoint a committee to investigate the legal problem. The Balkan states were urged to conclude treaties of extradition and judicial assistance.

M. Racoassa, of the Rumanian group, who read the statement on social policy, insisted on the necessity of the support of labor to the work of the Conference. He thought that serious attention should be given to the "precarious and difficult position of the industrial and agricultural workers in the Balkan countries." He believed that "the uniformity and internationalization of the legal protection of the worker would create similar conditions of production in all the countries and would greatly facilitate their political understanding." As a preliminary, M. Racoassa asked for ratification of the conventions and recommendations adopted by the International Labor Office at Geneva. Neither a new era nor a new life could begin in the Balkans "without the adoption of a courageous and wise social policy." Other problems were those of social insurance and equal treatment of nationals in all the Balkan countries, without regard to citizenship. The commission also directed the attention of the Conference to several other issues: improvement of working conditions for women and children, elimination of child labor, abolition of prostitution, and collaboration of sanitary services.

THE CONFERENCE PAVES THE ROAD TOWARD UNDERSTANDING— ITS SIGNIFICANCE

The closing session of the Conference was held on Monday, October 13, in the old Greek theater at Delphi—seat of the Amphictyonic League, the Balkan federation of the fourth century B. C.[42] Among

other things the Conference approved the permanent organization the statutes of which had been formulated by the Commission
on Organization.⁴³ A message was sent to the Balkan peoples re-
minding them that their welfare depended on a policy of peace,
collaboration, and union. The Conference called upon the Balkan
peoples and their governments "to forget old differences," and,
imbued with "humanitarian sentiments," to work "systematically
toward union." This would "constitute an important step" in Balkan history and "the point of departure for an entirely new state
of affairs in the Balkans." When the meeting came to an end, a
common enthusiasm was shared by all the delegates. A new ideal-
ism, expressed in the following message, seemed to have struck
root: "Nothing can prevent us from taking the new road which
we have traced for ourselves. Our union: that is the new ideal of
all the Balkan peoples."

The First Balkan Conference had adopted a series of splendid
resolutions touching on every phase of Balkan life—political, social, economic, and intellectual. Although these resolutions were
informal, that is, not binding on the Balkan governments, it was
not improbable that the governments would be influenced in some
degree by the actions of the Conference. It was felt, too, that the
semiofficial character of the Conference, rather than being a source
of weakness, might be an element of strength. Many of the delegates actually were leading political lights in their own countries.
The Conference did bring the representatives of the Balkan peoples together and demonstrated that they were capable of mutual
understanding and of approaching their difficulties in a friendly
manner. For the first time in history such a gathering had taken
place. If the mere fact that a meeting could be held may be viewed
as remarkable, the prevalence of a spirit of conciliation throughout
the serious discussions was, indeed, even more a triumph. Furthermore, the Conference did indicate the road to be followed in solving
the fundamental problems at issue. It "instituted a permanent
organism destined to serve the idea of a Balkan union." That the
road toward federation would have to be paved by gradual adjustment, and that it would be a long and arduous one, was certain.
The end of the road might not even be reached. But given good will

and intelligence, and a relative freedom from external interference, the goal might be approached, in view of the permanent nature of the Conferences. "The life of peoples is long. And the Balkan peoples cannot live or progress if they remain divided among themselves."[44]

NOTES TO CHAPTER II

¹ For the Little Entente in general see Florin Codrescu, *La Petite Entente* (Paris, 1932), 2 vols.; Aurel Cosma, *La Petite Entente* (Paris, 1926); Robert Machray, *The Little Entente* (London, 1929); and J. O. Crane, *The Little Entente* (London, 1931). The Portorose Conference, November, 1921, may be taken, perhaps, as another example of coöperation in the region. Cf. "The Portorose Conference," *International Conciliation*, No. 176 (July, 1922).

² The texts may be found in Aristide Briand, "Memorandum on the Organization of a Régime of European Federal Union, May 17, 1930," and "European Federal Union. Replies of Twenty-Six Governments of Europe," *International Conciliation*, Special Supplement (June, 1930) and No. 265 (December, 1930).

³ New treaties were being negotiated in 1933–34: Bulgaria with Rumania and Greece, and Albania with Jugoslavia, in particular.

⁴ For details see C. Petrov, "Commerce extérieur des pays balkaniques," *Bulletin de la Chambre de Commerce et d'Industrie Interbalkanique*, Nos. 4–5 (August, 1933), 25–40; "Les possibilités des pays des Balkans en matière d'échanges interbalkaniques," *ibid.*, No. 10 (March, 1934); Vuk Krajach, "Statistiques du commerce et de la navigation," *Les Balkans*, Nos. 14–15 (November-December, 1933), 1148–62; statistical tables, *ibid.*, Nos. 15–16 (December, 1931–January, 1932), 231–46; A. D. Sideris, "Les données économiques pour une Union balkanique," and C. Evelpidi, "La protection des produits agricoles des États balkaniques," *ibid.*, No. 1 (October, 1930), 10–17. See also C. Evelpidi, *Les États balkaniques*, 289–312; E. A. Avèrov, *Union douanière balkanique* (Paris, 1933); C. Gaziadi, *Les rapports des pays balkaniques et l'adoption des mesures les plus appropriées pour le développement économique de ces rapports* (Istanbul, 1932); Léon Savadjian, *Dossier économique des Balkans* (Paris, 1932).

⁵ See especially *Bulletin de la Chambre de Commerce et d'Industrie Interbalkanique* (March, 1934).

⁶ Evelpidi, 313–80; P. B. Dertilis, "Le problème de la dette publique des États balkaniques," *Les Balkans*, VI, Nos. 8–9 (August-September, 1934), 129–217; Nos. 10–11 (October-November, 1934), 563–98. *Les Balkans*, which publishes all the official materials of the Balkan Conference, is hereafter cited as LB.

⁷ This part of the discussion is based on *XXVIIᵉ Congrès universel de la paix. Tenu à Athènes du 6 au 10 octobre 1929. Documents officiels* (Geneva, 1930), 95–119, 189–97, 217–39.

⁸ *Ibid.*, 102. See also Léon Maccas, *Pour l'Entente balkanique* (Athens, 1929). For the text of the resolution adopted (No. 2), see the Appendix to the present work, Document I.

⁹ The institute was to be composed of a university and education, an ecclesiastical, a press and propaganda, a woman's, and a political section. A more detailed project was presented to the First Balkan Conference.

[10] *Première Conférence balkanique. Athènes, 5–12 octobre 1930. Documents officiels* (Athens, 1931), 17–21. Hereafter cited as I CB.

[11] I CB, 22–30.

[12] "Règlement provisoire des travaux de la Première Conférence balkanique," I CB, 32–38.

[13] A. Papanastassiou, "Les principes essentiels devant servir de base à l'Union balkanique," *ibid.*, 45–56.

[14] For the Maccas and Spiropoulos memoranda see I CB, 71–80, 87–90.

[15] These memoranda were prepared by J. Lambiris, D. K. Santis, A. Bakalbassis, S. P. Loverdo, and G. Pesmazoglou. I CB, 91–92, 135–47, 179–94.

[16] *Ibid.*, 198–218.

[17] *Ibid.*, 97–109, 121–24. The memorandum on education, by A. Delmouzos, is especially interesting. See also D. Calitsounakis, *Le règlement uniforme des questions ouvrières balkaniques.* Reprinted from *Le Méssager d'Athènes* (Athens, 1930).

[18] Th. Georgevich, "Le mouvement balkanique," I CB, 57–70. See also his "Le minimum des conditions politiques préalable pour la formation de l'Union balkanique," LB (February, 1931), 1–4.

[19] The memoranda of S. Gregorich, I. Mohovich, V. V. Georgevich, and Milan Vrbanich. I CB, 148–78, 195–97.

[20] Militza Bogdanovich, "La réforme de l'enseignement de l'histoire," and V. Jonich, "L'affinité mentale des peuples balkaniques," *ibid.*, 93–96, 110–20.

[21] *Ibid.*, 125–34. R. J. Kerner, *The Social Sciences in the Balkans and in Turkey* (Berkeley, 1930).

[22] D. Mishev and B. P. Petkov, *La fédération balkanique: Origine, développement et perspectives actuelles* (Sofia, 1930). Altogether, twenty-three memoranda were presented. Neither the Albanian nor the Turkish delegation appears to have prepared any.

[23] The *procès-verbaux* of the First Balkan Conference are in the *Méssager d'Athènes, Journal de la Première Conférence balkanique*, October 5–13, 1930, and in I CB.

[24] There were 98 official delegates, of whom 10 were Albanians, 11 Bulgarians, 30 Greeks, 7 Jugoslavs, 30 Rumanians, and 10 Turks.

[25] I CB, 221–24.

[26] I CB, 225–41.

[27] The six commissions were: (I) *Commission on Organization:* General principles of union, statutes; M. Papanastassiou, president. (II) *Commission on Political Relations:* Balkan Locarno, treaties of friendship, arbitration, and disarmament; M. Pella, president. (III) *Commission on Intellectual Cooperation:* Balkan institute, reform of instruction in history, exchange of professors; M. Hamdula Subhi Bey, president. (IV) *Commission on Economic Relations:* Economic understanding, common protection of agricultural products, bank and chamber of commerce, and agriculture; M. V.

Jonich, president. (V) *Commission on Communications:* Balkan postal union, improvement and development of the ways and means of communication; M. Natsi, president. (VI) *Commission on Social Policy:* Unification of social legislation, facilities of travel and labor; M. Sakazov, president.

[28] I CB, 241. See the project of M. A. Svolos, "Projet des statuts de la Conférence balkanique," *ibid.*, 80–86, and the provisional statutes, *ibid.*, 32–38. For text see below, Appendix, Document III. Each delegation is entitled to the presidency of one of the commissions and a vice-presidency of the Assembly and Council.

[29] A. P. Papanastassiou, *Vers l'Union balkanique* (Paris, 1934), 46–47. No regular or uniform method of constituting the national groups or delegations was yet determined, except as indicated. The subject was discussed at the Fourth Conference and was to be studied and referred to the Fifth Conference for solution.

[30] I CB, 243–60.

[31] *Méssager d'Athènes,* October 8, 9. At the dinner given to the delegates by the Greek government on Friday evening, October 10, M. Venizelos, the premier of Greece, said: "It would be chimerical to believe that it would be possible to realize the union of the Balkans before solving pending questions, and notably that of the minorities. When the minorities cease to be the cause of general dissensions the application of the treaties will be complete. When the treatment of the minorities is more equitable, they will be more loyal. And when we arrive at union, we will note that the minorities no longer are an element of dissension, but the greatest support for Balkan solidarity." Cf. I CB, 385–87.

[32] The resolutions are in I CB, 364–65.

[33] I CB, 266–76.

[34] I CB, 382.

[35] I CB, 260–66.

[36] I CB, 292–301.

[37] I CB, 276–92.

[38] *Ibid.* On request of M. Batzaria, of Rumania, concerning the meaning of the term "existing ethnic entities," M. Papanastassiou stated: "One must respect the minorities which exist, but not try to create new ones."

[39] I CB, 313–21.

[40] I CB, 322–48.

[41] He also suggested criminal prosecution of persons engaged in war propaganda, a principle already embodied, apparently, in Rumanian national law.

[42] I CB, 349–63.

[43] See below, Appendix, Document III.

[44] A. P. Papanastassiou, "La Première Conférence balkanique," *L'Esprit International,* V, No. 17 (January, 1931), 3–33. See also *Les Balkans,* Nos. 4–5 (January-February, 1931). For press comments see I CB, 412–31. The texts of the acts and resolutions are in I CB, 364–82; *Résolutions de la Première Conférence balkanique, 5–12 octobre 1930* (Athens, 1930). For the general resolution and the political resolution see below, Appendix, Document IV.

Chapter III

THE PRINCIPLES OF CONFEDERATION

The Second Balkan Conference (Istanbul, 1931)

NOT THE SMALLEST ACCOMPLISHMENT of the First Balkan Conference was the provision for a permanent organization with a Council, an Assembly, and a Secretariat. Like their greater prototype, the League of Nations, the Balkan Conferences were to be regular, periodic, and continuous. Balkan problems, like other international issues, could not be solved at a single gathering of minds, no matter how liberal or intelligent, or by a single stroke of the pen, however gifted.

CONSOLIDATING THE WORK OF THE FIRST CONFERENCE

Some time after the meeting at Athens, the third session of the Council of the Balkan Conference assembled from January 30 to February 1, 1931, to consider the particular problems remanded to it.[1*] The first of these was the uniformity of the organization of the national groups. On the basis of communications with these groups, M. Papanastassiou suggested that they should include organizations and associations which would contribute to the aims of the Conference. They should have branches and sections in all parts of the Balkan countries and should be organized into commissions of competent individuals and experts for examining the important problems confronting the Balkan Conferences. Another important question was the study of the nature of the future union. M. Papanastassiou, indeed, had prepared a questionnaire dealing with the precise nature and constitution of the proposed federation. Though he was merely attempting "to clarify the idea of the Balkan union so that all might know what they were talking about," there were several objections to the questionnaire.[2] Both the Jugoslav and the Rumanian delegation insisted that economic questions should have precedence over political issues. It was apparent at the Athens meeting that, although both Jugoslavia and

---

* Superior figures refer to notes which will be found at the end of this chapter.

[45]

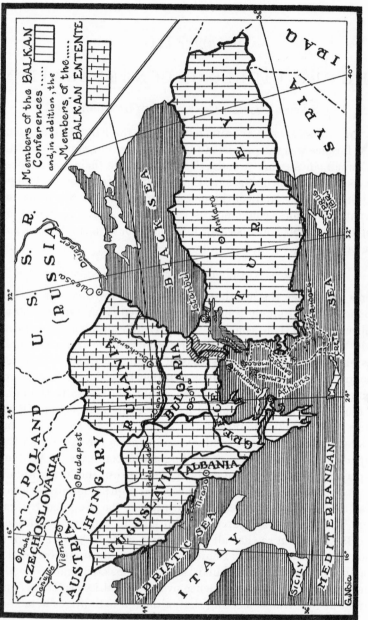

Map 3. The Balkan States and Turkey.

Rumania were favorably inclined toward Balkan coöperation, their position in the Little Entente and their other European connections made strictly Balkan affairs seem perhaps less essential. The Albanians believed that economic and political considerations went hand in hand, and the Bulgarian group favored immediate study of the political problem. M. Papanastassiou agreed with the Bulgarian group, but he did not wish to exclude the economic, social, or intellectual aspects of the matter. Nor did he wish to give the impression that "while we speak with so much enthusiasm on the necessity of the Balkan union, we take flight from fear immediately when we are confronted with the subject of its organization." He believed that "the realization of the idea of the Balkan union is a question not of a distant, but of a near future, as proved by all our efforts, our method of approach, the decisions we have reached and the statutes of our organization." In the end the Council decided to transmit the questionnaire to the national groups, which in turn were to send their responses to the Secretariat of the Conference at least a month before the next meeting.

The Council took several other important steps. It appointed a committee to study and prepare a draft of a Balkan political pact, another to examine the status of Balkan citizens, and a third to investigate the protection of tobacco.[3] The Council also decided to ask the Turkish foreign minister to call a meeting of the Balkan foreign ministers at Istanbul at the time of meeting of the Second Balkan Conference. All the national groups were urged to work for the adoption of the Balkan postal union.[4]

The final problem to be solved was that of the agenda of the next meeting. The only serious difficulty came when M. Kirov proposed to add consideration of the question of minorities at the next Conference. It will be recalled that the Bulgarian delegation had been only partly successful in obtaining a discussion of this problem at Athens, and then all controversial issues were studiously avoided. Although the Bulgarian group expressed a desire for an examination of the problem only "in principle," it felt that the delegates ought not to neglect "the most important problems." In order to conciliate the opposing groups, M. Papanastassiou finally proposed a formula, which was unanimously accepted, that the discussion of the minorities be considered in connection with the study of the application of the treaties.[5]

The Balkan Conference had given impetus to an actual movement toward some kind of federation, though vague and ill defined, among thinking circles of the peninsula. By the spring and summer of 1931, activity took shape in various forms. The fact that a Balkan Week was celebrated throughout the region testified to the vitality of the movement, though the observance in Bulgaria was not very wholehearted. Soon after the meeting of the Council at Salonica, as a matter of fact, M. Kirov and several members of the Bulgarian delegation were forced to resign because of their alleged failure to prosecute the question of minorities to a successful conclusion, and M. Sakazov became the chief of the Bulgarian group. In Albania, M. Konitza warned his colleagues that "the political difficulties reduce themselves to the problem of minorities. . . . To deprive the minorities of their rights, to oppress them, is to bring despair to them and consequently to create centers of danger; to accord them their due is to make loyal citizens of them."[6]

A very important step was taken in Istanbul when the Balkan countries sent delegates to the organization meeting of the first congress of the Balkan Tourist Federation, April 25–28. This gathering not only recommended the encouragement of tourist traffic, but also urged a thoroughgoing improvement of communications. Statutes for the federation, which were to be presented to the next Conference, were adopted.[7]

As significant as the meeting at Istanbul was the agricultural conference at Sofia, May 27–30, which brought together delegates from all the Balkan countries except Jugoslavia. Like the similar meetings recently held at Warsaw, Bucharest, and Belgrade, the conference at Sofia adopted several resolutions dealing with the collaboration of institutes for agricultural research, the problem of veterinary conventions, and the question of agricultural credit.[8]

Such progress had apparently been made that when the Twenty-eighth International Congress of Peace met in Brussels in September, 1931, it greeted "the success attained by the Balkan Conferences" with sincere enthusiasm and resolved that "the con-

ALEXANDER PAPANASTASSIOU
Former Premier of Greece

clusion of a Balkan pact of friendship, arbitration, and security would constitute a decisive step for the strengthening of peace and the constitution of the Balkan union."[9]

The controversy over the nature of the proposed union, however, continued. The primary issue was between the Jugoslav and the Greek conceptions of the ultimate aim. Dr. Th. Georgevich, of the Jugoslav group, felt that the meeting of the foreign ministers was an excellent proposal, and he favored the Balkan pact as a first step in the right direction. He recommended the improvement of communications and the development of a postal union. But Dr. Georgevich thought the final aim of federation was perhaps "very far from realization." He declared that the way to proceed was to "depolitize" the Balkans, the best means being to create a customs union. "The idea of a political union must be abandoned," since the entire plan was "too premature."[10] Naturally this attitude did not please M. Papanastassiou, who looked upon it as even more than damning with faint praise. While M. Papanastassiou did not minimize the economic problem, he did not believe that all effort should be confined to this realm. In other words, he did not accept the Jugoslav thesis that the Balkan Conference should not mix "into questions of political relations and should concentrate its exclusive attention on the economic question. . . . Our command must be: Forward for direct *rapprochement* and understanding under all forms."[11]

But this was not the only phase of the problem. If the Balkan Conference seemed to have accomplished something in the realm of the spirit, there was little actually to indicate it in the relations between the Balkan states. Few of the resolutions of the Athens meeting were carried into effect. No attempt appears to have been made to bring the Balkan foreign ministers together the first year. The formation of a political pact seemed a Utopian dream. None of the Balkan governments seemed to take into consideration any of the suggestions of the Conference. It was true that relations between Greece and Turkey were very cordial, as indicated in the exchange of official visits between M. Venizelos and Ismet Pasha. Jugoslavia and Rumania, of course, were quite friendly. But Greco-Bulgarian relations had been embittered by the question of reparations. The unsettled problem of minorities continued to trouble Bulgaria and Jugoslavia.[12] M. Neïkov, the Bulgarian minister to Greece, said that a solution of this problem was a

conditio sine qua non of the Balkan union. And this solution must be ... , if not prior, then at least parallel, to that of the other questions with which the Conference is occupied.... The Second Balkan Conference must canalize the problem, lay the foundations for its solution, and mark an appreciable and tangible step in this direction.

He doubted "if the pact could be accepted by everyone unless the question of minorities were settled at the same time."[13]

M. Papanastassiou was not unaware of all these difficulties and obstacles along the road of the Balkan Conferences. The First Conference had laid the foundations, but he was convinced that the second meeting would have "to submit the questions to a most serious study and arrive at more positive decisions." M. Papanastassiou wanted to see more concrete results in the realm of communications and economics, but, most of all, in connection with the postal union and the Balkan pact. Although he realized the tremendous difficulties involved in the question of minorities, he believed that "economic necessities, international conditions, the desire of the peoples to live in peace, the common lines which unite them—everything pushes the Balkan peoples toward understanding and union. The realization of this great ideal depends on the good will of their statesmen."[14] Would the Balkan Conference and the statesmen of the Balkan countries meet their opportunities and responsibilities? That, apparently, was the important question of the day.

THE PRINCIPLES OF CONFEDERATION BEFORE THE
SECOND CONFERENCE[15]

The Second Balkan Conference met at Istanbul, October 20–26, 1931, with almost two hundred delegates, experts, and observers attending. On the day preceding the formal opening, the Council met in the Yildiz Palace under the direction of M. Hassan Husni Bey, vice-president of the Grand National Assembly, and preparations were made for the deliberations of the delegates.[16] After definitely fixing the agenda,[17] the Council pledged its support to the coming Conference on the Reduction and Limitation of Armaments at Geneva and appointed two commissions, one to examine the obstacles to friendly relations among the Balkan peoples, the other to draw up a draft convention on the status of Balkan nationals.[18]

The first plenary session was held on October 20 in the Dolma Bagtche Palace.[19] Even in the opening addresses the delegates plunged into a serious discussion of the issues which had to be faced, but they did so, for the most part, with a spirit of tolerance and understanding. In the interim between the First and Second Conferences, the Bulgarians, as has been indicated, had succeeded in obtaining a more complete examination of the question of the minorities, and meant to make the most of it. It was the Albanian delegation, however, and not the Bulgarian, which took the lead in discussing this issue at Istanbul. In a response to the presidential address of welcome, M. Konitza, of Albania, at once raised the question of minorities. He did not approve the idea that only easy problems should be approached, because, he declared, "when one wishes to build a house, one does not begin with the doors and windows, but with the foundation, and the foundation of the common house which we wish to build is the equitable settlement of the rights of minorities." M. Sakazov, the new leader of the Bulgarian group, sounded much the same note. M. Papanastassiou believed that all the difficulties could be solved if the delegates would be sincere and frank with each other. "Our very presence here," he said, "proves that nothing is impossible, that there is no insoluble difference." The Conference was determined to move on to more concrete propositions, among these the study and adoption of a Balkan pact which would "facilitate the solution of all the other existing questions, including naturally the protection of minorities." M. Ciceo Pop, chairman of the Rumanian group, declared that a solution of the problem of minorities would not only promote peace in the Balkans, but would also contribute to "the peace and order of Europe." General Ismet Pasha, the Turkish premier, well summarized the situation when he declared in his address of welcome that "good understanding and Balkan solidarity" must rest on the two essential principles of the "absolute equality of states" and the mutual adjustment of conflicting interests. He was convinced that the Conference would facilitate and finally realize the ideal of Balkan unity.[20]

On the second day of the meeting the six commissions began their detailed examination of the questions to be studied. The Political Commission, under the presidency of M. Pop, considered the Balkan pact, the obstacles to political friendship, and the conference on disarmament.[21] Two Bulgarian memoranda, previously submitted to a special subcommittee which had studied the first two questions, dealt with the necessity of solving the problem of minorities as a vital part of the process of creating a federation along fundamental lines. M. Toshev wrote that the first great obstacle "which obstructs our road . . . is the question of minorities. . . . Without having settled it first we do not see how we can go further."[22] The Jugoslav memoranda stressed again the economic features of federation and union. Dr. Georgevich said that the political edifice could only be constructed "gradually." His delegation did not believe it possible to reach any political understanding as long as any state, either by itself or through organizations which it tolerated, interfered in the "internal life of neighbor states for the purpose of preventing their consolidation." Nor was it possible to build a union as long as some of the Balkan states were allied with "extra-Balkan states having designs of conquest or tendencies toward colonization in the Balkan countries and whose own territory or whose own forces and institutions are to be utilized against one or several Balkan states." The basis of all coöperation must rest on respect for national liberty and public security and the strict application of the principle of "the Balkans for the Balkan people." Quite evidently the Jugoslav memorandum was pointing directly toward the menacing position which Italy occupied in Albania, and toward the influence of the Macedonian Revolutionary Organization in Bulgarian governmental circles. The document brought on a serious controversy with the Albanian delegation, in which the Albanians accused Jugoslavia of ill-treatment of minorities, but it was perhaps significant that the Bulgarians did not join the controversy. Dr. Topalovich, one of the Jugoslav leaders, in a study of the Balkan pact, favored a permanent organization, and declared that in order to create a federation, everything must be done to settle "every litigious question among ourselves." He accepted the principles of non-aggression and mutual assistance, but was opposed to giving the organs of the confederation competence or jurisdiction over such serious problems as the minorities or frontier questions.[23]

M. Papanastassiou prepared a report on the application of treaties and the obstacles to Balkan friendship, in which he rejected at the outset any possibility of raising the question of treaty revision. Furthermore, he believed that such bodies as the Macedonian Revolutionary Organization would have to be dissolved. But the minorities should be given complete protection within the framework of existing treaties. The Balkan pact, he thought, was indispensable. "This pact, once realized, will serve as a sure basis for the pacific settlement of all the existing differences and for harmonious future collaboration among the Balkan peoples." Professor Spiropoulos, dean of the law faculty at Salonica, prepared the draft, founded on the well-known principles of outlawry of aggressive war, pacific settlement, and mutual assistance, which became the basis of discussion in the special subcommittee considering the subject. There was to be a "permanent commission of conciliation composed of members of the states signatory to the pact." Although questions concerning the territorial *status quo* were to be excluded from the procedures in the pact, that provision was not intended to signify the permanence of political frontiers. In the event of aggression, the Council of the League of Nations was to aid in determining the aggressor; in the event of flagrant aggression, then the parties themselves were to decide "whether they are in the presence of a violation of the obligation of non-aggression." It was thought unwise to make specific territorial guarantees similar to those embodied in the Locarno agreements, for the obvious reason that there would be grave objection on the part of some of the states, particularly Bulgaria.[24]

This short digest of the political memoranda indicates clearly the divergence of opinion among the groups. The subcommittee under M. Papanastassiou, however, accepted the draft of the Hellenic group in principle. With respect to the obstacles to political agreement, it suggested that "each delegation should propose practical solutions." An extraordinary session of the Council decided to appoint a special committee for the revision of the pact, "taking note of all the amendments presented, including those relative to the minorities." Awaiting the elaboration of the pact, the Council expressed a desire that the national groups of the interested parties reach direct agreements on the points at issue.

The two major problems which confronted the Commission on Intellectual Coöperation were the creation of a Balkan historical institute and the progressive unification of Balkan law. The only Albanian memorandum presented to the Conference stressed the necessity for changes in the teaching of history, economics, and geography in both primary and secondary schools, as well as the need for intellectual collaboration through newspapers, books, and the study of Balkan languages. A Bulgarian document pleaded for cultural freedom and sought "free diffusion of works of literature, science, and art of the other Balkan countries." The Turkish group urged that "the idea of the interdependence of Balkan interests" be introduced into school instruction. The Greek memoranda were for the most part limited to the several aspects of the unification of Balkan law. Unification of law would have a twofold usefulness: it would stabilize and promote relations among the Balkan peoples, and would move them farther along the road toward federation. For this reason there should be exchanges among students and professors of law, definite study of comparative Balkan law, and a meeting of the Balkan jurists. This was substantially the position assumed in a Turkish study of the same subject.[25]

In the discussions of the commission it was agreed that the question of legal unification should be referred to a special subcommittee before any definite conclusions could be reached.[26]

The Commission on Economic Relations discussed the protection of cereals and tobacco, the creation of a Balkan Chamber of Commerce and Industry, the collaboration of the institutes of credit, and the establishment of a Balkan bank.[27] The Hellenic group had made several studies for this commission. One report, dealing with bank facilities, urged the necessity of tax rebates, the opening of banking credits, and general coöperation among banks in promoting commerce. Another study pointed out the need for a customs union and a common commercial policy for the protection of agriculture and the sale of Balkan products. The Hellenic group also prepared a draft for the proposed Balkan Chamber of Commerce and Industry.[28] A Jugoslav memorandum traced the entire agricultural crisis to the fall in the price of wheat and said that the solution of the problem lay in a preferential customs régime. The tobacco question, only less vital than that of wheat, also demanded concerted action. Another Jugoslav report emphasized that only through some kind of economic union could the Balkan states "acquire complete economic independence and become very important exporters of agricultural products." Financial institutions would have to play their part in the promotion of definite commercial relations, and a Balkan bank, in which all the financial institutions of the region would participate, would have to be formed. Such organizations, it was contended, would be "the pioneers of the economic unity of the Balkans and become the link connecting the different national economies."[29] The Turkish memoranda dealt with all these problems. One stressed the stabilization of currencies, and, in spite of the obvious difficulties involved, favored general monetary union among the Balkan states.[30]

The Commission on Communications unanimously adopted the project for a postal union and studied further the problems of railway, air, telegraph, and telephone communications. The Balkan Tourist Federation, which had been founded in April, 1931, was also in session at Istanbul, and submitted resolutions to the commission, all of which were to be referred to the plenary session.[31]

No more important discussions, in the last analysis, concerned the Conference as a whole than those of the Commission on Social Policy. They involved the freedom of circulation and labor of Balkan nationals, the collaboration of the sanitary services, and the nationality of married women.[32] MM. A. Svolos and J. Lambiris, of the Greek delegation, who had outlined a draft convention on the status of Balkan citizens, proclaimed "the principle of free admission, free circulation, and free economic activity" for all Balkan nationals throughout the peninsula, on a basis of reciprocity. A Turkish report, generally sympathetic, proposed the appointment of a special subcommittee to study this subject. Two other memoranda submitted were limited to the problem of sanitary collaboration. Dr. Z. B. Markovich declared that this problem was one of peculiar importance, since the Balkan region, a highway between three continents, had brought diseases into Europe along with peoples and articles of commerce. Moreover, "the sanitary service [and] social medicine ... are the bases on which the aptitude of our Balkan nations for civilization can be measured."[33]

THE ISSUES BEFORE THE ASSEMBLY

The report of the Commission on Communications was the first to be considered by the second plenary session.[34] Although handicapped by the lack of experts in the national delegations, it did propose the connection of the main railways of the peninsula and the establishment of railway bridges across the Danube, and advocated the construction of a uniform railway connecting the Black Sea with the Adriatic. It urged the appointment of a special subcommittee to study aerial communications. The project of the Balkan postal union had already been prepared and was ready for adoption. This would constitute "the second practical achievement of the Balkan union"—the Balkan Tourist Federation had already been created. In the matter of highways, the Conference was asked to urge the various governments to give priority to the construction of great Balkan motor roads, especially one from Budapest to Athens and Istanbul *via* Belgrade, Bucharest, and Sofia.

The announcement of the formation of the Balkan Tourist Federation aroused general enthusiasm. M. Papanastassiou wished to see the immediate creation of the postal union also, and offered an amendment providing that it enter into force "as soon as two or three Balkan states have signed this convention," with provision for later adherence by the other states. The Conference, feeling that it was important to achieve something tangible, adopted the report, with the amendment, and the way was prepared for the establishment of the postal union.

The next item was the report of M. Akil Mukhtar Bey on behalf of the Commission on Social Policy. Basing its work on that of the Conference at Athens, the commission recommended the formation of a Balkan bureau of sanitary information and the publication of a bulletin in French under its direction. The bureau would be composed of one or two members from each delegation and its headquarters would be in Istanbul. The *rapporteur* also urged the creation of an autonomous commission on hygiene, of which competent physicians would be members, but the Conference thought it sufficient to create a subcommittee within the Commission on Social Policy.

The subcommittee on the unification of private law, now a part of the Commission on Intellectual Coöperation, was then ready to report. It was convinced that the achievement of the project, though extremely important, would be a long and difficult task, which would have to be accomplished through the establishment of chairs of comparative Balkan law in the universities and the exchange of professors and jurists among the Balkan countries. The preparatory work would have to be done by a Permanent Balkan Commission of Jurists. The commission thought that "every question of private law now attached . . . to other commissions [ought to be] remanded to the Permanent Balkan Commission on the Unification of Law for its advisory opinion." It also proposed the creation of a legal commission to examine all questions of law presented to the Conference. After much discussion it was decided to create a permanent legal commission and to give it a general jurisdiction.

M. Mylonas, of Greece, read the report of the Commission on Economic Relations. He recognized that the general economic crisis imposed the problem of "economic friendship." Special reports were to be presented on the questions of cereals and tobacco, as well as on the project for a chamber of commerce. M. Mylonas dealt particularly with the customs convention, which would lead to a Balkan *Zollverein*. It would involve regulation of the competition among countries which produce and export similar articles, and an *entente* concerning the exchange of industrial products. This would lead to the establishment of favorable tariff rates, and transport and financial and other customs facilities. In the end, rational division of labor, reasonable regulations of economic interests, and cordial economic friendship would follow. Midhat Bey then spoke for the Turkish delegation, chiefly about the project of the chamber of commerce. The task of this organization would be to work for closer economic relations, eliminate economic obstacles, organize fairs, and set an example for political friendship. It was proposed that the chamber be in "direct relations with the Balkan Conference," and that its decisions be communicated to it.[35]

The first report to be considered by the third plenary session,[36] on October 25, dealt with the nationality of married women, a problem which fell under the jurisdiction of the Commission on Social Policy.[37] The *rapporteur,* Mme Thiakaki, made reference to the general confusion of present legislation on the nationality of women, though almost universally the law forced a woman to lose her nationality of origin if she married a foreigner. In Turkey, however, a woman retained her nationality if she married a foreigner, even though the laws of her husband's country refused her this right. But a foreign woman marrying a Turkish citizen became herself a Turk. The problem of equality of women raised the question of nationality. A general Balkan rule making the regulations uniform throughout the peninsula was therefore a necessity—as much so as was uniformity in the codification of international law on that and other subjects. Three propositions were presented to the Conference : (1) adoption of the French position permitting a woman to make a formal declaration of nationality, either at marriage or within six months; (2) permission to the woman to keep her nationality or to change it to that of her husband by simple declaration; and (3) adoption of the proposal of the commission allowing a married woman to retain her citizenship with the right of changing it "on the same footing of equality as her husband."

Mme Thanopoulo, of Greece, supported the position of the commission because it would, she argued, clear up a confused situation and would recognize the equality of the sexes in the matter of nationality. Princess Cantacuzène pointed out that a very serious problem of international law existed, involving not only the husband and wife, but also the family as a social unit. But there was opposition to any consideration of the problem. M. Papanastassiou favored the principle of the equality of the sexes as a matter of social justice, but felt that the Conference should be prudent in such matters, even if it should also be a "promoter of social evolution." M. Topalovich announced that he also would vote for this proposition. Although he desired to be cautious, he did not wish to give the impression that the Conference was "opposed to the equality of the sexes." Finally, a motion was adopted permitting a married woman to retain or change her citizenship on an equal basis with her husband, as the commission had proposed.

The next set of measures approved by the Conference was that dealing with freedom of work and circulation. Admittedly, this was a very delicate problem in international relations, but the idea involved was of primordial importance. To carry out the policy of freedom of circulation and work, the commission recommended the abolition of the passport visa for Balkan nationals and confirmed the principle of "the unification of social legislation . . . guaranteeing freedom of work and association." It proposed the formation of a special committee to prepare a draft set of regulations covering freedom of circulation. In order to facilitate free circulation, a Balkan labor office was to be created.

The Assembly then proceeded to the propositions submitted by the Commission on Intellectual Coöperation. Some progress had been made in this realm since the Athens meeting. Several universities had arranged for exchanges of professors and conferences on Balkan union. The study of comparative Balkan constitutions was made obligatory for doctoral candidates in the University of Istanbul. Steps toward the creation of chairs of Balkan law had been taken in Turkey. It was reported that all the national groups had "taken the obligation . . . [to] . . . make not only history, but literature, geography, civic instruction, etc., serve the peaceful aims of Balkan friendship." The Balkan Press Association had been formed and national press organizations created. On the initiative of the Greek group, an Association of Hellenic Students had been organized for the purpose of founding "a greater union of all Balkan students." A similar student society had been founded at Istanbul.

But all these matters had been discussed before. M. Papanastassiou reminded the delegates that only two questions were before the Conference: the unification of law, which had already been approved by resolution, and the establishment of a historical institute. He did not feel that progress could be made by repetition of propositions already adopted at Athens, even if those resolutions had not been carried out. He therefore hoped that the Conference would approve the creation of an institute of historical research and "remand all the other proposals to the Council." The resolutions embodying the provisions for unification of law and the historical institute were adopted.

In the economic domain, the protection of tobacco and cereals remained for the consideration of the plenary session. The resolution adopted for the protection of tobacco called for the establishment of a Balkan Tobacco Office to coördinate and adapt tobacco production to the needs of the world market, carry on the necessary advertising, find new markets, and improve the quality of Near Eastern tobaccos. National tobacco offices were also to be created. The resolution which was sanctioned for the protection of cereals provided for the formation of national offices for the sale of cereals and a Balkan union of these offices, with a special grain exchange. Other parts of the resolution stipulated the organization of national and Balkan coöperative groups and laid the bases for the stimulation of a larger agricultural commerce within a partial customs union. The commission felt that "the organization for the sale of cereals on the basis of coöperation is a *sine qua non* for the solution of the wheat crisis."

The closing session of the Conference was held on October 26, at Ankara, in the hall of the Grand National Assembly.[38] President Mustapha Kemal was present and definitely encouraged the idea of Balkan confederation:

The present Balkan states, including Turkey, owe their birth to the historic event of the gradual displacement of the Ottoman Empire, finally interred in the tomb of history. That is why the Balkan nations, possessing a common history, were related for centuries. If this history presents painful and sorrowful aspects, all the Balkans share their responsibility for it, while that of Turkey has not been less heavy. That is why you are going to erect on the sentiments . . . of the past . . . the solid foundations of fraternity and open the vast horizons of union. . . . Since the foundation and aim of the union are collaboration in the economic and cultural domains of civilization, always respecting scrupulously mutual independence, it is not to be doubted that such an accomplishment will be received favorably by all civilized humanity.

The Ghazi wished the Conference "a most striking success."

On resuming work following Mustapha Kemal's address, the Assembly adopted a proposal of the Council that the Commission on Organization be transformed into a Legal and Organization Commission, to which would be given jurisdiction over matters of law as well as questions of organization.

The final issue to come before the Conference was contained in the report of the Political Commission, which studied the most difficult and complicated problems before the Conference. The heart of the whole political question was involved in the draft of a political pact, which had been studied by a subcommittee under the chairmanship of M. Papanastassiou. It confirmed "the necessity for the Balkan governments to conclude a multilateral pact of arbitration and friendship," and expressed the desire that "the interested parties agree directly on all questions which obstruct the moral *détente* among the Balkan nations."

The members of the commission unanimously approved the use of Professor Spiropoulos' draft of the pact. The differences in the commission arose over the method of determining the aggressor in the event of violation of the proposed pact: whether through recourse to a purely Balkan institution or to the good offices of the League of Nations. In presenting the report, Professor Spiropoulos declared : "I hope you will adopt [the resolutions] unanimously, [as] the Balkan nations are convinced that the Conference will mark the advent of an era when, by uniting their own vital forces, they will be in a position to break the course of death which war represents. . . ."

After a very brief discussion the Conference unanimously adopted the political resolutions. It remained for the next Conference to adopt the definitive text of a Balkan pact.

The Second Conference closed with a series of addresses expressing the spirit of the meeting. M. Pella, vice-president of the Rumanian delegation, voiced his faith in the kind of coöperation represented in the Conference. The delegates were trying to erect "a barrier against civil war, barbarism and anarchy," which might develop if they failed in their efforts. M. Hassan Husni Bey, the retiring president, felt that the Conference had produced some results, and that "in the struggle between faith and skepticism in our labors, we can clearly declare today that the victory of the first seems already assured."

As in the meeting at Athens, the Second Conference concluded with an address to the peoples, governments, and press of the Balkan states in which "the representatives of the Balkan nations" expressed their indomitable desire for the realization of an ideal "of which humanity will be proud," that of the Balkan union.[39]

THE PROGRAM ADOPTED AT ISTANBUL—THE ACHIEVEMENTS
OF THE CONFERENCE

One may be somewhat disappointed at the failure of the Second Balkan Conference to treat definitively of some of the pressing problems confronting it, but one should keep in mind that the Conference was only a private or semiofficial body, holding its second general meeting. And it did adopt some important resolutions, this time embodying more concrete and specific propositions than those approved at Athens. It was too early to expect that the resolutions would find practical application, but it was hoped—and not without justification—that they would have their benevolent influence on the attitudes and policies of the Balkan governments. At the first meeting the Greek government had taken a helpful part in encouraging the Conference. The participation of the Turkish government in the gathering at Istanbul was even more striking. Not only was it true that Ismet Pasha and President Mustapha Kemal addressed the sessions, but Tevfik Rushdi Bey, the foreign minister, appears on more than one occasion to have used his influence in conciliating conflicting opinions and interests.

That the Istanbul Conference seemed to have made some distinct advances over that at Athens may have been in part because it was the second, not the initial, meeting of persons interested in the problem of Balkan federation and union. There was, it would seem, a greater spirit of conciliation and understanding, and the Conference appeared to be better organized, with the delegations somewhat more balanced in composition. The members of the technical committees were successful in carrying a stage farther certain of the measures which had been studied at Athens and in definitely inaugurating a number of new proposals. Progress was made especially in the economic and other nonpolitical domains. The draft of the Balkan Postal Union was adopted and the way prepared for making that institution a tangible reality in the realm of communications. This was likewise true of the adoption of the draft of the Balkan Chamber of Commerce and Industry.[40] Together with the Balkan Tourist Federation, these institutions constituted important associations built upon and within the framework of the Balkan Conference itself. Falling also within the definitely practical domain were the measures taken for the protection of tobacco and cereals, including the establishment of Balkan offices for the purpose of such protection, and the outlines for the creation of a Balkan agricultural chamber. The resolutions pertaining to the unification of Balkan law and the development of a historical institute were also practical measures leading toward legal and intellectual collaboration along sound lines. In the realm of social policy, the recognition of the principle of the equality of women and the right of choice of nationality on a basis of equality with the husband, represented a substantial advance. Of the other resolutions in this domain, the one leading to the study and drafting of a document concerning the freedom of circulation and labor of Balkan nationals is very important.

If the Second Conference could hardly be said to have achieved anything outstanding in the political field, it did carry the discussions of the minorities problem and the political pact a step beyond the deliberations at Athens. Indeed, the major achievement in the political domain was the adoption of the principles of outlawry of war, pacific settlement, and mutual assistance, to be embodied in the future Balkan pact. The continued study of this proposed covenant among the Balkan states was to prepare the ground for its submission to and approval by the Third Conference at Bucharest. Moreover, the desire for the immediate conclusion of a Balkan pact, and the recommendation for direct understandings between interested groups on those problems which obstruct the path of friendship, were healthy signs.

In general, it appeared that the Conference was moving toward a partial customs union in the economic field, toward agreement in the realm of social policy on freedom of circulation and labor, and toward a political pact which would bring peace and security to the region.[41]

EDUARD BENEŠ
President of the Republic of Czechoslovakia

NOTES TO CHAPTER III

[1] For the minutes see LB, No. 5 (February, 1931), 25–33. See also *Le Temps*, January 30, 31, and February 3, 1931.

[2] The text of the questionnaire is in LB, No. 5, 31–32.

[3] The committee on the Balkan pact originally was to be composed of twelve members, two from each national group, under the presidency of M. Hassan Husni Bey.

[4] The Carnegie Endowment had offered $10,000 for the expenses of the Conference. M. Konitza announced that the Albanian government would offer £1,000 for the expenses of the Secretariat, and M. Hassan Bey declared the readiness of the Turkish government to do likewise. The other delegations were asked for similar support.

[5] Other questions placed on the agenda were: railway and telephone communications, freedom of circulation and labor, sanitary collaboration, protection of agricultural products, and organization.

[6] LB, No. 8 (May, 1931), 37.

[7] *Ibid.*, 39–40.

[8] LB, No. 9 (June, 1931), 48–50. A. Sideris, "Rapport sur les travaux de la Réunion agricole à Sofia," *ibid.*, No. 12 (September, 1931), 63–65. At the time of the celebration at Athens, resolutions were adopted: (1) that the problem of a Balkan Chamber of Commerce be studied; (2) that a Balkan fair be held at Salonica; (3) that a museum be organized in one of the principal cities of each Balkan country; and (4) that each group labor for the speedy development of economic relations. See also André Tibal, *La crise des États agricoles européennes et l'action internationale: Documents recueillis et commentées* (Paris, 1931), and Arnold J. Toynbee, *Survey of International Affairs, 1931* (London, 1932), 324–29.

[9] LB, Nos. 10–11 (July-August, 1931), 32–33.

[10] LB, No. 8, pp. 15–18.

[11] LB, No. 9, pp. 15–19; No. 8, pp. 1–15.

[12] LB, Nos. 10–11, p. 20.

[13] LB, No. 12, pp. 1–3.

[14] *Ibid.*, 3–6.

[15] The *procès-verbaux* of the Second Balkan Conference are in LB, Nos. 13–14 (October-November, 1931), 70–142, and *Le Journal d'Orient*, October 20–29, 1931. II CB contains only the memoranda and reports, not the minutes.

[16] The commissions were organized as follows: (1) Organization, M. Hassan Husni Bey, president; (2) Political Relations, M. Stefan Ciceo Pop, president, M. Papanastassiou, chairman of the committee on the Balkan pact; (3) Intellectual Coöperation, M. Mehmed Konitza, president; (4) Economic Relations, M. Papanastassiou, president; (5) Social Policy, M. Jonich, president; (6) Communications, M. Sakazov, president.

[17] The agenda was as follows: I. *Political:* (a) Balkan pact and discussion on the report of the committee on the application of treaties and the execution of the engagements arising therefrom, including those concerning minorities, and on all difficulties in way of political friendship; (b) the conference on disarmament. II. *Economic:* (a) Protection of cereals and tobacco; (b) creation of a Balkan Chamber of Commerce; (c) collaboration of credit institutions. III. *Intellectual:* (a) Creation of an Institute of Balkan History; (b) progressive unification of Balkan law. IV. *Communications:* (a) Railway junctions and construction of bridges for direct communication among Balkan capitals; (b) postal union and telephone and telegraph communications; (c) aerial communications. V. *Social Policy:* (a) Discussion and decision on reports of the committee on freedom of circulation and labor; (b) collaboration of sanitary services; (c) discussion on the nationality of married women.

[18] It was also decided that the plenary meetings were to be public, those of the commissions private.

[19] LB, Nos. 13–14, pp. 71–83.

[20] At a banquet tendered by the city of Istanbul on the evening of October 21, M. Topalovich said: "... we are not here to seek exclusively intellectual cooperation. We wish to prepare an *entente* of all our vital forces, economic, military and general." *Ibid.*, 83–90.

[21] *Ibid.*, 90.

[22] D. Mishev, *Mémoire présenté par le groupe national bulgare à la Deuxième Conférence balkanique au sujet des difficultés qui s'opposent à la détente morale et du rapprochement des États balkaniques* (Sofia, 1931) ; A. Toshev, *Exposé concernant la question minoritaire bulgare* (Sofia, 1931) ; B. P. Petkov, *Mémoire présenté par le groupe national bulgare à la Deuxième Conférence balkanique rélatif à l'application des dispositions du traité de Neuilly concernant la recherche et l'entretien des sépultures des officiers et soldats bulgares, ainsi que des internés civils des guerres de 1912–1918* (Sofia, 1931). See also LB, No. 12, pp. 24–28, and II CB, 65 ff., 75 ff.

[23] For the memoranda of Dr. Th. Georgevich and Dr. Zh. Topalovich see LB, No. 12, pp. 79–80, and Nos. 13–14, pp. 54–58; also cited in II CB, 107 ff., 110 ff. A dispatch in the London *Times*, January 22, 1932, declares that the Jugoslav delegation, in large part composed of members of the *Narodna Odbrana*, had instructions to oppose the conclusion of a Balkan pact and to work for an understanding with the Bulgarians. The Bulgarians stated that the essential conditions for an understanding were the recognition of the Bulgarian minority in Serbian Macedonia and the granting of political and educational rights to that group. The Jugoslavs insisted on the prior conclusion of a treaty of friendship. It seems that an invitation was issued to the Bulgarians to continue the discussions in Belgrade, but that M. Marinkovich, the Jugoslav foreign minister, did not approve of the conduct of the delegation. He insisted also on the liquidation of the Macedonian Revolutionary Organization.

[24] The Papanastassiou memorandum and the Spiropoulos draft of the pact are in LB, No. 12, pp. 31–44, and II CB, 92 ff.

[25] For discussion see LB, Nos. 13–14, pp. 90–93. The memoranda are in LB, No. 12, p. 23, pp. 48–57, Nos. 13–14, pp. 34–39, Nos. 15–16 (December, 1931–January, 1932), 213–15, and II CB, *passim*. See also G. Cassimatis, *L'unification du droit privé balkanique* (Paris, 1931).

[26] M. Clarnet, president of the Balkan Press Association, announced that his organization had drawn up a constitution and was attempting to encourage the idea of Balkan union. Cf. LB, Nos. 13–14, pp. 91–93.

[27] *Ibid.*, 93.

[28] For the Greek memoranda see LB, No. 12, pp. 25–29, 57–63.

[29] LB, Nos. 15–16, pp. 215–23, and Nos. 17–18 (February-March, 1932), 333–38.

[30] LB, Nos. 13–14, pp. 39–45; II CB, *passim*.

[31] Discussion in LB, Nos. 13–14, pp. 93–94. Memoranda, *ibid.*, 45–47, 69–78, and II CB, *passim*. See also G. Bouyoukas, *Considérations générales au sujet de l'amélioration de la communication ferroviaire interbalkanique* (Athens, 1931).

[32] LB, Nos. 13–14, p. 94.

[33] See LB, No. 12, pp. 44–48; Nos. 13–14, pp. 47–54; Nos. 15–16, pp. 223–29.

[34] LB, Nos. 13–14, pp. 94–108.

[35] The Rumanian delegation proposed that coöperative organizations be included in the membership of the chamber of commerce and industry.

[36] For the third plenary session see LB, Nos. 13–14, pp. 108–22.

[37] *Ibid.*, 108–17. Princess Cantacuzène proposed to amend the resolution with the suggestions: (1) that the married woman keep her nationality; (2) that the two parties change nationality only with mutual consent. M. Trajan D. Soimu suggested that the wife lose her nationality "only on condition of adopting the nationality of her husband, and keep her nationality if she thinks it her duty to make a special declaration on this subject." He also suggested that nationality be not changed during the marriage except by mutual consent, in order to guarantee "the institution of marriage and the family." The amendments were rejected and the Conference affirmed the original resolution of the commission.

[38] *Ibid.*, 123–31.

[39] *Ibid.*, 133. A final meeting of the Council was held on the train going to Istanbul. At this time it was decided to hold the next Council meeting in January, 1932, and the Third Balkan Conference in Bucharest in October, 1932.

[40] For the texts of the convention of the Balkan Postal Union and the statutes of the Balkan Chamber of Commerce and Industry see the Appendix to the present work, Documents V and VI.

[41] See *Le Journal d'Orient*, October 20–29, 1931, and LB, Nos. 13–14, pp. 2–25. The complete texts of the resolutions are in *Résolutions et vœux de la Deuxième Conférence balkanique* (Istanbul, 1931) and LB, Nos. 13–14, pp. 134–42. There is a good summary in Arnold J. Toynbee, *Survey* (1931), 324–40. The results were well received by the press and by all elements represented at the meeting. M. Konitza believed that "a forward step" had been taken on the political pact and the minorities. M. Sakazov declared that "one could not expect greater results" under the circumstances.

Chapter IV

THE POLITICAL PACT AND THE BALKAN UNION

TWO BALKAN CONFERENCES had now been held, one at Athens and the other at Istanbul. The meetings remained within the realm of private initiative, and though the governments looked with apparent benevolence on the idealistic labors of their nationals, they did almost nothing toward giving the resolutions of the Conferences the force of law. The fact that the Conference continued to function at all was, however, a symbol of faith and hope in the future; at any rate, the movement continued and preparations were made for the calling of the third meeting at Bucharest in the fall of 1932. Moreover, there had been some practical results from the first two Conferences. M. Papanastassiou, always the foremost protagonist of the idea of federation, has well summarized the achievements:[1*]

We already have the Balkan Press Association and the Balkan Tourist Federation. We have recommended the organization of the postal union, a chamber of commerce, an institute of historical research, a bureau of sanitary information, a bureau of labor, a central office for cereals, a grain exchange, a central union of national coöperative organizations, and a central tobacco office. We propose the creation of an agricultural chamber and a bureau of the postal union. Moreover, numerous special committees have been created for the examination of such questions as those of railroads, aviation, unification of law, and customs union, a certain number of which will constitute the cornerstone for the establishment of a permanent Balkan organism. . . .

All this convinces us that if the future labors of the Conference are pursued with equal success, and if the Balkan organizations which have already been created begin to function, we shall achieve union without knowing how we have done it. The conclusion of the Balkan pact, combined with the convention on the partial customs union and the agreement on the status of Balkan citizens, will constitute the first form of the union.

Certainly many obstacles still exist, and national egoisms, narrow conceptions, prejudices, and unilateral interests are still influential. But more powerful is the necessity for union, more dominant the desire of the peoples to guarantee peace and better conditions of existence.

* Superior figures refer to notes which will be found at the end of this chapter.

M. Papanastassiou may have been justified in his guarded optimism. Relations between Turkey and Bulgaria were very good; there had been no serious issues between them in years. A decision of the Permanent Court of International Justice (March, 1932) had brought some hope of settling the troublesome Greco-Bulgarian reparations issue. But Bulgaria and Jugoslavia remained so unfriendly that the committee on foreign relations of the Bulgarian Sobranje found it necessary to urge the Macedonian deputies "to use all their influence on their Macedonian cocitizens to induce them definitely to abandon armed struggle and thus to facilitate friendship between Bulgaria and Jugoslavia."[2]

All the Balkan governments announced their peaceful intentions at the Geneva Conference for the Reduction and Limitation of Arms which convened in February, 1932. Greece, Rumania, and Jugoslavia took similar positions, supporting in general the French thesis of security within the framework of a stronger League of Nations. Tevfik Rushdi Bey, the foreign minister of Turkey, asserted that his country had no territorial aspirations and wished only to live in peace. Turkey was "ready to undertake disarmament, but on the basis of the formula of equality of forces, taking into consideration the political, economic, and financial position of each country." As was to be expected, Bulgaria, one of the defeated powers in the World War, expressed discontent with the existing situation. "Disarmed and deprived of effective guarantees for her security," Bulgaria, thought M. Malinov, "would be happy to see positive improvements in international relations and progress in diminishing resentments among peoples."[3]

THE BEGINNINGS OF A POLITICAL PACT

It was in this atmosphere that the fifth meeting of the Council was held in Istanbul from January 28 to February 1, 1932.[4] The Balkan pact was its most serious problem. The Second Conference had referred this problem to a special committee, which was also to examine the question of the execution of the peace treaties, the issue of minorities, and the means for improving the relations of the Balkan states.[5] The committee met for an exchange of views in the afternoon of January 29. A long debate ensued over the Albanian proposal to create special offices for the adjustment of minorities disputes, the Jugoslavs being strongly opposed to this suggestion.⁶ Some way had to be found to satisfy the Bulgarian group, however, and, after deliberations lasting through several sessions of the committee, it was decided to follow the Greek draft of the pact as a basis. The new provisions, embodied in Articles XXI to XXVI inclusive, of the proposed Balkan pact, stipulated the formation of national offices of minorities and the creation of a Balkan commission of minorities, the latter to be composed of six members, one from each contracting state. Petitions might be submitted to the national offices, and, on the request of the Balkan commission, could be brought before that tribunal. The contracting states were to agree to accept any unanimous decision of the commission, but should differences of view develop, the matter was to be submitted to the League of Nations. The petitions were to be *bona fide* representations from the interested populations. The minorities were to be loyal to the state on whose territory they lived "and abstain from any action directed against the state." The states themselves agreed "to take the necessary measures for the purpose of preventing any kind of action which might disturb the peace and good relations among the Balkan peoples."⁷

Several other questions came before the Council. It framed the agenda of the next meeting of the Conference.⁸ Provision was made for the celebration of Balkan Week throughout the peninsula. The Council also appointed a committee to prepare the draft of a convention on the status of Balkan nationals, of which M. Topalovich, of Jugoslavia, was chairman. This convention would be an integral part "of the ensemble of projects involving the Balkan pact and the economic agreement on the creation of a customs union" and would come into force simultaneously with them.⁹

THE BALKAN SCENE IN 1932

Meanwhile, the need for solidarity, particularly in the economic realm, was being increasingly felt among the agrarian states in the Balkan peninsula.¹⁰ Many believed that economic salvation lay in the direction which the two Balkan Conferences had pointed out. When M. Papanastassiou transmitted the resolutions of the

Istanbul meeting to the Greek Parliament, he insisted that the Balkan governments ought to sanction the work of the Conferences, because economic and political conditions made some kind of union a necessity. A Balkan confederation would assure peace, improve the lot of the Balkan nations, and prepare a *rapprochement* among all the European peoples.[11]

It was thought that Greece and Bulgaria might seize the opportunity afforded by the Lausanne Conference on Reparations, in June, 1932, to enter into direct negotiations to liquidate their own disputes.[12] Jugoslavia and Bulgaria, in spite of their serious controversies, appeared to be on the verge of settling the question of "double properties" along their common frontiers, that is, properties which extended across the boundaries. In Greece, a political crisis in the spring of 1932 drove Venizelos from office and once more elevated M. Papanastassiou as head of the government. Another political upheaval, in Rumania, forced the resignation of Professor Iorga because of the failure to solve the financial problems of that country. Very cordial relations existed between Greece and Turkey, an important factor in the Balkan drama. The friendship of these two countries, which had been cemented by the political agreement in October, 1930, had been especially signalized in the exchange of official visits by Venizelos, Ismet Pasha, and Tevfik Rushdi Bey. As a direct result of the Second Balkan Conference the Turkish government had extended diplomatic recognition to Albania. Still another factor promoting the movement toward Balkan friendship was the entry of Turkey into the League of Nations on July 18, 1932. The absence of Turkey from the roster of the League would no longer be a barrier to her complete entrance into the Balkan federation, since all the members of the proposed association would have the same obligations as members of the League.[13]

On April 16 and 17, a meeting of the Bulgarian, Jugoslav, and Rumanian agricultural coöperatives was held. It was unanimously decided to recommend the establishment of "a common institution of a permanent character for the purpose of raising the value of cereals." The provisional location of this body was to be in Bucharest. This step, it was thought, might assist in the further economic collaboration of these states within the framework of the Balkan Conference.[14] The month of May saw a conference on the production of tobacco in Istanbul, in which representatives from Bulgaria, Greece, and Turkey participated. The delegates, who were official representatives of their governments, decided to create a permanent office in Istanbul, composed of functionaries of the participating parties.

Though the Bulgarians did not take part, the celebration of Balkan Week was much better organized than hitherto. The meetings in Greece were given over to a discussion of the medical and sanitary problems. The observance in Turkey was concerned with the development of the Balkan Chamber of Commerce and Industry, which actually was founded on May 27, 1932.[15] The Preparatory Balkan Committee of Jurists held its meetings from June 11 to 13, in Belgrade.[16] The Albanian group announced a series of meetings for the purpose of propagandizing the idea of Balkan union.[17]

But the great internal obstacle in the path of fundamental *rapprochement* remained the problem of minorities—and without some attempt at solution Bulgarian opinion could not be placated. In his statement to the *Sobranje* in May, M. Mushanov, the premier, declared that his people were, "without distinction of party, unanimous in demanding respect of the engagements assumed by virtue of the treaties." Unfortunately the hour was not propitious "for making these demands valid before the League of Nations." Bulgaria desired friendly relations with her neighbors, but "if the question of the national minorities prevents it, that is not the fault of Bulgaria." What the Sofia government desired was "the recognition of the ethnic and cultural rights of our conationals," and in raising the question, it did not seek to cause trouble. On the contrary, Bulgaria was merely trying "to find the means of creating normal and fraternal relations, as well as commercial contacts among the peoples whose relations are not yet determined."[18]

While final preparations were being made for the assembling of the Third Conference in October, the Stresa Conference for the Economic Restoration of Central and Eastern Europe met. It gathered under the auspices of the Commission of Enquiry for

European Union and as a direct consequence of the Lausanne Conference on Reparations which had convened in June, 1932. Greece, Bulgaria, Rumania, and Jugoslavia were the Balkan states represented among the sixteen national delegations. Included in the Stresa recommendations were provisions for the elimination of trade barriers, the revalorization of the cereals of eastern Europe, and the encouragement of a well-conceived plan of public works for improving economic relations, particularly for the disposal of agricultural products.[19] Although nothing immediate came from the Stresa meeting, some impetus was given for the solution of these same problems among the Balkan nations proper.

THE CRISIS AT BUCHAREST : THE BULGARIAN DELEGATION LEAVES THE CONFERENCE

When the Conference met in Bucharest, October 22–28, 1932, its agenda had been well prepared and many of the problems had been studied in some detail.[20] This was especially true of the Balkan pact (including the problem of minorities), economic collaboration, the status of Balkan nationals, and the unification of Balkan law. The Conference chose M. Ciceo Pop, president of the Rumanian Chamber of Deputies, as its presiding officer. The Rumanian group had issued an invitation to all the national delegations on October 14, and the president was especially happy that the Bulgarian delegation had accepted the invitation. He reported, however, that at the meeting of the Council on October 21, the Bulgarian group presented a letter announcing with regret that Bulgaria must withdraw from the Conference. This action had been taken because the problems of minorities and juridical equality of states, which the Bulgarian group had placed in the forefront of the questions to be considered, had not been solved in the interval since the last meeting.[21] The letter continued :

The Bulgarian national group believes that it is its duty once more to draw the attention of the Third Balkan Conference to the fact that without first solving the minority problem it scarcely sees any possibility of a favorable conclusion of the labors of the present Conference. . . . In the future, the fed eration of the Balkan states will be possible only if the obligations arising from the minority treaties are previously executed. . . . The Bulgarian delegation on this occasion makes the express reservation that the application of the provisions of the treaties relative to the minorities is a preliminary and essen-

tial condition to the acceptance of the Balkan pact. . . . The Bulgarian national
group finds it impossible to ask Bulgarian opinion to approve participation . . .
in a Third Conference which seems to register no progress either in the improvement of the condition of the minorities or in the establishment of new
and more direct relations among the Balkan peoples. . . .

Such are precisely the reasons which have forced the Bulgarian group to ask
the provisional adjournment of the Conference until next spring, in the hope
that by that time we may be able to achieve some improvement in the lot of the
minorities. . . . We hasten to assure you that as soon as the Conference is able
to take a first real step in the application of the rights of the minorities we will
be ready to associate our efforts anew in the work of lasting friendship and
cordial collaboration among the Balkan peoples.

This was, of course, a most emphatic reassertion of the original
Bulgarian position that the solution of the problem of minorities
must precede the creation of any fundamental kind of federation,
but such a severe proposal had not been expected, and the Bulgarian action was almost a bombshell. It was, moreover, a direct
challenge to the other delegations. Following the declaration, the
Council took note of the statements of the Greek, Rumanian, Turkish, and Jugoslav delegations that they would do everything possible to fulfill the Bulgarian *desiderata*. But the five national
groups naturally could not agree to suspend the sessions, which
had already begun. To have done that would have destroyed the
Conference itself.

The Conference at Bucharest opened with the customary cere-
monies. There were addresses of welcome and felicitation to which
the members of the delegations responded. M. Konitza, of Albania,
who had taken a leading part in the previous meetings, spoke of
the Balkan pact, which the Conference was expected to adopt :[22]

This pact, indeed, is the very basis of Balkan understanding: it will give
our peoples and governments the confidence without which all hope of *rapprochement* becomes vain. At the same time it will guarantee to the minorities
their natural rights and suppress the one serious obstacle to the understanding
of the peoples of the peninsula and contribute to their well-being. The Albanian
delegation declared at the beginning of the First Balkan Conference, and it
has not ceased to repeat since, that the solution of the question of the rights
of minorities was and remains the *conditio sine qua non* of the Balkan union.
A union without minority guarantees, if it were possible, would be of short
duration, since it would not be based on moral principles. It is true that the
decisions of the Conference do not bind our governments, but it would be ridic-
ulous to pretend that our national groups act independently of their governments. . . . Be that as it may, if the Balkan pact is not approved by our gov-

ernments before the month of October next, the Albanian national group . . . will not participate in the future labors of the Conference, as that body would no longer have any reason for existing.

M. Trifonov, of the Bulgarian delegation, emphasized even more strongly the importance of the problem of minorities.[23] The two main problems to be studied, M. Papanastassiou thought, were the Balkan pact and the program for greater economic collaboration. The Turkish leader, M. Hassan Husni Bey, declared not only that the Balkan Conference was a natural product of the historical development of the region, but also that the Conference "in the first place, ought to realize the Balkan union, which is the shortest road to a solution of all the difficulties."[24]

Granted the sincerity of the opinions expressed, the fundamental issue on which there was such critical controversy at the opening of the Third Conference thus appeared to be whether the difficulties were to be solved before or after the creation of a Balkan union. It was on this issue that the Bulgarians had left the Conference. Now the Albanians had threatened to withdraw if the Balkan states, within a period of one year, did not adopt a political pact which made provision for a solution of the question of minorities. Would the Conference at Bucharest meet this twofold challenge?

THE POLITICAL PACT AND THE OUTLINES OF THE BALKAN UNION

Following the opening session of the Conference, the various commissions began the study of the questions which were on the agenda.[25] The principal problem before the Political Commission, as we have seen, was the political pact, which already had been studied in detail. A report, drawn up by Professors Spiropoulos and Reshid Bey, pointed out that the new pact not only provided for a general Balkan security agreement, but also stipulated the creation of a permanent Balkan commission of conciliation, and arranged for a means of settling the problem of minorities. The stipulations concerning minorities were to fit into the other provisions for the pacific settlement of differences and mutual assistance. The committee felt that the critical situation in the Balkans made understanding and collaboration more urgent than ever and the acceptance of the pact much more likely. Approval of the new covenant would be "an immense contribution to the successful evolution of its work in the future."[26]

At the second session of the commission, M. Trifonov said that before proceeding to a consideration of the pact, "it would be indispensable to conform to the resolution and wishes of the Second Balkan Conference of Istanbul . . . relative to political *rapprochement* which stipulate the necessity of direct relations among the national groups." The Bulgarian delegation therefore proposed postponement of the discussions until the next Conference, "in the hope that in the interval meetings would take place which would lead to an understanding on the question of minorities." This position, as we have seen, was not shared by the other groups. M. Konitza announced that the Albanian delegation had come "with the mandate to demand the adoption of the pact [or] to withdraw." On the failure to accede to his point of view, M. Trifonov, in accordance with the Bulgarian communication to the Council, announced the withdrawal of his group, but said that it would maintain an observer to follow the debates. Meanwhile, the renewed Bulgarian request to the Council that the Conference be postponed was refused. It was then that the delegation, even without leaving observers, finally withdrew from the meeting.

After the Bulgarian withdrawal, the commission continued its examination of the pact. M. Spiropoulos, author of the first draft, urged the delegates to adopt the pact. But the conflict over Chapter IV, Articles 21–26, dealing with the minorities, was a very serious one, even though the pact as a whole had been accepted in principle. It was this chapter which set up a series of special national offices and a Balkan commission on minorities. The Jugoslavs objected to this provision because the commission, they contended, would be an institution outside the machinery already created by the minorities treaties, and would be a means for "encouraging turbulent minorities." The treaties were a sufficient guarantee for safeguarding the rights of minorities of language, race, and religion, and the League of Nations gave additional protection. Consequently, the Jugoslav delegation urged that the provisions be conceived in more general terms, thus:

It is left to the competence of the diplomatic conference among the Balkan countries to reach an understanding on the means of giving as effective protection as possible to the minorities, within the framework of existing treaties.

M. Papanastassiou took the more moderate view that there was no danger whatsoever in the proposed commission. Neither was there a conflict with the treaties or with the provisions within the system of the League of Nations.

Moreover, approval [of Articles 21–26 of Chapter IV, he continued] was decided in common agreement and with the participation of the Bulgarian delegation, in the subcommittee which examined the draft of the pact; we adopted Article 26, which imposes the obligations on the minorities and on the respective nations. In common agreement we also accepted the provisions of the draft concerning mutual assistance, which were accepted by the Bulgarian and Albanian delegations on condition that Articles 23, 24, and 25 be adopted by the Conference. If now after the departure of the Bulgarians we reduce the supplementary guarantees proposed by the draft, we would render still more difficult the resumption of Bulgarian collaboration and understanding among the Balkan countries in general.

The draft pact, with the provisions on minorities, was finally approved in the commission by a vote of twenty to five. M. Jovanovich's proposal to eliminate the section of Article 25 concerning appeals to the League of Nations was rejected. The other articles were adopted with only slight and unimportant modifications.

The Commission on Intellectual Coöperation, which met under the presidency of M. Mehmed Konitza, studied in particular the two important problems of the unification of Balkan law and the establishment of an institute of historical research.[27] It will be recalled that the Balkan Preparatory Commission of Jurists had met at Belgrade, June 11–13, to discuss the legal problem. The commission was divided into three subcommittees, on civil, commercial, and criminal law. In a concluding set of resolutions it expressed a wish that a complete review of Balkan law be published in French. It urged all the Balkan nations to participate in international legal congresses and recommended the exchange of law professors among the universities. At Bucharest the commission perfected a permanent organization for the purpose of carrying on its investigations in a more satisfactory manner.[28]

The second of the more important problems was the creation of a Balkan historical institute, the purposes of which were to promote research into the history of Balkan civilization and to publish documents and studies in this field.[29]

But there were other aspects of the intellectual approach to union. Once more, emphasis was laid on the translation of literary and dramatic works produced in the region, and use of both the radio and the cinema was stressed. The report of M. Clarnet, president of the Balkan Press Association which had been organized, declared that though the beginnings of that institution had been auspicious, not much had been accomplished. Only the Rumanian and Turkish press had remained true to the policy of conciliation, "while among the Bulgarians, the Greeks, and the Jugoslavs the polemical note has gained in force, virulence and acidity."[30]

A large number of important memoranda were presented to the Economics Commission. These studies were concerned particularly with the creation of a customs union and general economic collaboration, inter-Balkan coöperative relations, a chamber of agriculture, and coöperation of scientific agricultural institutes. Two memoranda discussed the customs union and economic collaboration. Both agreed on the necessity of collaboration, and one of them declared that "the Balkans will never belong to the Balkan peoples as long as they do not reach a common understanding." A Rumanian document concluded that "the Balkan states as a *bloc* can pursue a common commercial policy on the basis of the preferential system." A study of the agricultural problem urged the creation of a permanent Balkan coöperative union, which would establish direct relations among the national coöperatives and concentrate both export and import of coöperative products in these organizations. Relations among agricultural countries could also be encouraged and developed through the creation of a Balkan chamber of agriculture, which had been suggested at the Istanbul Conference, and for which a Rumanian document provided a draft set of statutes. The creation of a permanent organization of economists into an association or academy for the purpose of studying economic questions was also advocated. Another interesting study, by M. Chiritzescu-Arva, of Bucharest, took the position that internal reorganization in agriculture was just as important as international coöperation. He therefore proposed action along three general lines—geographical rationalization with adaptation of products to soil and climate, economic rationalization on the basis of scientific research, and technical rationalization. Under the last heading the author indicated that the small Balkan farms were unable to take advantage either of technical machinery or of intensive scientific agriculture. Only by associating these small farms into large coöperative farms could the Balkan peasant meet competition from the United States and other overseas regions or from Soviet Russia. A Jugoslav memorandum studied the development of agricultural credit, one of the most serious issues in agricultural economics. Although it considered the establishment of a Balkan agricultural bank rather premature, it did propose that the entire problem be investigated thoroughly. It will be remembered that a similar proposal was embodied in the recommendations of the Stresa Conference.[31]

These scientific studies prepared the Economics Commission for its deliberations. The proposal for a customs union was discussed at some length. M. Popescu, in particular, emphasized that there were at least two serious difficulties in the establishment of a preferential tariff régime: homogeneity of production, and the probable loss of the possibility of treating with other countries *en bloc.* He proposed that commercial conventions be made "between the Balkan *bloc* on the one hand and the industrial states on the other." There was general agreement that the trade possibilities between the Balkan states and the rest of the world would have to be studied seriously.

Four main problems were on the agenda of the Commission on Communications: development of maritime communications and transport, including the creation of a Balkan maritime office at Istanbul; new projects for joining the railway routes of the Balkans; prolongation of railways by automobile highways; and aerial communications. Not much had been accomplished in the realm of communications, however. The postal convention, for example, had been accepted only by Greece and Turkey.[32]

The committee on land communications concluded that it would be desirable to proceed as soon as possible to the joining of railways and highways connecting the Balkan capitals by the building of bridges and railway junctions which would facilitate direct connection. This was true particularly of railway communications between Belgrade and Bucharest and between Bucharest and Sofia. The committee on maritime communications urged the establishment of a maritime section in the Chamber of Commerce to make a general study of the problem. The committee on aerial communications discussed the conclusion of a Balkan aerial convention and urged the calling of a conference of aerial experts in Sofia in 1933. The committee on tourist traffic urged that the Conference support the resolutions of the Balkan Tourist Federation, that some of the Carnegie funds be placed at its disposal, and that the Conference request the Balkan governments to facilitate Balkan athletic gatherings, student visits, and tourist traffic.[33]

The discussions in the Commission on Social Policy were especially significant and led to a number of important suggestions.[34] A special committee, appointed at Istanbul to study the convention on the status of Balkan citizens, had accepted a Greek draft as a basis of discussion in January, 1932. The Greek project, which was concerned with the rights of Balkan citizens to travel and live without hindrance in the various states of the peninsula, had been amended in four particulars: (1) the Balkan states were to retain the right to regulate migrations into their territories, though such regulations were not to apply to changes of individual residence; (2) Balkan nationals in other Balkan states were not to be permitted to acquire land where state constitutions did not permit noncitizens to do so; (3) reciprocity was definitely stipulated; and (4) the committee decided to "make the draft convention an integral part of the Balkan pact and the economic pact." The acceptance of the project, however, was not to be interpreted as extending the rights of Balkan citizens to those of any other country. Another central proposal on the development of a unified social policy closely related to this pact was the creation of a Balkan labor office, for which M. Svolos drew up a draft set of statutes. The general purposes of the labor office would be to publish labor statistics and to give market information and instructions on the movement of Balkan population. In order to coördinate the social policy of the

Balkan states, the labor office would draw up draft conventions, assist in the application of labor legislation, and propose and organize investigations on labor questions and social policy.[35]

The protection of women and children was also seriously studied. It was agreed on every hand that the protection of children was a problem for the state, one writer urging the necessity of preparing a general Balkan convention for their protection. The problem of the equality of women, which had been studied at both the First and the Second Conference, attracted considerable attention. Princess Cantacuzène's memorandum declared that "the Balkan Conference must consider the freedom of the wife and mother as an essential reform and give her the place which is due her in the family, society, and the state." The question was a particularly difficult one in Jugoslavia, where six different codes of law dealt with the subject of women.[36]

The problem of medical coöperation, especially through the establishment of a Balkan medical confederation, was also definitely studied in the memoranda presented to the Commission on Social Policy. A Rumanian document, outlining in some detail the project for a medical union, gave as the aim of the federation, "Balkan sanitary collaboration and the improvement of the individual sanitary conditions of the Balkan peoples." Permanent national committees would be organized in each country, and all these committees, in direct communication, would constitute the Balkan medical federation.[37]

The discussion of these proposals produced a great deal of controversy within the commission, for they all were peculiarly delicate. After a long debate on the proposed convention on the status of Balkan nationals, the Greek draft on that subject was finally adopted, with an amendment stipulating that its provisions would "bear no infringement on the recognized right of each of the contracting parties to regulate movement of population by law, upon the advice of the Balkan labor office." The commission, however, did not recommend the creation of a Balkan labor office, important though the institution was. That question was to be referred to the next Conference. The proposal for the establishment of a Balkan medical union was accepted, but only on the condition that it should function as an independent institution affiliated with the Balkan Conference.

After the formal opening of the second plenary session on October 26,[38] M. Papanastassiou advised the Conference that the Bulgarian delegation had withdrawn "in order to protest against the failure to adopt its proposition to adjourn the discussion and vote on the draft of the [political] pact." He said that the Political Commission and the Council had examined the Bulgarian proposal sympathetically, but had found acceptance of it impossible. As he pointed out, "the Conference is not in a position to assume responsibility for the attitude of the governments." Further, M. Papanastassiou felt that "the adoption of the Bulgarian proposition would mean the abandonment of the method employed since the creation of our organization and would signify the very negation of the aim of our Conference." He hoped that the Bulgarian group would see its way clearly to accept the statement which he had outlined. He was convinced that "the adoption of the pact would contribute much to the creation of mutual confidence among the Balkan peoples, which would be the most solid basis for their mutual understanding and collaboration."

The Conference was now ready to consider the reports and recommendations of its various commissions. The first series of resolutions to be presented were those of the Intellectual Commission. The *rapporteur*, M. Cantacuzène, in advocating the acceptance of the suggestions of his commission, stressed the close intellectual and mental affinities of the Balkan peoples. Particularly important were the proposals for the formation of a historical institute and the preparation of a history of Balkan civilization, in which the idea of Balkan unity was to be predominant. M. Cantacuzène concluded that the book, the press, the university, the conference room, the cinema, and the radio were "the factors, which, in our day, prepare the ground for diplomatic understandings. We believe that before military, must come intellectual disarmament." All these recommendations, some of which indeed were repetitions of previous resolutions at the Athens and Istanbul meetings, were adopted by the Conference.

The Conference then discussed and adopted certain proposals

of the Commission on Social Policy. The first of these was the Children's Charter, based on the model provided by the League of Nations, and stipulating the formation of a special department for the protection of children in all the Balkan countries. The Conference also accepted the recommendations relating to the legal status of women. It approved the suggestions concerning the traffic in women and children. The introduction of a system of feminine police was urged as a restrictive measure, and it was recognized that coöperation was a prime requisite for any effective action.

The report of the Commission on Communications came up for consideration at the opening of the third plenary session.[39] The resolution concerning the postal convention, already adopted by Turkey and Greece, was unanimously approved. The proposals concerning maritime, land, and air communications also were accepted by the Conference, though the absence of experts in these fields created difficulties in the technical execution of the projects involved.

Noticeable interest was shown in the statement of the Preparatory Commission of Jurists for the unification of Balkan law. The Belgrade conference on law had recommended eight subjects with which unification might begin : marriage, letters of exchange, money orders and checks, extradition, judicial assistance, desertion of family, execution of judgments, and foreign arrests. In order to facilitate the study of legal unification it was decided to make a collection of the existing Balkan laws on these subjects, and the commission also recommended exchanges of law students and jurists among the Balkan countries.[40]

As we have already seen, the Economics Commission had prepared an important set of definite recommendations,[41] of which the resolution on the customs union and economic collaboration was the most significant. The examination of economic and financial matters at the first two Balkan Conferences had prepared the way for more concrete proposals. The report now presented was based on principles already adopted at previous meetings : institution of a contingent preferential tariff to favor the exchange of Balkan products, and a concerted commercial policy. The commission expressed the wish that states having no commercial treaties ought to conclude them immediately, and invited the Council to appoint a committee to coöperate with the Chamber of Commerce in drawing up a multilateral treaty of commerce based on a preferential tariff and a common commercial policy. A special committee for the purpose of studying the unification of tariff nomenclature was also recommended. Although the meeting at Bucharest did not adopt a proposal for a customs union, it cleared the way for the acceptance of a draft convention on regional economic understanding at the Fourth Balkan Conference in the fall of 1933.

The Conference was ready to accept the establishment of a Balkan Chamber of Agriculture and the proposal for the organization of scientific agricultural institutes. The question of agricultural credit was another serious issue, but it was felt that despite the need for such credit, the question ought to be referred to a committee for further study. A final problem was that of the Balkan coöperative organization. The suggestion of the commission that consideration be given to the formation of a Balkan Coöperative Office was approved. The National Coöperative Office of Bucharest was to draft a constitution for this new institution.

The suggestion of the Commission on Social Policy for the creation of a Balkan Labor Office was placed on the agenda for the consideration of the next Conference, but the draft convention on the personal status of Balkan citizens was accepted. This convention governed the rights and privileges of Balkan citizens in countries other than those of national origin. The Conference agreed, however, that the draft should be made "an integral part of the Balkan pact and of the economic convention, and in any case ... the acceptance of this project by the participating parties could not be interpreted as implying, *ipso jure*, the extension to citizens of other countries of rights accorded ... to Balkan citizens."[42] The foundation of an independent medical union was also approved.

Certainly the most serious issue at Bucharest centered around the adoption of the political pact.[43] This problem had been studied ever since the First Conference and a pact, modified after the Istanbul meeting, had been prepared by M. Spiropoulos. As M. Spiropoulos declared in the beginning of his address: "This problem of the draft of a Balkan pact is, in the opinion of everyone, perhaps the most important question on the agenda of the Conference this year."

The draft pact provided for a system of conciliation and organized security in the Balkans based on the principles of the League of Nations, the Geneva Protocol of 1924, and the Locarno agreements. The contracting parties agreed, in the first place, "to make no attack or invasion, or to resort to war in no case against another contracting party," but to submit "all questions of whatever nature" to the processes of pacific settlement. At the instance of the Rumanian delegation it was agreed that the principle of the outlawry of war did not apply to legitimate defense or sanctions under the Covenant of the League of Nations. The second principle was that of pacific settlement of disputes through a Permanent Commission of Conciliation, to be composed entirely of Balkan nationals. Each contracting party was to have in this Commission two representatives but only one vote. If the Commission did not succeed in reaching a settlement of a difference submitted to it, the controversy was to be taken before the Permanent Court of International Justice. The old distinctions between justiciable and nonjusticiable disputes were abolished. Every difference which might arise was to be submitted to the procedure of conciliation and judicial settlement. There were to be two exceptions to this rule : the territorial *status quo,* and cases "which international law leaves to the exclusive competence of the parties" were not to be included. The exclusion of the territorial problem, however, was not to signify the permanence of the *status quo,* since nothing in the pact would prevent "modifications as a result of an agreement between interested parties." The third principle, that of mutual assistance, stipulated concerted action against a Balkan aggressor. Article 19 declared that if one of the contracting parties believed a violation of the pact had been committed, the question should be submitted immediately to the Council of the League of Nations. If the Council declared by a four-fifths majority, excluding the votes of the parties in dispute, that a violation had occurred or was occurring, it was to give an opinion to that effect, and each party was "obligated to offer its assistance to the power against which the criminal act has been directed."

A fundamental part of the pact dealt with the problem of minorities. To give protection to the minorities, each contracting party was to create an Office of Minorities to which petitions concerning the application of the treaties concerning minorities could be addressed. Moreover, a Balkan Commission of Minorities was to be created, composed of six members, one from each state, which would meet annually in turn in each of the signatory states. At the request of the Commission the Offices of Minorities were to submit to it the petitions addressed to them, for the Commission's examination and decision. The parties were pledged to accept any unanimous decision of the Commission. If there should be a difference of opinion within the Commission, that body was to transmit the *dossier* to the Secretariat of the League of Nations. It was further stipulated that "petitions concerning the protection of minorities must give expression to the free will of the interested populations. The minorities must conduct themselves loyally toward the state on whose territory they live and abstain from any action directed against the state." The parties themselves agreed "to take the measures necessary for preventing any kind of action likely to disturb the peace and good relations among the Balkan peoples."

A final set of provisions declared that the pact was not to infringe on existing agreements providing for pacific settlement of disputes. Appeal to the Permanent Court of International Justice was stipulated where such procedure was necessary. Moreover, Article 36 declared, ". . . no stipulation of the present pact can be interpreted as restraining the League of Nations from taking appropriate measures at any time for safeguarding the peace of the world." No part of the pact was to be interpreted as "violating the obligations arising from the *Covenant* of the League of Nations. . . ."

Such was the political pact as outlined by M. Spiropoulos, who declared in summary :⁴

The conclusion of a general pact of nonaggression, arbitration, and mutual assistance by our governments may lead to a series of other agreements, political as well as economic, no less important for the development of our relations. . . . Of course, the draft . . . was not accepted unanimously, the Bulgarian delegation having withdrawn from our commission and our Jugoslav friends having made some reservations concerning the protection of minorities, and that has tended to weaken somewhat the value of the results obtained. But it would be going to the other extreme to underestimate its importance. It is now for our governments to act. Let them do everything possible to conclude and crown the work which we have begun.

M. Jovanovich then arose to state once more the position of the Jugoslav delegation on the question of minorities. In his opinion "it would be preferable to leave to the competent diplomatic services the problem of formulating the procedure necessary to assure a more effective protection to the minorities." M. Jovanovich wished to present his views to the plenary assembly, but M. Papanastassiou pointed out that the Commission itself did not share the Jugoslav view. The Conference then adopted the political pact.

The draft Balkan Pact which was adopted by the Third Conference did not contain anything which was unique or new in the annals of international organization. All its component elements were based on well-known principles of international law. Its machinery for conciliation was modeled on the system of the League of Nations. But the adoption of the pact was significant. It did propose to establish purely Balkan commissions or offices for the settlement of strictly Balkan problems. And it contemplated a solution of that most delicate of all Balkan problems, the issue of minorities, in a moderate, conciliatory, and constructive manner. For the first time in Balkan history representatives of the Balkan peoples, though they were not representatives of governments, had adopted a political agreement which was to govern all the states of the peninsula in their mutual relations. The farsighted leaders in the movement toward Balkan friendship apparently had met the challenge to adopt a pact. Would the Balkan governments accept their handiwork?

THE ACCOMPLISHMENTS AT BUCHAREST

The final session of the Conference was held on October 27 and was given over to the concluding addresses of the members of the different delegations.[45] M. Pella, chairman of the Rumanian group, was none too hopeful as a result of the meeting. "No one would doubt," he said, "that our Conference has tried to take a step forward in the three great economic, intellectual, and political domains of Balkan coöperation." Some progress had been made in the intellectual and economic realms, but little in that of politics. He did feel that the Balkan Pact represented an advance, for it was a draft "which the governments will have to discuss while considering the complex conditions and the real problems which exist in this region of Europe." M. Konitza, of Albania, believed that the meeting had moved forward in the approval of the Pact. "If this Pact is approved by our governments and put into force, it will lay the foundations on which the peoples of the Balkans will build their common house." He regretted that the Bulgarians had not supported the propositions in the Pact concerning the minorities. "Bulgaria is not small enough to count on the indulgence and protection of the family of nations and it is not large enough to rely on its own strength. [And] let our Jugoslav friends permit me to say that they would be much more appreciated and liked if they were less intransigeant."

M. Papanastassiou, who had done more than any other to promote the Balkan Conferences, was the next speaker to bid farewell. He, too, very much regretted the Bulgarian action. But he had faith in the future, and particularly in the Balkan Pact.

It is our profound conviction that this draft of the Pact once realized will have laid the most solid foundation for dissipating every distrust and assuring our collaboration. It marks a notable progress on the question of the protection of the minorities by the introduction of a procedure completing the existing treaties.

He was astonished that, in view of the added guarantees, the Bulgarians had left the Conference, but he believed that they would renew their participation. Finally, he added:

I know that there are many obstacles along our route. But I trust that no one will be discouraged; the great purpose which unites us will give us strength to surmount all difficulties. The idea of the Balkan union is on the march and nothing can stop it.

Rushen Eshref Bey, of the Turkish group, referred to the interest of the Turkish Republic in the preservation of peace and unity. M. Jovanovich, president of the Jugoslav delegation, saluted the achievement of the Pact—"despite the reservations formulated and the differences of view which had arisen in the course of our discussions. . . ." These differences, he felt, were inevitable, but not insurmountable.

The final address came from M. Ciceo Pop, the retiring president. He felt that the Conference had taken great steps forward in the formulation of the Balkan Pact and in tracing the general lines of economic collaboration, especially in the project for a partial customs union. Moreover, it had adopted a draft on the status of Balkan citizens and a series of important resolutions in the intellectual field. "But it is not enough to speak in favor of peace and friendship of peoples. Peace and friendship must be organized. The Conference is convinced that the only way to reach the goal will be to conclude such conventions as it suggests on political understanding, economic collaboration, and the recognition of the equal rights of all the citizens of our countries." M. Pop was sorry that the Bulgarian group had withdrawn, but he believed with M. Papanastassiou that the adoption of the Pact "doubtless will facilitate the solution of the differences which yet divide our peoples, in establishing a spirit of mutual confidence in their relations." He, too, was convinced that the Bulgarians would return to the Conference.

On October 25 the Council decided to hold the next meeting of the Conference in Belgrade.[46] Two days later the final session of the Council was held, all the delegations being represented, including the Bulgarian group. Although reiterating its faith "in the necessity for close coöperation among the six Balkan countries," the Bulgarian group once more insisted that the Conference could arrive at a real Balkan pact only after having prepared the ground through direct negotiations between the parties and through bilateral agreements settling the outstanding difficulties among the Balkan states. The other delegations, however, continued to stress the urgent necessity of the pact, hoping that the Bulgarian delegation also would adhere to it, as it had been accepted by the other five delegations. Furthermore, they repeated their declaration that "they would do everything possible" to reach a satisfactory understanding with Bulgaria; in return, the Bulgarian group promised to do "everything possible to give its adherence to the Balkan Pact."

The Third Balkan Conference thus came to a close. Its career had been a very stormy one, with both the Bulgarian and the Jugoslav delegations assuming an intransigeant attitude. But it had achieved some progress, even if the governments had as yet taken no serious action in the directions pointed out. The Conference had adopted a Balkan Pact which opened a way to settle even the problem of minorities, and which provided the machinery for the peaceful settlement of all other questions. It had traced the general lines of a partial customs union and economic collaboration. And finally, the Conference had approved a draft convention on the status of Balkan citizens and laid the foundations for a Balkan medical union. Future developments toward definite confederation would have to be built on these economic, social, and political bases. Added to the other resolutions which had been adopted, these achievements constitute no mean advance in the direction of Balkan friendship and coöperation.[47]

NOTES TO CHAPTER IV

[1] A. Papanastassiou, "La Deuxième Conférence balkanique," *L'Esprit International*, No. 22 (April, 1932), 229–30. See also Ettore Rossi, "La seconda conferenza balcanica," *L'Europa Orientale*, Nos. 1–2 (January-February, 1932), 1–28.

[2] LB, Nos. 17–18, pp. 302–03.

[3] See especially League of Nations. *Records of the Conference for the Reduction and Limitation of Armaments. Series A. Verbatim Records of Plenary Meetings*, Vol. I. February 2nd–July 23rd, 1932. IX. Disarmament. 1932 IX. 60. (Geneva, 1932), 111–14, 128–31, 135–38, 149–50, 177–79.

[4] The Council minutes are in LB, Nos. 17–18 (February-March, 1932), 320–27.

[5] This committee included, among others, Hassan Husni Bey, chairman, M. Konitza, J. Sakazov, A. Papanastassiou, and J. Spiropoulos.

[6] The Albanian proposal called for a commission of government representatives, presided over by the presidents of the respective national groups, which would examine questions relative to the application of the minority and other provisions of the treaties. There was also to be a national commission in each state.

[7] LB, Nos. 17–18, pp. 322–23. A. Papanastassiou, *loc. cit.*

[8] The agenda for the Third Conference was: I. Regulations for procedure in the assembly and commissions. II. The Balkan pact. III. Statutes of the institute of historical research; elaboration of a manual of the history of Balkan civilization, translation of literary and dramatic works, use of film and radio. IV. Convention on general economic collaboration and customs union; coöperation in scientific research in agriculture, development of agricultural credit. V. Development of land and sea communications; building of railways, construction of roads, improvement of harbors, Balkan public works system. VI. Convention on personal status of Balkan nationals; Balkan labor office, children's charter, question of women, sanitary and veterinary convention, struggle against tuberculosis.

[9] LB, Nos. 17–18, pp. 324–25.

[10] *Ibid.*, 329.

[11] *Ibid.*, 330.

[12] LB, Nos. 19–20 (April-May, 1932), 370.

[13] See League of Nations. *Official Journal. Special Supplement No. 102. Records of the Special Session of the Assembly*. II. July, 1932 (Geneva, 1933), 17, 21–23.

[14] LB, Nos. 19–20, p. 380.

[15] The Balkan Chamber of Commerce and Industry now publishes a monthly *Bulletin*.

[16] The report of this meeting is in III CB, 17–20. A session of the *Conférence des tabacs d'Orient* was held in Istanbul, May 15–22, 1932.

[17] LB, Nos. 19–20, p. 380.

[18] LB, No. 21 (June, 1932), 407.

[19] See League of Nations. Commission of Enquiry for European Union. *Report by the Stresa Conference for the Economic Restoration of Central and Eastern Europe*, C. 666. M. 321. (Geneva, 1932.) See also Miloslav Matich, *L'Union danubienne d'un point de vue yougoslave* (Paris, 1933), 139–247.

[20] The complete minutes of the Third Conference are in *Journal de la IIIe Conférence balkanique* (Bucharest, 1932), *L'Indépendance Roumaine* (Bucharest), October 21–28, 1932, and LB, Nos. 1–2 (October-November, 1932), 70–199. III CB contains only the documents and the minutes for the opening and closing sessions.

[21] LB, III, Nos. 1–2, pp. 73–77. See also *L'Indépendance Roumaine*, October 24, 1932.

[22] LB, III, Nos. 1–2, pp. 86–88.

[23] *Ibid.*, 88–89.

[24] *Ibid.*, 89–98.

[25] *Ibid.*, 99–104.

[26] Cf. J. Spiropoulos and Reshid Bey, *Pacte balkanique* (Bucharest, 1932), and J. Spiropoulos, "Rapport sur le Pacte balkanique," III CB, 13–17.

[27] LB, III, Nos. 1–2, pp. 104–08.

[28] *Commission préparatoire interbalkanique de juristes*. I. Belgrade, June 11–13, 1932. II. Bucharest, October 22, 1932. (Mim.) The commission met again at the time of the Salonica Conference. See LB, VI (December, 1934), 786–96.

[29] See especially the reports of C. C. Giurescu and N. A. Constantinescu in III CB, 21–25, 25–35.

[30] Reports in III CB, 35–49. *Les Balkans* has published many translations of Balkan literary and dramatic works.

[31] Memoranda in III CB, 51–135. See also the two mimeographed reports of Dr. Cvetko Gregorich, *Sur la convention économique interbalkanique*, and Alexander Jovanovich, *La collaboration des pays balkaniques à l'étude scientifique des problèmes économiques* (Belgrade, 1932). Commission discussions, LB, III, Nos. 1–2, pp. 108–11.

[32] *Ibid.*, 111–16.

[33] Memoranda in III CB, 137–77. Mimeographed Jugoslav reports: Slavko Sirishchevich, *Le problème des communications aux pays des Balkans;* St. Josifovich, *Rapport sur les routes;* M. Trebinjach, *Rapport sur la communication fluviale* (Belgrade, 1932). See also A. Tibal, *Les communications dans l'Europe danubienne* (Paris, 1933).

[34] LB, III, Nos. 1–2, pp. 117–21.

[35] Memoranda in III CB, 179–94. See especially the reports of A. Svolos and G. Vladescu-Racoassa.

[36] Memoranda in III CB, 194–273. Mimeographed Jugoslav reports: Z. V. Markovich, *Le problème de la protection de l'enfant en Yougoslavie*, with annex; Vera Kichevats, *La législation se rapportant à la réglementation de la prostitution et à la traite des femmes et des enfants en Yougoslavie* (Belgrade, 1932).

[37] Memoranda in III CB, 273–302.

[38] LB, III, Nos. 1–2, pp. 122–37.

[39] *Ibid.*, 137–58.

[40] *Ibid.*, 139–40. See also G. Cassimatis, "Les traits généraux des droits positifs des pays balkaniques"; "Rapports soumis à la commission pour l'unification du droit par le groupe hellénique, le groupe turc et le groupe yougoslave sur les constitutions, le droit pénal, le droit civil et le droit commercial"; G. Cassimatis, "Sur l'unification des législations balkaniques—lettre de change, billet à l'ordre, chèque"; LB, No. 22 (June, 1932), 469–503; No. 24 (September, 1932), 693–94.

[41] LB, III, Nos. 1–2, pp. 140–46.

[42] *Ibid.*, 154–58. See the Appendix to the present work, Document IX.

[43] *Ibid.*, 146–53.

[44] See also Stevan Petrovich, *L'Union et la Conférence balkanique* (Paris, 1934), 82–203, and the brief comparative analysis in N. J. Padelford, *Peace in the Balkans* (New York, 1935), 49 ff., which appeared since this study went to press. For the text see below, Appendix, Document VIII.

[45] LB, III, 154–70.

[46] *Ibid.*, 170–71.

[47] For the resolutions and acts of the Third Conference see LB, III, Nos. 1–2, pp. 172–96; III CB, 347–72.

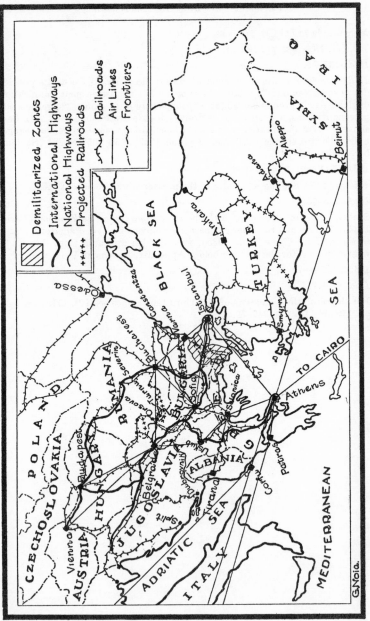

Map 4. Balkan and Near Eastern Communications.

Chapter V

ECONOMIC AND SOCIAL UNION

THE FOURTH BALKAN CONFERENCE (SALONICA, 1933)

THE FOURTH BALKAN CONFERENCE, scheduled to meet in the middle of September, 1933, at Salonica, was postponed on account of the inability of the national groups to reach satisfactory conclusions on certain problems. It was evident that the Conference had reached a crisis at Bucharest. Although that meeting had accepted drafts of a customs convention, of a pact on the personal status of Balkan citizens, and of a Balkan Pact, it had also witnessed an open break with the Bulgarian delegation, and even the Albanian group had threatened to bolt the movement if more tangible results should not be forthcoming by the fall of 1933. Furthermore, there were serious *lacunae* within the organization of the Balkan Conference. The weakest point was, of course, that the resolutions generally were not executed by the governments. This was true in the economic, social, and intellectual fields, as well as in the political. Again, the Conference often adopted resolutions without counting the cost, in money or in effort, of putting the measures into effect. In the third place, the memoranda submitted by the various groups were sent in so late as to preclude the careful study which they required. The national groups themselves were not so constituted as to give the best possible service to the idea of Balkan union in all its ramifications. Finally, while there were provisions for a permanent secretariat and a permanent headquarters, these actually did not exist. The immediate problems before the Balkan Conference were, therefore, those of repairing political fences, smoothing over the difficulties which had developed within the machinery of the Conference, and attempting to bring about tangible results.[1*]

THE LITTLE ENTENTE AND THE BALKAN CONFERENCE

The Council of the Conference, which had its special problems to solve, did not convene until the middle of March, 1933.[2] The first

* Superior figures refer to notes which will be found at the end of this chapter.

question to be considered was that of the practical application of the resolutions of the previous Conferences. M. Ciceo Pop, the president, stated in his opening remarks that in spite of all the difficulties, the people of the peninsula were deeply conscious of the fact that "their safety lies in their political and economic solidarity." He did not believe that the Balkan peoples could go back on the work accomplished by the Conferences "without compromising themselves, and without prejudicing at the same time their collective interests." But it was one thing to pass resolutions and quite another to carry them into action. All the delegations, consequently, pledged themselves to do everything to influence their governments to act on the resolutions of the Third Conference. M. Papanastassiou desired immediate application of these resolutions, even if only two governments were ready to proceed, especially in the three basic matters of the Balkan Pact, the customs union, and the convention on the personal status of Balkan citizens.

Another important issue concerned the holding of the next meeting. It was decided that the Fourth Conference, which was to have met in Belgrade, should convene in Salonica, which was situated centrally for most of the delegations. The major item on the agenda appeared to be the final adoption of a convention for regional economic understanding.[3]

To give satisfaction to the wishes of the Bulgarian group concerning bilateral discussions for the examination of differences among the Balkan countries, three meetings were held, one at Bucharest and the other two at Sofia. At Sofia both the Greek and the Turkish group conferred with the Bulgarians and reached a decision, on March 21, to work toward the improvement of their mutual relations and toward the practical application of the wishes of the Conferences. A meeting between the Jugoslav and Bulgarian groups in Bucharest, however, reached no general agreement.

Since there had been some misgivings about the effect on the Balkan Conference of the consolidation of the Little Entente on February 16, 1933, Jugoslavia and Rumania being members, M. Papanastassiou asked the representatives of those countries to explain their position. The Council accepted their assurances that the new development did not change the political direction of their

NICOLAE TITULESCU
Minister of Foreign Affairs of Rumania

countries in respect to the Balkan movement and that "the new pact of the Little Entente [did] not constitute any obstacle to the political *rapprochement* pursued by the Conference." It was believed, in fact, that with their experience in the Little Entente, Rumania and Jugoslavia "could contribute much to the realization of the Balkan idea." In his valedictory, M. Pop declared that the Little Entente could only "rejoice in our action" and see in the proposed Balkan Pact "an eminently peaceful factor." M. Pop was confident that even the troublesome question of the minorities could be solved. Moreover, in view of the pressing international crises in European politics, he was happy to declare that "important Bulgarian statesmen are persistently working for Bulgar-Jugoslav understanding."

The meetings of the Council closed with a dinner given by M. Titulescu, the Rumanian foreign minister, at which the Balkan diplomatic representatives were present. In the course of his address M. Titulescu declared that the pact of the Little Entente "is only a defensive agreement and is not at all of a nature to prevent the realization of the Balkan union."[4]

THE POSTPONEMENT OF THE CONFERENCE

Events on the larger stage of world politics, which were to prove determining factors in the Balkan scene, were also delaying the calling of the Balkan Conference. Apparently a policy of watchful waiting was to be pursued. The advent of Adolph Hitler in Germany produced a tremendous reaction all over Europe and had a direct bearing on the consolidation of the Little Entente.[5] The continued failure of the Geneva Arms Conference and the breakdown of the London Economic Conference were other contributing factors in the Balkan maladjustment. The London meeting, however, did see a certain unity of action on the part of the Balkan states, which participated in an agrarian *bloc*.[6] At London, too, Soviet Russia showed signs of returning to the European polity and of playing an increasing part in Central European and Balkan affairs, as exemplified in the treaties of July 3–5, 1933, in which Turkey, Jugoslavia, and Rumania participated, and which gave guarantees for preservation of the territorial *status quo*.[7]

While the London Conference was in session, the Commission on Communications of the Balkan Conference held a meeting in Sofia (June 15–17) and adopted a program calling for the construction of highways, bridges, and railways in the Balkan peninsula. Somewhat later, September 11–13, the first meeting of the Balkan Medical Union was held in Belgrade, and an important series of discussions about Balkan medical problems was held.[8] In these fundamental matters the work of the Balkan Conference was proceeding without interruption.

In the Balkan region itself there was feverish diplomatic activity. The political maneuvers which were to lead to the signature of the Four-Power Balkan Pact of February 9, 1934, had already begun.[9]

The fact that the Fourth Conference did not meet until November 5, 1933, was not of serious consequence. The delay in meeting made it possible for the national groups to watch the trend of events in European and Balkan diplomacy, and enabled the leaders to conciliate restive elements.[10] When at last the Conference did open, the delegations were prepared for very effective work.

The Council held its opening session on November 4, with M. Papanastassiou as president, since the Conference once more was assembling on Greek soil, at Salonica. Almost immediately the question of minorities arose when M. Jovanovich, of the Jugoslav delegation, challenged the timeliness of mentioning "especially the minorities [on the agenda], since those resolutions are not the only ones which have not been applied." It was well, he thought, "not to place too much emphasis on questions which are irritating." Naturally, M. Sakazov, of the Bulgarian group, could not agree, for he pointed out that the question was of peculiar importance to the Bulgarian group, and his delegation had returned to the Conference only "on the condition that all the differences which prevent *rapprochement* among the Balkan peoples be examined." The Jugoslav delegate did not take specific exception to these remarks, and the Council passed to the question of the modification of the statutes of the Conference—a problem which was to assume significance in these sessions. On the proposal of the president, the Council decided to charge the Legal Commission with the study of the unification of consular conventions. It also agreed that the problem of a Chamber of Agriculture should be studied by the Economics Commission and referred to the Fifth Conference.[11]

THE LARGER PROSPECTS OF THE CONFERENCE

At the first plenary session of the Conference it was apparent that there was a greater optimism for the future than had been true in the past.[12] M. Papanastassiou sounded the note of hope and enthusiasm in his address of welcome:

These meetings will lead to the signature of identical protocols, according to the terms of which the groups assume the obligation to do everything possible for the application, in their respective countries, of all the resolutions of these Conferences, in order to bring about an early settlement of economic, political, and financial differences between their countries, and the general *rapprochement* of all the Balkan peoples.

Although the Balkan Conferences were unofficial, and although many of the resolutions had never been executed, the president saw a good omen in the fact that "outside this movement, another official Balkan movement of considerable importance, which has its source in our own organization, has been outlined in the course of this year." Furthermore, the Greco-Turkish agreement which had been signed within recent weeks was an auspicious sign in the direction of Balkan good will. Nevertheless, M. Papanastassiou recognized that these events did not institute "a systematic collaboration of all the Balkan peoples" and "could not be compared to a multilateral Balkan political pact, such as the draft elaborated by our Conference." The speaker concluded by alluding to the general failure of the Conference to bring about the periodical meetings of the Balkan foreign ministers. He was not unaware of the problems yet to be solved. "Certainly the task which we have undertaken is arduous. But our faith, the faith which moves mountains, will help us to surmount all obstacles."

The speakers who followed were hardly less enthusiastic. M. Maximos, the Greek foreign minister, expressed his hope for "the most brilliant success" of the meeting. Dr. Natsi, of the Albanian group, was gratified at the recent diplomatic events in the Balkans. He felt that "the aim pursued by the Conference is to form a *bloc* which would assure all the Balkan frontiers against any eventual aggression coming from a member of the Balkan family or from the outside"—the European situation, however, looked very black to him, and he did not believe that "fine speeches and half-measures can change this situation." M. Sakazov affirmed that "governmental policy has already advanced some steps toward the idealistic program which we are pursuing." In the opinion of the Turkish leader, Hassan Husni Bey, the ideal of the Conferences was not to constitute "an aggressive *bloc,* or a factitious and precarious alliance of the governments, but an intimate union of the nations, seeking only their safety and prosperity in a mutual understanding." "We live at a time," he said, "when more than ever we need peace. The Balkan states are doing everything to assure peace in a definite manner; therefore, all our understandings . . . must be based on a political understanding." M. Jovanovich, of Jugoslavia, reëchoed the sentiment of union :

> The Balkans must remain for the Balkan peoples. But to attain this end we must not occupy ourselves with questions in which agreement appears difficult, not to say impossible, but must deal with those which facilitate *rapprochement.* The Jugoslav group . . . is entirely devoted to the study of questions of a social, cultural, and economic order. . . . The first step would be the establishment of commercial relations. . . . The second would be a partial customs convention.

Beyond that M. Jovanovich would not go, of course, for such had been the position of his delegation since the inception of the movement. But it is fair to say that a spirit of enthusiasm and tolerance was to pervade the atmosphere of the Conference as it moved into the more serious work of deliberating on the problems which confronted it.

THE CONFERENCE AT WORK

The various commissions of the Fourth Conference began their discussions on November 6. The primary concern of the Political Commission, under M. Pella, of Rumania, was to study the application of principles already formulated by the three previous Conferences, particularly the resolutions calling for periodical meetings of the foreign ministers and the official adoption of the Balkan Pact.[13] Although the importance of such a procedure was recognized, M. Sakazov expressed the fear that such meetings would be in large measure academic. In his view it was "impossible to develop the idea of Balkan understanding without a previous settlement of differences"; he therefore proposed "the meeting of the ministers of foreign affairs by groups of two states, the states interested in the questions to be examined." But the other delegations did not approve the suggestion, which was similar to the Bulgarian proposals at the other Conferences. M. Pella believed that the difficulties of which the Bulgarian leader had complained could best be solved through the meetings of all the Balkan ministers in common council. M. Sakazov, however, stood his ground, declaring that

bilateral meetings are more practical. We Bulgarians are of this opinion because Bulgaria is not in the same situation as the other Balkan countries. We do not have disputes with all the Balkan states and what interests us especially is the solution of the differences which divide us from certain countries.

He was willing to accept the Pella compromise, which provided for bilateral agreements within the larger Balkan organization, a position which met with M. Papanastassiou's approval.

In the discussion of the Balkan Pact, M. Sakazov reiterated the Bulgarian reservations to the Bucharest project, particularly on the solution of pending questions and the problem of minorities. There were also reservations relating to Chapter IV of the Pact on the technical procedure in the settlement of the minorities question and on the issue of the equality of the Balkan states. M. Sakazov repeated that "in certain respects all the Balkan states are not equal. So long as this is true we cannot adhere to the Balkan Pact." M. Papanastassiou, however, objected that these reservations were not well founded "because the draft of the Pact is based on the absolute equality of the six countries and consequently one cannot justly formulate any complaint of inequality in connection with the Pact." The Jugoslav group accepted the principles embodied in the document, "including those concerning minorities." Reservations on Chapter IV referred only to "the procedure to be followed."

The major work of the commission, M. Pella thought, was in the assertion of the principles of a multilateral agreement. Since Turkey, Rumania, and Jugoslavia had signed the convention of London with Soviet Russia relative to the definition of an aggressor, M. Pella declared that "the provisions of this convention ought to be introduced into the [Balkan] Pact." The Greek delegation, however, objected on the ground that such action would lead to dissensions in the Conference, particularly with the Bulgarians. M. Pella's proposition had to be referred to the Council, which was called into special session.

At the Council meeting the Bulgarian group again raised the minorities issue, but agreed to make no mention of its reservations if the Council should decide to create a special commission for adapting the draft pact and especially the provisions concerning minorities. This proposition was not accepted. Finally, it was agreed that the commission should renew its approval of the pact unanimously, the Bulgarian delegation merely "repeating its declarations concerning the equality of states and the protection of minorities."

At the last session of the Political Commission on November 9, it was decided to support the proposal for periodical meetings of the Balkan foreign ministers and to ask the governments "to conclude a multilateral pact based on the principles of the draft adopted by the Third Conference." The Bulgarian group was to present its reservations on the floor of the Conference.

The major issue before the Commission on Economic Relations was the convention for a regional customs union. This problem had been studied thoroughly ever since the beginning of the Conferences, and now, apparently, the delegates at Salonica were prepared to take definite action. M. Simonides, a member of the Superior Economic Council of Greece, had prepared a memorandum and a draft convention for a customs union, in which he laid down the general and specific principles on which he thought such a union should be based. He believed that the Balkan states should adopt a preferential quota system in their reciprocal economic relations. The Rumanian delegation, too, was interested in this problem, and several memoranda pointed out the difficulties involved. The road toward a regional agreement would be a long and hard one. Dr. Florin Codrescu's study concluded that communications would have to be greatly improved and that it would be necessary "to establish through common agreement direct tariffs for all articles, the exchange of which can be facilitated among the Balkan countries." All the writers were agreed that the anarchy in commercial relations would have to be ended if prosperity were to come to the peninsula.[14] M. I. Sakazov wrote:

> The formation of the Balkan agrarian *bloc* is necessitated by the fact that the agricultural crisis in the Balkan states has actually attained its paroxysm; and aggravation of the present situation is a great danger for the existing economic and legal order. This situation imposes very heavy responsibilities which rest entirely on the governments themselves. . . . In the west it is still felt that the industrialization of the Balkan agricultural countries is an abnormal and useless phenomenon, and for this reason customs barriers are raised in those countries. However, in the present state of agricultural production, none of the Balkan countries can permit the luxury of allowing free entry to the industrial products of the west.

Agricultural credit, in which the Balkan states were very weak, attracted serious attention. One excellent study, by M. Alivisatos, of Greece, stressed the fact that the problem of credit was intimately intertwined with all the fundamental questions of agriculture. To solve the problem, he proposed, among other things, the unification of the credit system in all the Balkan countries, the enlargement of the coöperative base, the organization of state agricultural insurance, the use of deposits in national agricultural credit institutions, and the unification and simplification of the legal rules regulating agricultural credit. Finally, he suggested the creation of a permanent Balkan council to coördinate all these activities. Certainly these were definite and important suggestions of far-reaching significance. A Bulgarian memorandum declared that sufficient credit was "a condition necessary to the development and prosperity of agriculture in the Balkans." Bulgaria, with its facilities centered in the Agricultural Bank, it was contended, had gone farther in this direction than the other countries.[15]

The question of coöperatives was studied in some detail. One writer emphasized that there were already more than 17,000 coöperative organizations in the Balkan region, and urged the creation of a coöperative office of the countries of Central and Balkan Europe. In accordance with the recommendations of the Third

Conference, the Rumanian delegation drew up a set of statutes for a Balkan Coöperative Office, which would compile statistics, publish a bulletin, and assist in the exportation of coöperative products.[16]

All these studies were thoroughly discussed in the Economics Commission.[17] The first problem considered was that of the customs union. In a formal statement for the Turkish delegation, M. Midhat Bey declared that "Balkan commerce must be regulated by principles of a close collaboration within a partial customs union or even a complete one." For economic relations with the outside world "a common policy" was necessary. M. Codrescu indicated that the Rumanian delegation could accept the idea of preferential tariffs, but would have to prepare a memorandum on quotas. The Jugoslav, Turkish, Greek, Bulgarian, and Albanian groups were ready to accept the system of preferential tariffs.

After continued discussion in the session of November 7, the Bulgarian delegation presented a declaration on the customs union :

The Bulgarian delegation renews its declaration ... accepting in principle the idea of a Balkan customs union, but it regrets not being able even to enter into the discussion of the project ... before the previous conclusion ... of bilateral treaties of commerce on the basis of preferential tariffs.... Consequently, the Bulgarian delegation expresses the desire that its wishes for an early conclusion of bilateral commercial treaties as well as the expected settlement of all the economic differences among the Balkan countries be mentioned in a special resolution of the plenary session....

This was similar to the Bulgarian attitude concerning the political pact, and it was not viewed with favor by the other national groups. The discussion continued in the afternoon, with important differences of opinion developing between the Greek and Jugoslav delegates. The Jugoslav delegation objected to any kind of permanent economic commission as the supreme organ of the union "which would infringe the national sovereignty." Later the idea of a permanent body was accepted, provided its functions should be purely "advisory." At the final session on November 9, the project of the customs union, based primarily on the Greek and Jugoslav drafts, was approved.

The convention for a regional economic understanding, like the political pact adopted at Bucharest, was a document of fundamen-

tal importance.[18] It was based on the desire to develop exchange of
Balkan products among the Balkan countries and to promote cooperation for the protection of Balkan commerce in the markets of
the world. The contracting parties were to grant mutual most-
favored-nation treatment in their tariff arrangements. A system
of quotas was to be arranged, subject to revision as conditions demanded. Moreover, "special treatment and preferential rights"
were to be granted with respect to articles which "are particularly
necessary in their national economies." Special arrangements were
to be made for products which were not included in the preferential system and for merchandise under the control of a state monopoly or *Régie*. Provision was also to be made for the unification of
tariff nomenclature and customs formalities. Article 8 provided
particularly for the development of a common economic policy
and the protection and promotion of Balkan products on the markets of the world. The signatory states, for instance, agreed to "combine their efforts for the most effective protection and defense of
their foreign exports, in order to assure the largest possible outlet
of the principal products of the Balkan countries." Before concluding a commercial treaty with an extra-Balkan state, the signatories were to proceed to a mutual exchange of views. They were,
moreover, pledged to consider in common "the practical measures
to be adopted" for concerted action for the protection of their principal products. The contracting parties also agreed to offer mutual
assistance "to facilitate the export of their products abroad by
assuring them free and direct transit under the best conditions, on
the basis of equality of treatment."

Perhaps the most important section of the convention (Articles
9–11) was that which set up a Permanent Balkan Commission for
International Commerce. The Permanent Commission was to be
made up of three delegates from each signatory state, the presidency to be filled annually in turn by the first delegate of each of
the signatory parties. The Commission was to be set up for the
purpose of assembling the necessary documents and of advising
concerning the means of encouraging the foreign commerce of the
signatories, and especially their mutual trade. Acting on its own
initiative, on the proposal of the national groups of the Balkan

Conference, or on the request of one of the participating parties, the Permanent Commission was to examine questions concerning the commercial relations of the Balkan countries, especially with respect to the application of preferential treatment and the coördination of their commercial policies, to draw up advisory opinions, and to formulate concrete proposals. The primary task of the Commission was to advise concerning the means of eliminating the obstacles to intra-Balkan trade and to advance the economic coöperation of the Balkan countries. In this connection it would submit proposals to the governments of the participating states for treaties and other measures for the development of the national economies and the improvement of mutual commercial relations. In order primarily to provide for the transition period, a Chamber of Compensations for the International Commerce of the Balkan Countries was to be created within the Permanent Commission.

The Balkan regional economic convention was to be of unlimited duration. It could be denounced after a trial period of two years, after a previous notice of twelve months.

Few matters were brought before the Intellectual Commission which had not been discussed before, and neither the memoranda nor the discussions in the commission went beyond the reassertion of previous suggestions.[19] This was likewise true of the Commission on Communications. A large number of studies had been presented to it, emphasizing the general necessity for improvement in railway and highway communications. All were agreed that there was much to be done, and that relatively little had been accomplished by the Conferences. Technical and financial considerations, as a matter of fact, prevented any real achievement in this realm until the governments themselves were definitely prepared to act.[20]

Several important matters confronted the Commission on Social Policy, and it was prepared to make some definite recommendations.[21] Among the memoranda on social questions those on sanitary and medical issues were especially interesting. Dr. Vayanos, of Greece, for example, presented an excellent study on a program of rural hygiene, in which he contended that "rural hygiene must be based on effective medical assistance and the creation of health centers . . . analogous to those in Jugoslavia." Another document stressed the necessity of a thorough, simple, and unified system of social insurance throughout the peninsula. A third memorandum, by Dr. Akil Mukhtar Bey, was concerned with the Balkan Medical Union, founded by the Third Conference. He believed that the union ought to center its attention on the publication of sanitary information and the exchange of physicians and students. The most important immediate problem before the commission was the formation of a Balkan labor office, the establishment of which had been recommended at Bucharest. A draft of statutes for this office had been prepared by MM. A. Svolos and A. Zaccas, of Greece, but the Jugoslav delegation was opposed to it. One Jugoslav study declared that the establishment of the office was not "of such an urgent nature," and that the governments would not be "disposed to assure the financing of the different organizations which we are creating." After some discussion in the commission, however, the draft for the creation of a Balkan labor office was approved. A subcommittee was to be created for the study of veterinary questions.

Very significant were the projects which were examined by the Organization and Legal Commission.[22] One of the new proposals accepted by the commission was embodied in a study by M. Spiropoulos, of Greece, who suggested that inasmuch as there were "no special consular conventions among the Balkan nations," one ought to be drawn up for all the countries of the peninsula. A general consular convention would work toward closer political and economic relations.

But the problem which was to bring about much future thought and discussion in the circles of the Conference was that which concerned the fundamental nature of the organization. In behalf of the Jugoslav delegation, which more than once had shown its displeasure with the trends of the Balkan Conference, Dr. A. Novakovich presented a memorandum with a systematic plan for a complete reorganization of the Conference.[23] He moved in his report that the Conference henceforth be called the "Union for Balkan Understanding," and that the national groups simply become "Associations for Balkan Understanding." The delegations would be chosen by members of the associations, and persons and organizations pursuing aims contrary to those of the Union would be excluded from the associations. All decisions of the Union would have to be *unanimous*. The general effect of these changes would apparently be to weaken the structure of the edifice which had been built up in the period since 1930. This was pointed out in a memorandum by M. Papanastassiou, who favored keeping the Conference on an unofficial basis, but desired that the membership, in large part, come from parliamentary bodies.[24] He was opposed to the Jugoslav proposal dealing with unanimity in voting because the Conference was not an official body and the principle of unanimity would have prevented many of its decisions. Moreover, it would block future action. M. Papanastassiou summed up :

> If the Novakovich project were accepted it would have the effect of giving the Conference an entirely private character which would weaken its authority. . . . Experience has proved that it is necessary to modify the statutes of the Conference, but these modifications must take place in such a way that the authority of the Conference will be enhanced. This can be attained if the Conference acquires a more parliamentary character, while not excluding the participation and activity of persons outside parliament. Otherwise, if the decisions of the Conference are not rapidly applied, we incur the risk of greatly lowering the prestige of the Conference. Consequently, the greatest participation of parliaments and members of parliaments, which represent their peoples, is necessary.

M. Papanastassiou was supported by the two Rumanian delegates, MM. Raducanu and Pella. M. Popovich, however, moved that the Conference proceed to the study of the Jugoslav proposal, which contained "practical ideas," but the motion was opposed by the Hellenic group. M. Papanastassiou very pointedly remarked that the proposal was "not at all reconcilable with his own proposal to give the Conference a more parliamentary and more official character." Finally, a committee was appointed which formulated the following acceptable resolution :

> The commission believes that the statutes of the Conference ought to be revised in order to assure as large a participation as possible to parliamentary members within the national groups and in the Conferences. The Council is charged to constitute a committee for the revision in order to give effect to this decision. Consequently, the project submitted by the Jugoslav delegation, as well as any other proposed amendments to the statutes, will be sent to the said committee.

THE CONFERENCE COMPLETES ITS LABORS

The Conference was now ready to consider the recommendations of its commissions. At its second plenary session, on November 9,[25] it adopted the suggestions of the Commission on Intellectual Relations dealing with language instruction, the Balkan Week, and collaboration of Balkan athletic associations. The next item of importance was the adoption of the program for the development of a sanitary convention and a multilateral veterinary agreement. The Assembly also decided to study a project for rural hygiene. The next session saw the approval of the report on communications.

As was natural, the endorsement of the suggestions and recommendations of the Political Commission occasioned much comment and some controversy. M. Maccas, who served as the *rapporteur* of that body at the third session,[26] admitted that the labors in this field had not been "as fruitful as those of certain other commissions." He did note, however,

that in the political field the official diplomatic movement lately has been very active in the Balkan Peninsula and that it is inspired by the ideal of our Balkan Conferences—so much so that we can take pride that we have really been the precursors of the present diplomatic movement. It is our duty to coördinate and generalize this official Balkan movement, to give it that character of Balkan universality which is yet lacking, perhaps, and which is at the basis of our political work.

M. Maccas then presented the resolutions calling for the periodical meetings of the Balkan foreign ministers and the conclusion of the multilateral pact among the Balkan states, both of them propositions as old as the Conference. He recalled both the Jugoslav and the Bulgarian reservation concerning the political pact which had been adopted at Bucharest. It was suggested that the Greek government might facilitate matters by calling the Balkan foreign ministers together. M. Aurel Cosma, of Rumania, reminded the Conference that the Balkan Pact

must be based on respect for all the national interests of each participating country. The structure of this Balkan Entente must satisfy the aspirations of the Balkan peoples and must harmonize the general interests of the peninsula with the special interests of all the contracting states.

M. Sakazov declared that the proposed resolutions did not satisfy the Bulgarian group:

The Bulgarian delegation, relying on the principles of nonaggression, pacific settlement of international conflicts, and mutual assistance, accepts a Balkan Pact under the following reservations:

(1) The recognition of the principle of full legal equality for Bulgaria in its relations with the other Balkan states.

(2) The loyal and integral application of the provisions of the clauses of the minority treaties assuring the Bulgarian minorities in the Balkan countries full and complete legal, moral, and cultural protection.

In making these reservations M. Sakazov asserted that the Bulgarian group remained faithful to the ideals of the Conference. M. Papanastassiou was satisfied with the Bulgarian declaration, but believed that the proposed pact itself was a good compromise and a decisive step toward the solution of Balkan problems. This likewise was the position of M. Pella, of Rumania, who was convinced that the pact would "contribute to the disappearance of the moral frontiers which separate our peoples." Finally, both the political resolutions were accepted in unanimity, since the Bulgarian group was content with a declaration of reservations.

As the third session came to a close, the Conference adopted the report of the Legal Commission providing for a study of changes in the constitution and statutes of the organization. The project for the establishment of a Balkan labor office, proposed by the Commission on Social Policy, was also approved.

The next plenary session continued the discussion of social policy and adopted the report on female labor.[27] The Assembly also approved the suggestions of the Economics Commission which called for the establishment of a Balkan coöperative office and the adoption of the draft convention on economic collaboration.

THE SIGNIFICANCE OF THE FOURTH BALKAN CONFERENCE

The work of the Conference at Salonica now drew to a close. The final session was held on November 11.[28] In summing up the achievements of the Fourth Balkan Conference, M. Papanastassiou, the retiring president, declared:

Our agreement on political *rapprochement* and the respective resolutions, adopted in unanimity, would be sufficient to give this Conference an exceptional place in the series of Conferences. Our resolution on economic coöperation proves what a forward step we have taken here at Salonica. The other resolutions are no less important. . . . Moreover, we have noted among the delegates this time a greater proportion of high state functionaries and parliamentary members. We rejoice in the presence of a larger number of parliamentary members, for our ambition is to become, little by little, a true parliament of the Balkan peoples. . . . Our satisfaction is also greater this time because the Balkan governments have felt the necessity of following the road which we have outlined.

The feeling that much had been accomplished was echoed in the speeches of other members. M. Natsi, of Albania, declared that his government was desirous "of seeing the union of our countries accomplished . . . and would be happy to enter into contact with the other governments if they are animated by the same thought."

M. Sakazov, who led the Bulgarian group, said:

This Conference has been the most fruitful of all. Our aim is broad; it is to unite six peoples who have a great past, so full of differences, into a political and economic union. . . . We have now collaborated, we Bulgarians, in all the labors of the commissions. If we have obtained much in all the commissions, let us recognize that in political matters we remain somewhat behind. However, we must strive to succeed in this domain. . . . Let us hope that in the interval before the Fifth Conference public opinion in our countries will be sufficiently prepared for satisfactory solutions in the political realm. The ground will then be entirely ready to raise the edifice of federation, of Balkan union.

Other speeches expressed much the same sentiment of enthusiasm and hope. M. Pella, of Rumania, declared that his country would "give its loyal and unlimited collaboration to the efforts of the Balkan Conferences." M. Mihailovich, of Jugoslavia, was no less sanguine concerning the achievements:

Like masons of the great common edifice of economic coöperation in the Balkan countries . . . , we have laid solid foundations, and have built the first floor of this monumental structure. The foundation is the application of the most-favored-nation treatment for all those of our countries which do not yet have regular economic relations. But we have not rested, we have gone further . . . , we have opened the possibilities for preferential treatment for the purpose of favoring a wider exchange of our Balkan products. A permanent commission of experts, named by our governments, will be formed to study and assemble the documents on all questions of our common commercial policy, and in a short period of time we hope to be able to put the roof on this new building: The Balkan Customs Union.

In closing it was announced that the next meeting would be held in Belgrade. Finally, a message to the Balkan peoples declared: "Our supreme duty is to advance still more quickly in that direction which illumines the ideal of the complete union of the six Balkan nations."

The achievements of the Fourth Balkan Conference mark it as the most successful of the meetings which had thus far been held. This was true both in the realm of the spirit and in the domain of the resolutions which were adopted. The Bulgarian delegation returned to labor in the movement, and the meetings were conducted in a broad spirit of tolerant give-and-take. In the practical aspects of the measures which the Conference sanctioned, the delegates adopted principles which seem to lead concretely into the fundamental issues of Balkan unity. The resolutions dealing with intellectual problems had reëmphasized the necessity of preparing the mental and moral background for a really vital sentiment of Balkan friendship and federation. The decisions relative to communications not only stressed the improvement and perfection of railways and highways, but also called for the definite creation of a maritime section in the Balkan Chamber of Commerce and Industry, which was already doing effective work in the economic sphere. The resolutions on social policy took concrete form in the decision to establish a Balkan labor office, with a draft set of statutes already adopted. Further, the Conference urged the study of the problem of rural hygiene and fostered the idea of a general Balkan sanitary and veterinary convention. It also advocated special protection for women in industry, and gave its support to the general principle that women should be placed on an equal basis with men in social and economic life.

The Conference was prepared, after four years of labor, to study its constitution with the prospect of strengthening its membership by including more parliamentarians and more officials. This problem was to confront the next Conference. Provision had also been made for examining the question of the adoption of a uniform Balkan consular convention.

The economic decisions were more precise and definite, for the Conference approved the draft agreement providing for general economic coöperation, and ultimately for a Balkan customs union. The project for a Balkan coöperative office had been accepted, with the expressed wish that agricultural credit be facilitated through the establishment of agricultural banks. A final provision dealing with Balkan agriculture and international commerce

TEVFIK RUSHDI BEY
Minister of Foreign Affairs of Turkey

looked toward a revalorization of agricultural products through the creation of a common front, and toward the completion of the Balkan commercial treaty structure. The resolutions in the economic realm stand out as the most important achievements of the Fourth Conference.

The political recommendations reaffirmed the necessity for periodical meetings of the foreign ministers; and more important, they restated approval of the draft Balkan Pact. Moreover, the Bulgarian delegation, far from disapproving the idea of a political accord, contented itself with a declaration of reservations designed only to remove the obstacles in the path of full coöperation.

It has been suggested that the Balkan Conferences were pointing the way toward Balkan union along three fundamental lines— political, social, and economic union. By the end of the Fourth Conference, the outlines of a possible future federation were becoming increasingly clear in these essential directions. The real issue now had become: Would the Balkan governments follow the lead of the Balkan Conferences? An answer to this question will be indicated in the pages which follow.

NOTES TO CHAPTER V

[1] See M. Papanastassiou's statement in *Méssager d'Athènes*, November 7, 8, 9, 1932, and his account of the Third Conference in *Vers l'Union balkanique*, 123–45.

[2] The minutes of the Council, March 17–20, 1933, are in LB, III, 542–55.

[3] The agenda was as follows: I. Modification of the statutes; model statutes for the national groups. II. Application of the resolutions of the preceding conferences, including those concerning minorities; unification of consular conventions. III. Instruction in Balkan languages; the Balkan Week; creation of a subcommittee for coöperation of physical and athletic educational organizations. IV. Draft convention for Balkan economic coöperation; statutes of the maritime section of the Balkan Chamber of Commerce; agricultural questions—agriculture credit, Balkan agriculture and world commerce, chambers of agriculture, draft statutes of the Balkan coöperative office. V. Improvement of civil aviation; constitution of a program of highways connected with international highways; revision of conclusions of previous conferences on land, sea, and air communications, and tourist traffic. VI. Statutes of the Balkan labor office; sanitary and veterinary conventions; protection of female labor. Rural hygiene.

[4] LB, III, 554–55. M. Papanastassiou made a similar statement in the *Méssager d'Athènes*, March 23, 1933, declaring: "For a moment the pact of the Little Entente caused the fear that Rumania and Jugoslavia were abandoning the effort for Balkan union. But this fear was dissipated. The Jugoslav and Rumanian delegations, and the Rumanian minister of foreign affairs, with all his great authority, gave the assurance that the pact of the Little Entente, which is a world organism for the safeguarding of peace, does not prevent these two countries in any way from participating in the Balkan movement, and that the Rumanian government is resolved to work more actively for the idea of the Balkan union." M. Papanastassiou was also impressed that "in Bulgaria the ground is more favorable to the *rapprochement* of the Balkan peoples." He concluded: "It is time that the governments, which have been so prodigal in good words, pass to acts. That is what the Balkan peoples expect. They wish nothing more ardently than to have peace assured and to create more favorable economic conditions, a thing which the coöperation of the six peoples alone can guarantee." See also Papanastassiou, *Vers l'Union balkanique*, 144–45, 149–63.

[5] This discussion is continued more in detail in the next chapter, which deals with the Balkan Pact of February 9, 1934.

[6] See the statement of Dr. Beneš in *L'Echo de Belgrade*, June 21, 1933.

[7] Cf. Mabel S. Ingalls, "The Balkans in the World Crisis," *Foreign Policy Reports*, IX, No. 20 (December 6, 1933).

[8] See Reshid Saffet Bey, "Rapport sur les communications"; "Rapport au IVe Conférence de la Fédération balkanique de tourisme"; "La semaine médicale balkanique" (report of the meeting of the Balkan Medical Union), LB, V (January-February, 1934), 161–67; (May-June, 1934), 537–650.

[114]

[9] New York *Times*, October 1, 1933. See Chapter VI for further details.

[10] *L'Echo de Belgrade*, September 7, 13, 20, 1933. Note also the discussions relating to the Balkan Conference in the Greek Parliament on September 1, 1933, and the letters exchanged between the heads of the Balkan governments, LB, IV (September-October, 1933), 652–669.

[11] The minutes of the Council are in LB, IV (November-December, 1933), 992–95; the minutes of the entire Conference, *ibid.*, 992–1104.

[12] *Ibid.*, 995–1014.

[13] For Political Commission see *ibid.*, 1015–21.

[14] The memoranda of the Economics Commission are in LB, IV, 852–56, 1116–18; V, 126–31, 179–84, 192–95. See especially those of MM. B. Simonides, S. Marodich, I. Sakazov, and D. P. Mihailovich.

[15] For the memoranda on agricultural credit see LB, IV, 747–52, 753–80; V, 113–25, 706–10.

[16] The memoranda on coöperatives are in LB, IV, 724–46; V, 132–36.

[17] For discussions in the Economics Commission see LB, IV, 1022–33. See also Petrovich, 204–38.

[18] See the Appendix to the present work, Document X, for text.

[19] The memoranda, which are in LB, IV, 711–17, 1130–34 and V, 136–60, 171–75, contain four excellent Bulgarian studies on Balkan law. For discussion see LB, IV, 1033–37. See also Petrovich, 242–55.

[20] The memoranda on communications are in LB, IV, 718–20, 1119–29; V, 161–67. See also André Tibal, *Les communications dans l'Europe danubienne* (Paris, 1933). The discussions in the commission are in LB, IV, 1037–39.

[21] See LB, IV, 1037 for discussion in the Commission on Social Policy, and LB, IV, 691–706, 836–44, 1135–47; V, 163–67, 196–98 for the memoranda.

[22] Discussions of the Organization and Legal Commission are in LB, IV, 1039–41; the memoranda, *ibid.*, IV, 673–85, 845–51, 686–90. See also A. Papanastassiou, *Vers l'Union balkanique*, 215–19; Petrovich, 39–81.

[23] Dr. A. Novakovich, "La modification des statuts de la Conférence balkanique," LB, V, 352–68.

[24] A. Papanastassiou, "Modification du statut de la Conférence," LB, IV, 686–90.

[25] LB, IV, 1041–1047.

[26] *Ibid.*, 1047–65.

[27] *Ibid.*, 1065–72.

[28] *Ibid.*, 1072–86.

Chapter VI

THE FOUR-POWER BALKAN PACT, 1934

BY THE FALL OF 1933 the Balkan Conferences were but part of a more general and official movement looking toward a definite political *rapprochement* among the Balkan states. On February 9, 1934, as we shall see, a political pact was signed by the representatives of Greece, Jugoslavia, Rumania, and Turkey. It will be the purpose of this chapter to trace the history of the diplomatic movement which produced the Four-Power Balkan Pact, to relate this movement to the work of the Balkan Conferences, and then to point out its significance in the recent trends toward regional security on the continent of Europe.

THE EUROPEAN BACKGROUND OF THE BALKAN PACT

The trend toward regional security in the Balkan Peninsula has its background in postwar attempts in Europe to find some sort of unity whereby disarmament, arbitration, and security could be obtained. The League of Nations in its origin bade fair to fulfill this need in the European system, but the absence of certain Great Powers like the United States and the Union of Socialist Soviet Republics weakened the League from the beginning. The weaknesses of the League of Nations made possible a return to a system of alliances not unlike that which prevailed in prewar Europe. The French alignment, for example, is familiar to all students of recent European politics. Moreover, the League *Covenant* itself, in Article 21—a provision in which Americans were much interested—stated that nothing in the *Covenant* should "be deemed to affect the validity of international engagements, such as treaties of arbitration or regional understandings like the Monroe Doctrine, for securing the maintenance of peace." The Little Entente (1920–21), composed of Czechoslovakia, Jugoslavia, and Rumania, represented a fundamental attempt, within the framework of the League of Nations, to find protection and peace in a restricted area. An effort was made in 1924, through the so-called Geneva or Beneš Protocol, to fill in the gaps of the *Covenant,* but in

March, 1925, the British government, now turned Conservative, denounced the Protocol and called for more localized or regional pacts of security. The Locarno Agreements followed, and went into effect with the German entry into the League in 1926. The Treaty for the Renunciation of War as an instrument of national policy and the General Act of the League of Nations, which provided model agreements for mutual assistance and nonaggression, typify further endeavors to organize the peace structure of the world. As will be indicated later in this chapter, the movement now became (1933–35) more definite than ever, with developments not only in the direction of a Balkan pact, but also of a Baltic pact, an Eastern European Locarno, and a Mediterranean security agreement.

More recently the rise of Adolph Hitler in Germany has been an important factor in promoting the *rapprochement* of the European powers, bringing them together in an attempt to secure their territorial frontiers. The reaction in Western Europe has been tremendous. One attempt was centered in the proposal of Signor Mussolini for a Four-Power Pact, including France, England, Italy, and Germany. After months of discussion the Pact of Rome was signed on June 7, 1933. In the original proposals of Mussolini in March, 1933, the Four-Power Pact would have constituted a European directory of the great Powers, somewhat supplanting even the League of Nations. These plans, however, had encountered the severe objections of the Little Entente and Poland, and as a result the final pact, representing a French victory, placed the scheme within the framework of the League. Moreover, France had promised her Central European allies that the question of frontiers would not be considered without consultation with the states concerned.[1*] Nevertheless, the Italian scheme aroused the fears of such states as Czechoslovakia, Jugoslavia, Rumania, and Poland. The estrangement between France and Poland, which has been so pronounced in recent months, had its beginnings in this episode.

One of the important results of these diplomatic maneuvers was the transformation of the Little Entente into a permanent diplo-

---

* Superior figures refer to notes which will be found at the end of this chapter.

matic federation in February, 1933.[2] The newly developed organization, which had grown out of the original treaties of 1920–21, included not only a permanent political body with a secretariat, but a standing economic council as well. It was designed, of course, to consolidate the positions of the three member states in Central Europe, now apparently threatened anew by the developments in Hitlerite Germany and by the effort of Italy to establish her hegemony through the Pact of Rome.

The movement was further accentuated by the increasing evidence of the failure of the Arms Conference at Geneva, which had begun its sessions in February, 1932. Owing to the increasing political tensions in the world, with Japan advancing into Manchuria and Mongolia, and Germany threatening the peace structure in Europe, that Conference apparently had been doomed from the beginning. More and more there developed among some of the powers represented at Geneva the feeling that the problem of security had to be solved before that of reduction of arms could be approached. This had been the French thesis from the very inception of the Conference. By the time of the London Economic Conference of June-July, 1933, these trends were taking definite shape. The London Conference indicated the return of Soviet Russia to the political system of Europe. Threatened in the Far East and in Europe, the U. S. S. R. now sounded the same note of political security which France had upheld since the days of the origins of the League of Nations. The result was the signing of a series of nonaggression agreements on July 3, 4, and 5, 1933. On July 3, the U. S. S. R. signed pacts with Afghanistan, Esthonia, Latvia, Persia, Poland, Rumania, and Turkey. On the next day similar agreements were concluded with Czechoslovakia, Jugoslavia, and Rumania, as members of the Little Entente. To these agreements Turkey likewise was a party. The Soviet Union also concluded a treaty with Lithuania. It is interesting to note that the definition of an aggressor (Article II) in these almost identical pacts followed the Politis Report of May 24, 1933, and read:

... The aggressor in an international conflict, with due consideration to the agreements between the parties involved in the conflict, will be considered the state which will be the first to commit any of the following acts:

1. Declaration of war against another state;

2. Invasion by armed forces, even without a declaration of war, of the territory of another state;

3. An attack by armed land, naval or air forces, even without a declaration of war, upon the territory, naval vessels or air craft of another state;

4. Naval blockade of the coasts or ports of another state;

5. Aid to armed bands formed on the territory of a state and invading the territory of another state, or refusal, despite demands on the part of the state subjected to attack, to take all possible measures on its own territory to deprive the said bands of any aid and protection.

Very significant was the declaration in the next article that "no considerations of a political, military, economic or any other nature can serve as an excuse or justification of aggression. . . ."[3] Not only did the making of these treaties at the London Conference indicate the desire of Russia for the security of her frontiers; they also tended to make that country a defender of the territorial *status quo* against any upset by force of arms.

The import of the agreements for the Balkan region was appreciably large. The treaty with Turkey was doubtless merely an extension of treaties going back as far as 1921 and 1929, but for Rumania the convention helped to solve the question of Bessarabia and to lessen any tension bearing thereon in the Little Entente. Since Section 5 of Article II defines as an aggressor any state which offers its support to armed bands which make incursions across the frontiers of other states, the treaties had a great bearing on the Macedonian question between Jugoslavia and Greece on the one hand and Bulgaria on the other. This would mean that the Soviet Union would offer no support to such incursions from Bulgaria into Jugoslav territory. It might finally lead to a solution of that troublesome issue if Bulgaria adhered to a similar pact. A contribution of appreciable importance would then have been made to the solution of a problem which had caused friction in the Balkan Conferences from the beginning.[4] There were indications, however, that the Bulgarians were not prepared to sign such a pact in its existing form, in view of the possible implications with respect to the *status quo* in Macedonia.

BALKAN DIPLOMACY PREPARES THE WAY

The road toward official *rapprochement* among the Balkan nations was even more rocky than the one which was being paved by the Balkan Conferences. Steps toward a solution of many of the problems, however, had been taken over a long period of years. A brief résumé of the treaties and agreements is both impressive and instructive, and furthermore it will indicate that the moves which were made on the diplomatic chessboard in the fall of 1933 and the winter of 1934 were not the product of a single day's dream. Jugoslavia and Rumania had signed a treaty on May 21, 1929, within the framework of the Little Entente, and, as has been seen, this structure was completed by the pact of organization of the Little Entente in February, 1933. A Greco-Rumanian treaty of arbitration was signed on March 22, 1928, and a Greco-Jugoslav treaty of friendship, conciliation, and judicial settlement was signed on March 27, 1929. Turkey had signed a treaty of neutrality and conciliation with Bulgaria on October 25, 1929. A glance indicates that Bulgaria was as yet not a party to any of these agreements except the treaty with Turkey. The fall and winter of 1933–34 were to see the culmination of these attempts to consolidate Balkan friendship in the conclusion of a Greco-Turkish pact (September 14, 1933), a Turco-Rumanian agreement (October 18, 1933), and a Turco-Jugoslav treaty of friendship (November 27, 1933), not to mention the renewal of the Bulgar-Turkish treaty of 1929. It was this diplomatic movement which finally led to the Four-Power Balkan Pact of February, 1934. To an examination of these developments in the Balkan Peninsula our study now turns.

The first definite move in the direction of a more complete friendship among the Balkan nations was the conclusion of the Greco-Turkish pact of September 14, 1933. Greece and Turkey had been bitter enemies for centuries, and had recently fought the destructive war of 1918–22, following the World War. They had, however, settled many of their outstanding difficulties through the exchange of Greek and Turkish minority populations, as provided by the Treaty of Lausanne. This was a major contributing factor to the *rapprochement* of 1933. The new treaty guaranteed their mutual frontiers and took steps to formulate a common policy through common representation at certain international conferences of limited membership. For example, Article III declared:

> In all international conferences of limited representation Greece and Turkey agree that the delegate of one of them will have the mission of defending the common and special interests of the two parties and they agree to unite their efforts to assure this common representation either to each in turn, or in cases of special interests, to the country most concerned.

The treaty aroused some apprehensions in Bulgaria over the ultimate designs of the two signatories, but the object seems primarily to have been to cement their mutual relations and to promote a common international policy. Both countries gave evidence of a desire for a general Balkan adherence to the pact or for the signing with them of similar agreements. Indeed, both Greek and Turkish statesmen visited Sofia, but the only result of the journeys was the renewal of the Turco-Bulgarian treaty of 1929.[5] The difficulties between Greece and Bulgaria were not so amenable to adjustment.

The second piece of evidence pointing in the direction of some kind of *détente* in the mutual relations of the Balkan states was that series of events which led to the meetings of the Balkan sovereigns in the fall of 1933. Superficially, these meetings seemed but the attempt of the Balkan monarchs to bolster up their positions. Actually, the import was far deeper if one takes into account all the developments which were bringing the rulers together. On October 1, King Alexander of Jugoslavia and his queen visited in Bucharest with King Carol, and two days later they were being received by the sovereigns of Bulgaria. It was the first time in more than twenty years that a Serbian monarch had touched Bulgarian soil. M. Mushanov, the Bulgarian premier, told the press: "We must consider that this visit will advance the desired *rapprochement* between the two Slav peoples," even though Bulgaria was not ready to sign a political pact. The official policy was one of peace with all neighbors, but in full independence. On October 4, the Jugoslav sovereigns visited Istanbul, where they were welcomed by Mustapha Kemal, and then proceeded to Athens on their way home. On October 9, it was announced that the definitive text of a pact of friendship with Turkey had been initialed.[6]

Somewhat later, on October 28, King Boris attested to the new feelings of official friendship in his speech from the throne at the opening of the *Sobranje:*[7]

> We are ... particularly happy about the visit which the King and Queen of Jugoslavia have paid us at the chateau of Euxinograd. We see in it the expression of a cordial friendship. In the course of these last months the government has been happy to receive visits from the president of the council and the minister of foreign affairs of the Turkish Republic, the minister of foreign affairs of the kingdom of Rumania and the president of the council and minister of foreign affairs of Hungary.

In the response to the throne there was general agreement on foreign policy. Dr. Danev declared that Bulgaria's policy must be animated by "a spirit of peace and understanding," but insisted:

> One important question to be settled in this domain is that of the minorities to whom our neighbors have not given rights according to the treaties. But the application of the clauses relative thereto is an indispensable condition to the improvement of the Balkan atmosphere. To the neighboring countries desirous of concluding pacts, Bulgaria must recall that they have to conform especially to Article 19 of the *Covenant* of the League of Nations. Of course, the problem of a Bulgarian outlet to the Aegean Sea must be settled.

The same note was sounded in the address of M. Mushanov on November 23:

> The policy of the Bulgarian government is a policy of peace and understanding with all. ... This preoccupation has found an expression in the *Covenant* of the League of Nations, a *Covenant* which looked precisely toward the creation of conditions for peaceful development and the triumph of justice and equity.

Bulgaria was a member of the League and an adherent to the Paris Pact for the renunciation of war. The recent meetings of the Jugoslav and Bulgarian kings led the premier to note the "existing unity between the king and the people, which is in my opinion a gage of the solid basis of the state and of the normal and happy development of the country." Moreover, it was "a new fact which can only make us rejoice and give us reasons to believe that the contacts between the two peoples will be reëstablished and again become normal." Likewise the meeting with King Carol on October 31 and the visits of M. Titulescu, the Rumanian foreign minister, and of the Turkish statesmen were happy auguries for the future. M. Mushanov did not expect results of vast importance, but he did look for something tangible.[8]

Meanwhile, the Turco-Jugoslav pact of friendship was signed in Belgrade on November 27. It was an agreement of nonaggression, judicial settlement, arbitration, and conciliation. The treaty was hailed as a constructive achievement on the road to the pacification of the Balkans. Three days later, M. Tevfik Rushdi Bey, the Turkish foreign minister, explained in Sofia that the pact was not designed against anyone. Among other things the Turkish statesman declared :⁰

We Turks are in fact antirevisionists. We ask nothing of anyone and on our part we give nothing to anyone. Our desire is to live peacefully and freely without being troubled within the limits of our territory. Now we desire an absolute peace in the Balkans. Thus we consider that the spirit of the treaties constitutes the best basis of good international relations. We see no other means of assuring a normal world life. On the other hand, Bulgaria also has always given her word that she believes in respect for treaties. But on this basis everyone can sign.

Turkey had taken her stand definitely with those European powers which were defending the territorial *status quo*.

Preparations were now being made for the visit of the Bulgarian royal party to Jugoslavia, which took place from December 10 to December 13. At a great state banquet on December 11, King Alexander declared, in raising his glass to his guest, that only "a policy of peace and consolidation of the existing order can truly assure to our peoples the full guarantee of a better future." He saw in King Boris "the great artisan of the same ideas and a powerful factor in their realization." King Boris reciprocated these peaceful sentiments, but, of course, could not endorse the "existing order," for Bulgaria had protested against the Treaty of Neuilly ever since its signature in 1919. An official *communiqué* issued at the close of the visit stressed "the identity of their views on the necessity of peace and understanding among the Balkan nations," and concluded :

The ministers have noted the necessity for a sincere and continuous collaboration for the establishment of increasingly friendly and cordial relations between the two countries, and have agreed to negotiate a treaty of commerce and a veterinary convention, to simplify passport formalities in order to facilitate relations between the two peoples, and to develop and improve the means of communication between the two countries. They are persuaded that the lines of friendship between Bulgaria and Jugoslavia constitute a valuable contribution to the maintenance of peace among the Balkan nations and facilitate their [i.e., the Balkan nations'] agreement.

M. Mushanov believed that the visit would work toward the "reenforcement of peace in the Balkans," though no political compact seemed immediately possible. There is no doubt that the meeting produced a feeling of good will among the peoples of both countries.[10]

Shortly after this, on December 21, M. Maximos, the Greek foreign minister, arrived in Belgrade for conversations concerning the coming Balkan Pact, which was now very much in the air. Upon being questioned concerning the probable attitude of the Little Entente toward the proposed treaty, M. Jevtich, the Jugoslav foreign minister, declared:[11]

> The work of the Balkan Entente is parallel to the policy of the Little Entente in Central Europe and is bound to it by reason of the Balkan members of the Little Entente [Jugoslavia and Rumania]. ... Both policies aim at agreement and coöperation among the peoples who have as a principal aim the maintenance of the necessary peace in the Balkans as well as in Central Europe.

With these assurances from his conversations in Belgrade, M. Maximos journeyed to Paris, London, and Rome in the interest of the proposed Balkan Pact, and early in January the Greek ministry of foreign affairs issued a formal statement on the proposal:[12]

> Concerning the question of the Balkan Pact, M. Maximos has expressed his conviction that the pact will be concluded. "I am certain ... that the great powers, Italy, England, and France will approve the pact and will make it a useful instrument for the consolidation of peace. The pact will provide for the consolidation of the *status quo*, to which Greece adheres. Her position is that the treaties must remain untouched. Such is also her point of view in regard to the Treaty of Neuilly, particularly concerning the clauses relative to the outlet of Bulgaria on the Aegean Sea."

The next move of importance was the meeting of the Council of the Little Entente at Zagreb, January 8–11, 1934. Among the matters to be discussed was the project of the Balkan Pact. The idea of the pact was accepted in principle, but it was necessary to await the interviews between King Boris and King Carol in order to know whether Bulgaria would remain outside or sign the agreement. The Little Entente was in favor of the limited objectives of the Balkan Pact and looked forward to coöperation with a Balkan

Entente in their respective policies. The Little Entente took another step of outstanding significance at this meeting when it voted that its members should begin negotiations for the resumption of diplomatic relations with Soviet Russia.[13]

On January 25, King Boris and his queen visited Bucharest. At the state banquet on the next evening King Carol emphasized his conviction that "only a policy of sincere understanding and consolidation of the existing order" could lead to peaceful collaboration. King Boris, too, desired peace and spoke of "a policy of understanding and confidence serving the vital interests of our peoples." As in Belgrade, he did not endorse the "existing order." The official *communiqué* which summarized the results of the conferences spoke of the important issues between the two countries—the application of the agrarian reforms in Rumania, the payment of pensions, and the minorities. The governments were convinced that the settlement of these problems would "assure the establishment of a still closer friendship between the two neighboring countries," which would contribute to the peace of the peninsula. But in all this there was no specific mention of the Balkan Pact.[14] Bulgaria was not prepared to sign a Balkan Pact.

THE CONCLUSION OF THE FOUR-POWER BALKAN PACT

Preparations had now been made for the definite conclusion and signing of the Four-Power Balkan Pact. From February 2 to February 4 the Balkan foreign ministers were in Belgrade formulating the final text. It was announced in Istanbul that the contents would be communicated to Bulgaria and that an acceptable formula would be prepared for her adherence. Nevertheless, it was clear that there would be a clause on the inviolability of the frontiers, since the four Balkan powers initiating the agreement stood on that basis. On February 4, an official *communiqué* announced that the ministers had paragraphed "the definitive text of the pact of the Balkan Entente" and that the official signatures would be affixed at Athens within the week.[15] There was little prospect, however, that Bulgaria would adhere to the new instrument, and Albania, on account of her peculiar relations with Italy, was not even asked to sign—evidently the four Balkan powers desired to do nothing which would offend fascist Italy. The semiofficial Belgrade journal, *Politika,* complained on February 3 about the absence of these two Balkan states :[16]

Bulgaria and Albania ought to face reality and not see in the agreement merely the satisfaction of others, but also and indirectly their own interests. Albania and Bulgaria must understand that a perfect example of a regional agreement is given by the Little Entente, whose strength lies in the good will of its members, always ready to sacrifice their particular interests for the good of the community. Such a conception must predominate in the Balkans and Balkan understanding will be perfect.

News of the paragraphing of the definitive text was received with varying sentiments in the European capitals. Paris was very favorably impressed, since the treaty was based on the preservation of the *status quo,* and both Jugoslavia and Rumania were within the framework of French alliances. Rome was both skeptical of the proposition and opposed to the very principle of the pact. Italy could not look with favor on any consolidation of the Balkan region which would not only strengthen the hands of Jugoslavia by associating her definitely with Greece and Turkey, but would also offer a prospect of removing both Albania and Bulgaria from their Italian moorings. London viewed the new agreement with reserve and circumspection. On February 5, Sir John Simon told the House of Commons that[17]

His Majesty's Government would welcome any pact between the Balkan states tending to general pacification and coöperation provided that it is not directed against any other power or powers. It would for this reason be desirable that the terms of the pact should, if possible, be so drafted as to secure the accession of Bulgaria.

Soviet Russia, like France, and especially since July, 1933, appears to have been much in favor of the new pact. Indeed, the formation of a Balkan Entente with Soviet Russia's old friend, the new Turkish Republic, as a member, might lead to a Near Eastern *bloc,* whose primary aim would be to insure the freedom of the Dardanelles in the event of war. But the pact was certainly not of a kind to please the Sofia government, which contended that it could not waive rights under the Balkan agreement which were guaranteed under Article 19 of the *Covenant* of the League of Nations.[18]

The pact of the Balkan Entente was formally signed in Athens on February 9, 1934. It provided that "Greece, Jugoslavia, Rumania, and Turkey guarantee mutually the security of all their Balkan frontiers." The parties engaged to concert on the measures necessary to carry out the agreement. They bound themselves "to undertake no political action toward any other Balkan country nonsignatory of the present treaty, without previous mutual agreement and to assume no political obligation toward any other Balkan country without the consent of the other contracting parties."

A so-called "secret protocol," also signed on February 9, gave further clarification to the terms of the treaty. An aggressor, for example, was defined in accordance with Article II of the London Conventions of July 3–5, 1933. Another article declared: "The Balkan Pact is not directed against any country. Its direct object is to guarantee the security of Balkan frontiers against aggression on the part of a Balkan state." The four powers were definitely pledged to take united action against any threat from a Balkan state. Conventions for the execution of the terms of the pact were to be concluded within six months. The pact was not to be in contradiction with existing treaties previously contracted by the signatories. Finally, the protocol emphasized that "the Balkan Pact is a defensive instrument," and that "the maintenance of the territorial *status quo* actually established in the Balkans is final for the contracting parties."[19]

In the course of an official dinner on February 9, the ministers of the four Balkan nations made some significant comments concerning the agreement which they had just signed. M. Maximos, the Greek foreign minister, declared that they had "certainly not been able to realize all the results which our peoples and the apostles of the Balkan idea have asked of us," but added:

We have built on a solid basis: the reasoned defense of our common interests. We have begun by establishing the scrupulous respect of our rights on the land of our hearths as a point of departure of our common life. . . . Does this affirmation of our common interests imply malevolent or aggressive intentions toward the other countries? To affirm such an absurdity would be not only to mistake our true intentions, but especially to impute to the other countries aspirations which they certainly could not have. . . . The example of our four countries . . . enjoying the fruits of their common labor in order and peace, cannot fail . . . to convince all the Balkan peoples of the advantages which they may draw from this close solidarity.

M. Titulescu, of Rumania, stressed even more pointedly the conservative nature of the new agreement:

> The first stability which a state requires, not only in its own, but in the general interest, is the stability of its frontiers. . . . But as long as uncertainty exists on the question of the state frontiers, the complete duty required by the international community is not possible. . . . The treaty of Athens is a gesture commanded especially by the instinct of conservation. . . . But we are ready to undertake, with all those who will recognize definitively and loyally our frontiers, a vast labor of economic and political *rapprochement*, which devalorizes the frontiers. . . .

M. Jevtich, the Jugoslav foreign minister, sincerely hoped that "all the Balkan peoples would join in this work of Balkan understanding in order to contribute to the creation of an atmosphere of international confidence." The Turkish minister, M. Tevfik Rushdi Bey, declared that the dominant note was "to safeguard and defend as the most sacred thing the rights of the society to which we belong; to respect with the same force and conviction the legitimate conditions of the coexistence of each state."[20]

Such was the interpretation given to the pact by those who had signed it. It was natural that there should be a major sentiment in favor of the treaty among the signatory countries, but it was not unanimous. The Jugoslav press almost universally supported the idea of the pact, and this was likewise true in Rumania, though there was some opposition among those Rumanians who felt that their country was more a Central European than a Balkan power. With respect to the purely defensive character of the pact, M. Titulescu declared in an interview:[21]

> This treaty is in fact one of the most powerful instruments of peace which we can offer. The aim of the authors is to relieve the signatory nations from the care of their frontiers, in order that they may devote themselves to creative work, which alone can enable the world to emerge from the grave crisis which threatens it. . . . Our treaty remains open to the adherence of all the Balkan peoples who wish loyally to accept its stipulations.

In Turkey the attitude toward the pact was uniformly favorable, and the Turkish government was the first to ratify the treaty, on March 7, 1934. In a lengthy address before the Grand National Assembly, on the occasion of the ratification, M. Tevfik Rushdi Bey said:[22]

The Balkan Pact ... constitutes a happy manifestation of the policy of peace, security, and good neighborhood which we have always pursued in this region, and the sign of a happy development in Balkan history, as well as of the inauguration of a new era of fraternity among the Balkan peoples. ... It is our principal hope to pursue a policy of good neighborhood with Bulgaria, with whom we are mutually bound by a treaty of neutrality in case of aggression, and to maintain constant good relations between the two peoples. ... [The pact] is not in contradiction with [Turkey's] existing friendship with Soviet Russia and other friendly states. ...

In Greece the Balkan Pact became the center of a heated political controversy. M. Venizelos, who was one of the architects of the Balkan League of 1912–13, led the opposition to its ratification. The distinguished wartime leader of the Greeks was especially critical of the pact because, he contended, it would involve Greece in controversies with great powers, particularly with Italy. This might happen, he thought, in the event of an aggression against Jugoslavia on the part of a Balkan state (Bulgaria perhaps), in which Italy might take part. Or it might happen if Italy attacked Jugoslavia through Albania, and was supported by Bulgaria. The newspaper controversy was very bitter, and it took several conversations among the party chieftains to achieve a satisfactory formula. M. Papanastassiou played a notable rôle in trying to conciliate the opposing groups. The treaty finally was unanimously ratified by the Chamber of Deputies on March 15, and by the Senate on April 2. In the course of his remarks on the pact, M. Maximos stated that the agreement was "a contract of definitive peace among the Balkan states," to which he hoped Bulgaria would adhere as a fifth state, since it was "not directed against anyone." He concluded:

The aim of the pact tends particularly to discourage definitively any intention on the part of anyone to overthrow the existing *status* in the Balkans and to arrest thus in its genesis any future intention to provoke any disorders. Greece believes with conviction, and this conviction is shared by all the governments of the contracting states, that the union of their efforts for the safeguarding of Balkan interests will furnish to each of them a new authority in international society. The pact has strengthened their collaboration and will put a definite end to uncertainties of every nature. ... However, the absence of Bulgaria constitutes a serious *lacuna,* which we hope will disappear with time. From the very beginning of the elaboration of the pact, the four contracting parties wished to give tangible proofs of their friendly attitude in communicating to Bulgaria the text of the pact, after the preliminary communications which had already been made, drawing her attention to the benevolent consideration which would be given to any proposition of adherence on her part. We have received favorably her proposal for the conclusion of a pact of nonaggression, and we hope sincerely that this proposition will be realized.

In response to a question of M. Papanastassiou's, the foreign minister declared that "the Balkan Pact had in view only the guarantee of the security of Balkan frontiers in relation to another nonsignatory Balkan state," and that "there would be no difficulty with a great power in execution of the engagements assumed by the pact."[23]

The political agitation in Greece over the ratification of the Pact, and the interpretation placed upon it by the government, produced repercussions in Jugoslavia and Rumania, which were not allayed by the news of the ratification. The treaty came before the Jugoslav Chamber of Deputies on March 12, when M. Jevtich explained that, though it was open to objection because neither Bulgaria nor Albania had adhered to the agreement, it was the "first and only effective attempt to arrive at a durable organization of peace and security in the Balkans. The Pact constitutes the maximum of what could be realized under present conditions."

We must accept this Pact loyally and reject all *arrières-pensées* in its interpretation if we desire truly to appreciate the exact value of the constructive policy it must serve. . . . One cannot say that Jugoslavia is not in friendly relations with all the Balkan states without exception. The Jugoslav government will continue this policy of friendship and closer collaboration with the Balkan peoples.

La Bulgarie, the official journal in Sofia, rightly declared that M. Jevtich's speech was couched in the most conciliatory terms. The Jugoslav foreign minister followed his address in the Chamber with one in the Senate on March 27. It was in part a response to the recent moves in Central Europe which had produced the Italo-Austro-Hungarian agreements of March 17. The Rome Protocols, following hard on the liquidation of the socialists at the hand of the Dollfuss government and the development of a fascist Austria, provided for close political and economic relations among Italy and Austria and Hungary. Italy was looking forward to an ever-expanding influence in Central and Balkan Europe, and in the Near East and Africa as well. Already a great military high-

way, the Packstrasse, was being constructed across Austria to con-
nect the borders of Italy and Hungary, the implications of which
were plain to the Belgrade government. On March 18, just one day
after the signing of these significant agreements, Signor Mussolini
declared that "of all the great western powers in Europe the near-
est to Africa and Asia is Italy.... A few hours on the sea and a
fewer still in the air are enough to unite Italy with Africa and
Asia." While he denied any intention of political expansion or
territorial conquest, Il Duce entrusted this "natural expansion
leading to collaboration between Italy and the people of Africa
and the eastern nations" to "the present Italian generation and to
that of tomorrow."[24]

Not until April 4 was the Four-Power Balkan Pact presented to
the Rumanian Chamber of Deputies. On that occasion, M. Titulescu delivered a most important declaration of policy in which
he outlined his firm opposition to any revision of the treaties, de-
nying even that there was any principle within Article 19 of the
Covenant of the League of Nations, which had been invoked by
Bulgaria, to support the idea of territorial revision. No frontiers,
he contended, could be altered without the consent of all parties
concerned. He also emphasized the eminently conservative and
constructive character of the Pact, which he linked closely to that
of the Little Entente. The ministers of the Balkan Entente, now
engaged in a "work of political realism" through their periodical
meetings, would promote "economic,, commercial, and cultural
relations among the Balkan states."[25]

No further discussion concerning the new treaty took place in
the Jugoslav or Rumanian parliaments, and very quietly by royal
decrees the two governments ratified the Four-Power Balkan Pact
on June 16, 1934.

Meanwhile, what of the Bulgarian attitude? As early as February 1, M. Mushanov, the premier, told the foreign affairs committee of the *Sobranje* that Bulgaria could not adhere to the Four-
Power Balkan Pact because it violated the provisions of Article
19 of the *Covenant* of the League, and Bulgaria could not "renounce ... rights which the League *Covenant* confers on her." The
premier declared, however, that the government was determined

to follow its policy "of peace and understanding." It had proposed to the Rumanian government that "a pact of nonaggression between the two respective countries be signed, which would guarantee the neighboring kingdom of the north against any aggression on the part of Bulgaria, while awaiting the peaceful revision provided by the treaties of peace." But Rumania had rejected this proposal. Later in the month, King Boris, while in Paris, after attending the funeral of King Albert of Belgium, is reported to have told M. Barthou that though Bulgaria had not so far signed the pact, "that did not obviate her adhering to it at a later date."[26] Apparently the question was still open.

The Bulgarian attitude was more clearly and fully defined in M. Mushanov's statement of policy before the *Sobranje* on March 30. He declared that the Four-Power Balkan Pact was "superfluous," since peace was not threatened by anyone. A friendly settlement of outstanding difficulties, he thought, was much more to the point.

> [Moreover] to adhere to the Pact would mean our renunciation of a solemn stipulation of the *Covenant* of the League of Nations contained in Article 19. . . . I could say that the Pact concluded at Athens is not in harmony with the ideas which prevailed at the creation of the League of Nations or even with the spirit of its *Covenant*. . . . The Pact was communicated to us when it was paragraphed at Belgrade and we learned of its conclusion and definitive text through the journals. But even today we do not know the authentic and complete tenor of the Pact, because it possesses, as is already known, a secret annex. . . . I declare here, however, that we are not alarmed and that we are not suspicious; strong in our love of peace and in our loyalty, we look into the future peacefully. On the other hand, we are convinced that even if they have mutually agreed to keep secret the so-called secret protocol, the governments signatory to the pact will deem it necessary to publish it, for publication is required by Article 18 of the *Covenant* of the League of Nations.

The premier did not, evidently, see much danger in the possibility that Bulgaria would be isolated in the Balkans, though this fear had been expressed in some Bulgarian circles. Nor did Bulgaria, by remaining aloof from all attempts toward Balkan friendship, intend to promote disunity within the peninsula. Moreover, M. Mushanov was convinced that a considerable *détente* already had developed, even if all the problems had not been settled in a short space of time.[27]

THE FOUR-POWER BALKAN PACT AND THE BALKAN CONFERENCE

The conclusion of the Balkan Pact was a partial achievement of one of the fundamental aims of the Balkan Conference, but at the same time it constituted one of the grave problems of that organization. The Four-Power Balkan Pact did not include all the Balkan states, since neither Albania nor Bulgaria was a party to it. Furthermore, to all intents and purposes, it seemed to be purely political, whereas the Balkan Conferences looked toward a more fundamental and comprehensive union of all the Balkan peoples, politically, economically, socially, and intellectually. The Pact provided for the security of Balkan frontiers, but it instituted no machinery for the solution of outstanding problems.

While the Balkan diplomats were gathering in Belgrade for the initialing of the Pact on February 4, M. Papanastassiou, who had presided over the destinies of two Balkan Conferences and who was the guiding spirit behind the entire movement, sent a letter to the Balkan foreign ministers urging that they take into consideration the proposals for a political pact which had been embodied in the draft adopted by the Third Balkan Conference at Bucharest. Specifically, M. Papanastassiou declared :[28]

Before proceeding to the adoption of the pact of guarantee of frontiers, be content for the moment with the conclusion of a pact including provisions of nonaggression and the pacific solution of differences. On such a pact, it has been demonstrated since the Second Balkan Conference that the six Balkan countries are in agreement. There will be no inconvenience in inviting Albania also to participate in such a pact, since the obligations are of a general nature. Such a pact will mark the beginning of a new era in the Balkans and of an understanding and systematic collaboration of the six Balkan nations.

Although the governments did not follow these suggestions, since the question of territorial security seemed more important, M. Papanastassiou said he felt that the Four-Power Balkan Pact was, nevertheless, a good beginning.

But the Pact negotiated is limited to the single mutual guarantee of the Balkan frontiers. This clause differs from that of the mutual assistance contained in the draft adopted by the Conference; mutual assistance guarantees the contracting parties against an attack coming from one of them, while the guarantee clause of the frontiers applies in the case of attack even on the part of noncontracting Balkan states. This clause is doubtless broader and guards the interests of peace, but it has produced the impression that it excludes the application of Article 19 of the *Covenant* of the League of Nations; on the other hand, the haste in concluding a pact containing only the single guarantee of the frontiers renders more difficult the general *entente* of the Balkan peoples. . . . The four signatory states are in accord in manifesting their opposition to the revisionist movement recently noted. But . . . this opposition could be indicated without having recourse to the hasty conclusion of a pact containing only the guarantee of the frontiers.

After the signing of the treaty, M. Papanastassiou again communicated with the signatories, directing their attention to the resolutions of the Balkan Conferences, and asking them to take into consideration certain principles at the first meeting of the Council of the Balkan Entente, namely, the provisions of the draft Balkan Pact adopted by the Conference; the projects for economic coöperation; the draft on the status of Balkan citizens; the creation of the Balkan Labor Office; the Balkan Postal Union; and the Chamber of Commerce and Industry.

When the Council of the Balkan Conference met at Athens from March 31 to April 3, there were two major issues to be considered.[29] The first was the problem of the Balkan Pact. The second was the amendment of the statutes of the Conference, with the Greek and Jugoslav delegations presenting fundamentally opposing projects.

The major controversy naturally centered around the Four-Power Balkan Pact. In the course of his opening remarks, M. Papanastassiou complimented the Bulgarian delegation on its attitude toward the Conference. In response to a telegram from the Albanian group announcing its refusal to attend on account of the Pact of February 9, he affirmed that the Balkan Conference could not be held responsible for the attitude or the actions of the governments in adopting the new political Pact. M. Papanastassiou did not believe that the Albanian delegation would remain outside the movement, nor did he think that the work of the Conference had been finished. On the contrary, it was more necessary than ever "to complete the work already accomplished, which is in reality only a beginning." He further declared that the foreign ministers of the signatories of the Pact had assured him "that they will do everything possible to complete it according to the desires of the Conference. . . . Despite its defects, the Pact signed constitutes a point of departure for official Balkan collaboration." The Jugoslav delegation took the definite position, indeed, that the signing of the Pact had completed the work of the Conferences and that there was no further need of annual meetings. M. Papanastassiou denied this assertion:

Even if the Pact had been signed by the six [Balkan] countries, the Conference would always have a task to fulfill. Peace is not assured and consolidated by the signature of a single pact for the guarantee of frontiers. We must create a community of sentiment and organize collaboration among the peoples. The Conference will not have finished its task before the Balkan Union is created. The statutes require annual meetings. A decision to suspend these meetings would be contrary to the statutes and the Council is not competent to make such a decision.

But the most serious episode developed when M. Sakazov arose to present the views of the Bulgarian delegation. It was well known that Bulgarian circles were not at all pleased with the terms of the Four-Power Balkan Pact. Once before, the Bulgarian delegation had withdrawn from the Conference—and it had taken that action on account of the adoption of the draft political pact at Bucharest. Would the Bulgarians again withdraw, this time in protest against the action of four Balkan governments? M. Sakazov expressed the Bulgarian view very succinctly:

What is the real contribution which the Balkan Conference can now make to the work of *rapprochement* and peace in a new situation in which the states of the peninsula pursuing the same ends ... have believed that they must form a sort of coalition for the defense of the frontiers established as a consequence of the last wars? Our country came out of these wars not only with important territorial losses, but also with a gravely compromised economic balance. Lands incontestably a part of the national Bulgarian patrimony were taken from us for purely strategic reasons. More than a million of our conationals whose cultural, social, and legal interests cannot leave us indifferent, have remained under a foreign domination, deprived of their rights. ... Politically we continue to be placed in a condition of juridical and moral inequality, notwithstanding the principle of the equality of states in their cultural, social, and economic relations. The obligations which the treaties have imposed on us have been executed and we continue to execute them at the price of superhuman efforts which exhaust our national economy. But the obligations assumed by the other countries are unfortunately a dead letter.

The Balkan Conferences first met four years ago and many fine resolutions had been adopted, but M. Sakazov wondered what the results of those meetings had been, in spite of the efforts put forth.

And it is precisely in the midst of all these efforts that the four Balkan countries reach an agreement in order to prepare a great surprise for us and no less a deception: the conclusion of a pact of mutual assistance and reciprocal guarantee, the tendency of which is to affirm forever the right of the stronger in opposing readjustments by pacific means provided by general treaties, in eluding obligations arising from the pacts such as those concerning the protection of the minorities, in attaching, in a word, no importance to the interests of the two other Balkan countries which have not adhered to the Pact. Will not this flagrant contradiction, which offends the most elementary sentiment of justice, result in paralyzing all our noble efforts to create a fine, healthy, and durable institution, harmonizing all the Balkan interests? It is the striking contradiction between the aspirations of the Conference, on the one hand, and the work of the four governments, on the other, which obliges the representatives of the Bulgarian national group today to put to the delegations of the other Balkan countries the following questions:

1. Do they approve—yes or no—the Pact which has been signed, now a partial Balkan Pact, directed against the other countries of the peninsula?

2. Are they disposed to uphold, in the light of the secret clauses of the Pact, the contradictions existing between its stipulations and the aspirations of the Conference, and if so, do they wish to take on themselves the obligation to recommend to their respective governments the conclusion of pacts of non-aggression which would permit the Conference to persevere in its efforts to bring about the early conclusion of the customs union and the political unity of the Balkan countries? The attitude of the Bulgarian delegation will depend on the response of the other delegations to these questions.

Certainly the position of the Bulgarians was clear. It offered the prospect of putting the other delegations in a dilemma. According to the Bulgarian position, the other national groups must accept either the Four-Power Balkan Pact or the work of the Balkan Conferences. The Bulgarians contended, in view of the alleged contradictions involved, that the other delegations could not have both the Balkan Conference and the new political agreement. M. Papanastassiou, who was glad to see such clarity of thought in the Bulgarian statement, reminded his colleagues, however, that the Conference was not an official organization and that it could not be held responsible for the attitude of the governments. The essential task of the Conference was "to create a movement of *rapprochement,* to study questions of common interest, and to prepare the ground for collaboration among the states," and it should not lose sight of the final aim, "the creation of a Balkan federation." Moreover, the question of the Four-Power Pact could be placed on the agenda of the next meeting.

But what of the next meeting—the Fifth Balkan Conference? M. Jovanovich, of Jugoslavia, had already suggested that it be postponed for one or two years so as to give Bulgaria and Albania time to adhere to the new political agreement, and now that he had listened to M. Sakazov he was more convinced than ever that the next Conference should be delayed. M. Pella, of Rumania, could not favor adjournment of the Conference, for he believed that adjournment would only increase the distrust. He felt that the Balkan Pact was not contrary to the spirit of the Conference; it was only a beginning of the work of collaboration. "To suspend the Conferences is to bury the idea and to assume that the governments have done everything," leaving nothing for the Conferences, which ought to pave the way toward unity. When the proposal to postpone the Conference for a year was brought up for decision, only the Jugoslav and the Bulgarian groups voted for it.

The discussion which followed centered about the reorganization of the Balkan Conference itself and the establishment of a permanent headquarters. M. Pella had suggested the necessity of a permanent headquarters and a definite staff, and was supported by M. Papanastassiou, who did not believe, however, that the Conference need always meet in the same place. This problem, apparently, did not concern the Jugoslav delegation, for M. Jovanovich explained that "since the signature of the Pact of the Balkan Entente, the propaganda provided at the beginning of the work of the Balkan Conferences is less necessary." M. Sakazov desired to know something of the nature of the headquarters and the staff to be established. It was explained that there would be six secretaries, their duties being to assemble the archives and carry on the correspondence of the Conference. The task could be accomplished, M. Papanastassiou thought, if the governments would designate consuls or other diplomatic officials for such work.

The Conference voted that the next meeting be held in Istanbul, and that Istanbul henceforth should be the permanent headquarters of the organization. On the proposal of M. Papanastassiou, it was decided, in spite of opposition, to call the organization "The Balkan Parliamentary and Social Union," signifying both the more official and the broader social character of the institution.

The remaining two days were in large part given over to questions of procedure. On April 2, M. Penakov, of the Bulgarian group, proposed to supplement the provisions for the protection of minorities in Chapter IV of the draft Balkan Pact adopted by the Conference at Bucharest with the establishment of bilateral minority offices. After some discussion it was decided that this suggestion be studied.[30] In response to a question of M. Papanastassiou, the Bulgarian, Jugoslav, and Rumanian delegations gave assurance that their respective governments were disposed to adhere to the Balkan Postal Union, which Greece and Turkey had approved and ratified.

THE REGIONAL SECURITY MOVEMENT IN EUROPE

It was apparent after the signing of the Four-Power Balkan Pact of February 9, 1934, that the next major step in the direction of Balkan friendship would be in the improvement of the official relations between the members of the new Balkan Entente on the one hand and Bulgaria and Albania on the other. The most serious issue, of course, was between Bulgaria and Jugoslavia. Happily, as we have seen, there were real indications that the relations between these two Slav countries were on the mend. This, likewise, was true of Jugoslav-Albanian relations, the new trend being especially noticeable in the signing of two commercial accords in April and May, 1934.[31] Early in April M. Mushanov, the Bulgarian premier, visited M. Jevtich in Belgrade, and later in the month he promised M. Barthou, the French foreign minister, that though Bulgaria could not sign the Balkan Pact, everything would be done to bring about the establishment of friendly relations with Jugoslavia. M. Barthou and M. Titulescu discussed, on April 18, the possibility of Bulgaria's signing a pact of nonaggression with her neighbors. At the same time, M. Jevtich was cementing Turco-Jugoslav friendship by his visit to Ankara. On his way back through Sofia, M. Jevtich told Bulgarian journalists of his hopes and declared that "all the questions between Bulgaria and Jugoslavia can be settled. For this purpose nothing more than good will is necessary."[32]

Early in May, M. Jevtich paid an official visit to Sofia, where he engaged in conversations relative to the settlement of Jugoslav-Bulgarian differences. An official *communiqué,* issued on May 9, stated that the ministers of the two governments were examining questions of passport facilities, commerce, and communications. The visit produced a favorable impression in both countries, and on May 24, a commercial treaty was signed.

The Bulgaro-Jugoslav *rapprochement* was much simplified by the *coup d'état* of May 19 which brought the semifascist ZVENO government of M. Kimon Georgiev into office. The new government was determined to effect a thorough "renovation" of the Bulgarian parliamentary system and a reorientation of Bulgarian foreign policy. On foreign affairs it issued the following manifesto : "Peace and good relations with all the Great Powers and *especially with our neighbors;* reëstablishment of our relations with Soviet Russia." The fact that the government also decreed the "reëstablishment of the public authority over the entire extent of the territory" indicated that it was prepared to liquidate the Internal Macedonian Revolutionary Organization (IMRO). Indeed, it at once proceeded to reorganize the local government into seven departments, with governors of far-reaching authority. Included, of course, was the Petrich district, hitherto dominated by the Macedonian revolutionaries. This was a step taken not only to reassert the authority of the Sofia government, but also to liquidate the outstanding difficulty in the relations with Jugoslavia. The fact that M. Constantin Batalov, the Bulgarian minister in Paris, became the minister of foreign affairs, indicated an orientation in foreign policy which was not hostile to France, as well as a policy based on friendship with Jugoslavia. There was to be coöperation with all the Balkan countries, and negotiations were to be begun immediately for the settlement of all questions. With reference to the Four-Power Balkan Pact, however, M. Batalov declared on May 26 that "the viewpoint of Bulgaria . . . is well known and remains unchanged." But the new government was ready to renew the offer of bilateral pacts of nonaggression and to conclude a similar multilateral pact.[33]

It was at this time that the diplomatic scene shifted to the broader stage of world politics and the program for Balkan *rap-*

prochement began to fit into the movement for regional security in Europe. The rise of Adolph Hitler, the withdrawal of both Japan and Germany from the League of Nations, the failure of the Disarmament Conference at Geneva, and the threat to the entire system and the machinery of peace—all these were forcing the European powers toward a new alignment and toward an attempt to attain their security through regional political agreements. As we shall see, the Balkan Pact was but one of these, for soon we have proposals for a Baltic pact, an Eastern European Locarno, and a Mediterranean agreement. France will be seen drawing close first to Soviet Russia and then to Italy, and all these states, considering their territories threatened, will be grouping themselves in accordance with their interests.

French foreign policy, under the direction of M. Louis Barthou, looked definitely toward friendship with Russia and the membership of the latter in the League of Nations. Late in April, M. Barthou visited Warsaw in order to tie Poland more completely to France, since Poland appeared to be moving toward Germany, as evidenced by the German-Polish treaty of nonaggression in January, 1934. But it was no secret that the French foreign minister was not successful in his mission.[34] M. Barthou went to Prague on April 26 to cement the French alliance with Czechoslovakia. Nearly two months later, he traveled to Bucharest, where the conference of the Little Entente was being held from June 18 to June 20. The Little Entente not only endorsed the conclusion of the Balkan Pact of February 9 and the normalization of Soviet Russia's relations with Czechoslovakia and Rumania, which took place on June 9, but also announced its support "of all European forces, particularly the conclusion of security pacts, which were strengthening security among the Central European nations."[35] Following a significant speech before the Rumanian parliament on June 20, in which he declared that France stood definitely on the basis of the territorial *status quo,* Barthou was made an honorary citizen of Rumania.[36] On June 24, he visited Belgrade in his endeavors to hold Jugoslavia within the French orbit of alliances. In both Jugoslavia and Rumania, apparently, he was successful, though his remarks in neither country helped the French cause in Bulgaria.[37]

Meanwhile, the Conference for the Reduction of Armaments had resumed its sessions in Geneva on May 29, with little prospect of constructive achievement. It seemed clear, indeed, to the majority of the Continental Powers represented, that any reduction of armaments should be preceded by political agreements on the security of frontiers. This view was now supported in its entirety by Soviet Russia. Turkey, fearful of the possible designs of fascist Italy in the Near East and particularly in the Straits, informally communicated to the Balkan states her desire for the right to fortify those strategic waters. On June 1, Tevfik Rushdi Bey submitted a resolution asking the Conference "to enter without delay upon an exhaustive study of the problem of security," for the purpose of arriving, especially in Europe, "by general or regional agreements based on the principles set down in the Treaty of Locarno and in that of the Balkan Entente, at such solutions as might be best calculated to make it possible to conclude [agreements] for the reduction and limitation of armaments." The Turkish resolution also suggested that a committee be appointed for the study of the proposal on security pacts.[38]

Among its resolutions, the Conference provided for a commission to study the entire question of security agreements. By June 25 this commission had ended its sessions and prepared a report. The document, submitted by M. Politis, of Greece, who had studied the problem for years, endorsed the whole program of regional security, and in the main provided:[39]

1. Regional security agreements should conform to the rules laid down in the great general pacts such as the Covenant of the League of Nations and the Pact of Paris, and be brought into line with the special agreements previously concluded by the contracting parties, either among themselves or with third states.

2. Such agreements should not be directed against any power or group of powers. . . .

3. The expression "regional security agreements" does not necessarily imply that the application of such agreements is strictly confined to a certain region. It may also be applied to agreements concluded among a very large number of states.

4. The Committee of Arbitration and Security declared in 1928 that it is useful even for states nonmembers of the League of Nations to participate in these agreements.

5. In seeking the most appropriate formulas for facilitating the conclusion

of such agreements there should be borne in mind, in addition to the Rhine Pact of Locarno and the Model Treaty of Mutual Assistance of 1928, agreements since concluded which are at present in force, such as the London Pacts of 1933 among twelve states on the definition of the aggressor, one of which is open to accession by all states, and the Balkan Pact concluded in 1934 among four states, which has been left open for the accession of other states in the same region.

It is noteworthy that although the British delegate did not accept the definition of the aggressor contained in the Soviet treaties of July 3–4, 1933, he did not object to its adoption by the other countries. The French, Russian, and Little Entente delegates considered the report "very satisfactory."

Some days later, on June 29, M. Litvinov made an extended comment on the fundamental ideas embodied in the conception of regional security. He pointed out that "the idea of regional pacts of mutual assistance was born out of the universal sense of insecurity, out of the uncertainty that in general, and particularly in Europe, peace would be maintained." The specific causes, he thought, were "well enough known." He himself had proposed such a pact to cover the Baltic region in April, but Hitlerite Germany had rejected it. Likewise, he had suggested one to Japan, with similar success.

So long as security is uncertain, it is quite natural that those states which are sincerely anxious to spare their own peoples and other peoples the horrors of war should be seeking new means to insure security for all and particularly for the weakest states, those which may find themselves in the first line of fire and be swept off the map of Europe.

In the present situation, the Soviet commissar felt that disarmament could "hardly be regarded as a guarantee of security." Nor did he feel that the *Covenant* of the League of Nations or the Briand-Kellogg Pact offered sufficient guarantees. This, likewise, was true of bilateral nonaggression pacts, concluded by some states to free their hands "and secure their rear or flanks for an attack on other states." Of course, the policy of military alliances and armaments offered no solution at all. Consequently,

By a policy of elimination we thus arrive at another means, namely, pacts of mutual assistance, which must by no means be regarded as an attempt to encircle anyone, since every state belonging to a given region may join in these pacts. Having equal rights and obligations and equal measures of security, not one signatory of such a pact should be considered encircled or subject to any danger if only he shares the other signatories' desires for peace. *Of course, it is different when any state, anxious to have free hands, deliberately refuses to participate in the proposed regional pact; but in this event it has no right to complain of encirclement if, in accordance with its own desire, the pact is concluded without it.*

M. Litvinov had in mind the proposal for an Eastern European Locarno when he made this statement, and he insisted that there was no necessary connection between this suggestion and the Balkan Pact, but he did declare that "it would be reasonable to apply regional pacts to other parts of Europe as well, and even to other continents." Soviet Russia was prepared to play her rôle in the movement of regional security, and in this connection, to enter the League of Nations.[40]

Truly, Europe as a whole was facing a very grave situation in the summer of 1934. Unrest prevailed everywhere—even authoritarian governments such as that of Hitlerite Germany were showing signs of weakness. On June 30 came the "blood bath" in Germany in which General von Schleicher and Captain Roehm were eliminated. There were fears that the French general staff might seize this opportunity to put an end to the possible menace from across the Rhine. Scarcely a month later the chancellor of Austria, Dr. Engelbert Dollfuss, was assassinated, and there was threat of a Nazi *putsch*, which the Italians were prepared to answer with a march into Austria. An incident might start the war machines.

It was in these general circumstances that Dr. Eduard Beneš, the Czechoslovak foreign minister, appeared before the parliament in Prague on July 2 to discuss a new phase of the struggle for European balance.[41] In his address he laid particular stress on the development of schemes for regional security. He believed that Europe stood "at the parting of the ways and the path which shall be followed will lead either to serene and tranquil heights or to a new abyss of conflicts, disorders, and crises." The critical situation had been brought about by the weakening of the League of Nations through the withdrawal of Germany and Japan, and by the failure of the movement for the reduction of armaments. M. Beneš further declared:

Europe, since the end of 1933, rightly or wrongly has felt itself threatened with serious conflicts. Its vigorous reaction to this threat has taken the form of incessant and feverish diplomatic negotiations; a new grouping of European forces is consequently being prepared, a regrouping which, in the last few weeks, may be said to have brusquely and unexpectedly become apparent to everybody and which appears to be of a nature to change, to a certain degree, all the previous relationships on the Continent.

As a consequence of the new trend of affairs, the reorganization of the Little Entente in 1933 was part of this realignment. This, likewise, was true of the Four-Power Balkan Pact.

In fact we should not consider that the chief significance of the Balkan Pact lies in political or military agreements relative to the frontiers of the Balkan States or that it is aimed against Bulgaria. What has been realized in the form of a pact of guarantee is of infinitely greater importance and meaning, like that which has been and still is the principal meaning of the Little Entente: the Balkan Entente is in fact the putting into practice of this principle—the Balkans for the Balkan peoples. By this pact, for the first time in contemporary history, the Balkan States are organizing themselves by pacific means and are demanding of the Great Powers that they leave the Balkans to themselves. ... It is a sort of evolution in Balkan policy; it is an event of the first magnitude in European politics, an event which with perfect logic arrays itself among the contemporary postwar evolutionary tendencies. ... There will be no war in the Balkans if there are no rivalries there among the Great Powers. Then only will the famous historic word "Balkanization" lose all meaning. Under these conditions no local quarrel among the Balkan States will again provoke a European conflict.

M. Beneš believed that the new Bulgarian government would coöperate with the new Balkan grouping, "even if that coöperation should not take the form of direct adhesion ... to the Balkan Pact." The close connection between the Little Entente and the Balkan Entente, under the influence of "French policy," M. Beneš thought, would "furnish one of the new important guarantees of peace." Moreover, Czechoslovakia was prepared to coöperate with Italy to insure economic assistance to Austria "in order to eliminate the imminent danger of *Anschluss*."

The trend toward the establishment of an Eastern European Locarno, in which Soviet Russia was to play such a part, was saluted by Dr. Beneš. The return of Soviet Russia to the European system, as a consequence of the German and the Japanese threat, would aid in the consolidation of peace. The question of the Eastern Locarno was not that of aligning one group against another

DEMETRIUS MAXIMOS
Minister of Foreign Affairs of Greece

in the form of military alliances, but was a measure to attain security, "to place all the nations on the same footing in relation to each other and at last to establish equilibrium in Europe."

With the development of the movement for security it was natural that both Great Britain and Italy should be forced to take positions with reference to the problem. Certainly neither country could remain outside, though both were anxious to avoid complicated and extended obligations reaching beyond their original commitments in the Locarno Agreements of 1925. Italy, indeed, was so much opposed to the Barthou program in Central Europe, where France and Italy had struggled for supremacy ever since the end of the war, that, partly in response to the French overtures, an Italian fleet had sailed into the Albanian port of Durazzo in the last days of June, leaving only on July 1. It appeared that the Italian government had demanded that Albania refrain from joining the Balkan Pact and that its relations with Jugoslavia become "less close."[42] On July 9, M. Barthou arrived in London, soon after the visit of General Weygand, in order to determine the exact position of the British government toward his proposed system of security pacts and particularly toward the Eastern European Locarno. He received his answer in the statement of Sir John Simon and the debates in the British House of Commons on July 13.[43] All the elements in the House of Commons supported the scheme, even including Sir Austen Chamberlain and Winston Churchill, who now appeared in the rôle of supporters of Soviet Russia. Sir Austen went so far as to say that "if Germany refused the reciprocal arrangement she could not complain if those whose advances she had declined, then provided for their own security and if in so providing they clearly indicated that they had Germany's policy in mind." Sir John Simon made it clear that Great Britain could not "lend any countenance or any encouragement or moral support to new arrangements between States in Europe which would be of a definitely selective character in the sense that they were building up one combination against another." Sir John also declared that Great Britain would assume no new obligations under the pact, but he was happy to endorse the idea. He was ready to welcome Soviet Russia into the Council of the League of Nations.

Moreover, the British foreign minister read a statement from Rome indicating that Italy was prepared to assume a like attitude on these problems.[44] The state of mind of British officialdom was given perhaps even more definition in the debates on the provisions for air defense on July 30, when the acting premier, Mr. Stanley Baldwin, warned the House of Commons that "the well-being of this country depended on the well-being and security of Europe," and declared that "when you think of the defense of England, you no longer think of the chalk cliffs of Dover, you think of the Rhine."[45] Threatened now by a possible German menace from the air, as once she had been on the seas, Great Britain, apparently, was no longer content to remain a passive spectator of European events. It seemed clear that the might of Britain would be thrown into the scales against a violent rupture of the *status quo*.

When the League of Nations convened for its annual session in September, the movement toward regional security had gained much ground. The Balkan Pact was already an accomplished fact, and even the Bulgarian government, though there were no signs of any desire to adhere to the treaty, was certainly moving in the direction of friendship with its neighbors, especially Jugoslavia.[46] A Baltic Pact among Latvia, Esthonia, and Lithuania was signed at Geneva on September 12. Both Great Britain and Italy had approved the principle of an Eastern European Locarno, and France and Italy were on more friendly terms than ever before in the postwar years. But Poland, now between the states of the Baltic group and the Little Entente and anxious to play an independent rôle, presumably as a Great Power, was not at all enamoured of the idea of an Eastern Locarno. Poland was definitely moving away from her French orientation.[47] On September 10, Germany formally rejected the Eastern Locarno on the ground that the problem of mutual military assistance presented insurmountable difficulties, and that her central position among the heavily-armed powers would make Germany the battleground of Europe. Furthermore, the Hitler government denied that there was any real "political need" for special guarantees by France and Russia, and that in any event, Germany could not expect to profit by them. In place of the pact, Germany proposed bilateral pacts of nonaggression and consultation.[48] Germany's position in her demand for equality and in her opposition to a multilateral pact was not unlike that of Bulgaria with reference to the Four-Power Balkan Pact.

Several problems came before the members of the Little Entente and the Balkan Entente, which held sessions on September 13 and 14, at the time of the meeting of the League of Nations. Both groups endorsed the entry of Soviet Russia into the League, the idea of security pacts, and the principles involved in the minority treaties. The Little Entente took a definite stand in favor of "the complete independence of all the states in the Danubian basin." The Council of the Balkan Entente considered favorably "the proposed pacts of security, or those which are in the process of negotiation, and especially the Mediterranean Pact, which it wishes to see concluded at an early date." The Balkan Entente was looking forward to the announced visit of the Jugoslav sovereigns to Sofia, Bulgaria.[49]

It was at this session of the League of Nations, on September 18, that Soviet Russia was admitted to membership and elected to the Council. Though there was, inevitably, much of the old diplomacy, and though Soviet Russia entered the Geneva organization from purely utilitarian motives, her action was viewed as a fundamental contribution to the organization of peace.[50] M. Litvinov, who was already the virtual dean of Geneva diplomatists, in his remarks accepting membership, significantly declared :

We must establish that any state is entitled to demand from its neighbors, near and remote, guarantees for security and that such a demand is not to be considered as an expression of mistrust. Governments with clear consciences and really free cannot refuse to give in place of declarations, more effective guarantees, which would be extended to themselves and give them also a feeling of common security.

Shortly after the meeting of the League of Nations it became evident that the movement for reduction of armaments was "as dead as the dodo," at least for the time being. The principal reason was the fear of Hitlerite Germany. The Arms Conference was postponed until November, and then the path toward peace was to proceed along the road of a series of interlocking security pacts with international supervision of the manufacture and accumulation of arms. The regional security pacts would be composed of the Four-Power Balkan Pact, and the proposed Mediterranean, Baltic, and more general Eastern European Locarno pacts. This was the French scheme, and the French believed that Poland would be forced into line, that Great Britain and Italy would join because of their fears of Germany, and that even the United States would look with objective sympathy on this conception of the organization of European peace on the basis of the *status quo*. By such action Germany, as a consequence of her utter isolation, might eventually be brought back into the fold of the League of Nations.[51]

There now remained two other tasks essential to the completion of these aspects of the security program. The first was to cement even more closely the *rapprochement* between Jugoslavia and Bulgaria, which had been begun in the fall and winter of 1933. The second was to solve the difficulties between France and Italy and bring about friendship between Italy and Jugoslavia. If these things could be accomplished, Louis Barthou's program of an organized peace on the basis of the Versailles system of treaties would be well-nigh fulfilled and the Balkan region itself could be pacified.

On September 27, the day when the fifteenth session of the League of Nations ended, King Alexander and Queen Marie of Jugoslavia arrived in Sofia to return the visit which the Bulgarian sovereigns had made in the previous December. The principal purpose of the sojourn was to attempt to cement the new friendship by the settlement of certain outstanding difficulties. A *communiqué* issued on September 30 declared that the two governments were prepared to reach an agreement on such matters as railway communications, passport formalities, and economic exchanges. It was also emphasized that it was indispensable to promote and strengthen the cultural ties between the two countries—a commercial and veterinary agreement had been signed in May, and already there were indications of improved relations. It may be, too, that some form of political connection was worked out, without formal adherence of Bulgaria to the Four-Power Balkan Pact. While this move toward friendship fits within the plans developed by France, there seems no doubt that the two countries were also attempting to work independently toward genuine Balkan coöperation. There were fears, however, that unless other developments intervened, *rapprochement* between Jugoslavia and Bulgaria might be the beginning of a Slavic *bloc* in the Balkans, with possibilities of an alliance.[52]

About one week later, King Alexander began his fateful trip on the *Dubrovnik*, to France, where he was going for a thorough discussion of France's new policy of close collaboration with Italy, as well as to report on his conversations in Bulgaria. Jugoslav newspapers had unleashed a bitter attack against Italy within the week, and Mussolini himself had warned the Jugoslavs that these attacks must cease.[53] Indeed, there was grave opposition in Jugoslavia to the French maneuvers in the direction of Italy, and many felt that it would be very difficult for France to conciliate the antagonisms of Central Europe, just as it was difficult to reconcile the position of Poland with the newly formed friendship between France and the Soviet Union. There were signs that even Rumania might strain at the leash within the Little Entente. Perhaps Hitlerite Germany might break through the new ring now forged about her—a ring partly of Germany's own making. Moreover, there were indications that Hungary, the erstwhile economic and political friend of fascist Italy, was becoming alarmed at the new trend of affairs at Rome. Political relations in Central Europe seemed to be in a state of flux. Perhaps King Alexander's trip would have served to stabilize the situation and quiet these fears, for following that visit, M. Barthou was to go to Rome for conversations with Il Duce. But within a few minutes after King Alexander landed on French soil he was shot down by an assassin, and with him died Louis Barthou.[54] Was the movement toward regional security to stop here?

NOTES TO CHAPTER VI

[1] For the text of the pact and the French explanations see *L'Esprit International*, No. 27 (July, 1933), 477–84.

[2] See *ibid.*, No. 26 (April, 1933), 325–27, for the text. There is an excellent discussion of Czechoslovak foreign policy in Dr. Kamil Krofta's *A Short History of Czechoslovakia* (New York, 1934), Chap. XIV.

[3] See *The Soviet Union Review*, XI (July-August, September, and October, 1933), 166–71, 192–93, 216–18, for texts and interpretations. The text of the Pact of the Soviet Union with the Little Entente and Turkey, London, July 4, 1933, is in the Appendix to the present work, Document XII. For the background of the definition of the aggressor see League of Nations. *Records of the Conference for the Reduction and Limitation of Armaments. Series B. Minutes of the General Commission.* II. December 14, 1932–June 29, 1933. IX. Disarmament. 1933. IX. 10. Litvinov's statement of February 6, 1933, is contained in pp. 234–38. Kemal Husni Bey's statement requesting full Turkish sovereignty over the Straits is on pp. 364–67. On May 24, 1933, the Politis Commission on Security made its report [pp. 494–502]. Great Britain, Italy, and Hungary were opposed to the definition. M. Malinov, the Bulgarian delegate, declared on May 29 that the definition "might conflict with justice and leave the door open to abuse in complicated and difficult cases. ... The Bulgarian government could not accept the criteria for the automatic designation of the aggressor contained in Article 1 of the Act in question. In would be glad, however, to support any text giving a general definition of the article in question" [551–52].

[4] Albert Mousset, "Les Balkaniques à la Conférence de Londres"; Charles Loiseau, "Les Balkans et l'U. R. S. S."; *L'Europe Centrale* (July 1, 29, 1933), 410–12, 473–75. President Roosevelt's statement of May 16, 1933, and Ambassador Davis' remarks at Geneva on May 22 emphasize the idea of non-aggression. Likewise, the implication of the Roosevelt statement of December 28, 1933, that 90 per cent of the people of the world were satisfied with existing boundaries, is significant.

[5] New York *Times*, September 17, October 1, 1933. The text of the treaty of September 14, 1933, between Greece and Turkey may be found in LB, IV (September-October, 1933), 624–29, and in the Appendix to the present work, Document XII. A Turco-Bulgarian veterinary convention was signed on December 22, 1933; *La Bulgarie*, July 28–31, 1934.

[6] *L'Echo de Belgrade*, September 7, 13, 20, October 4, 1933; *La Bulgarie*, October 19, 1933. Also M. S. Ingalls, "The Balkans in the World Crisis," *Foreign Policy Reports* (December 6, 1933).

[7] Texts in *La Bulgarie*, October 28, 1933.

[8] Texts, *ibid.*, November 15, 25–30, 1933.

[9] *L'Echo de Belgrade*, November 29, December 6, 1933; *La Bulgarie*, November 30, 1933. See also Leon Savadjian, "La politique extérieure de la Turquie et le problème de la paix balkanique," *L'Europe Nouvelle* (December 16, 1933), 1206–09.

[10] *L'Echo de Belgrade,* December 13, 20, 1933; *La Bulgarie,* December 9–14, 1933.

[11] *L'Echo de Belgrade,* December 27, 1933.

[12] *La Bulgarie,* January 10, 1934.

[13] *L'Echo de Belgrade,* January 17, 1934.

[14] *La Bulgarie,* January 27, 29, 1934.

[15] *L'Echo de Belgrade,* February 7, 1934.

[16] See also G. Hateau, "La Bulgarie et le 'Pacte balkanique,' " *L'Europe Centrale,* January 27, 1934.

[17] The London *Times,* February 6, 1934.

[18] See *La Bulgarie's* editorial comment, February 8 and following, and the excerpts from other Bulgarian journals. M. Mushanov declared on February 5 that Bulgaria was still ready "to conclude nonaggression pacts with all Balkan countries within the framework of the League of Nations *Covenant* and in the spirit of the Kellogg Pact." See New York *Times,* February 6, 1934.

[19] The text of the Four-Power Balkan Pact of February 9, 1934, may be found in LB, V (January-February, 1934), 92–93, in English in the New York *Times,* February 18, 1934, and is reprinted in the Appendix to the present work, Document XIV. A summary of the alleged secret protocol was first published in the Bulgarian journal, *Zora* (Sofia), March 18, 1934. The alleged text was published in *La Macédoine* (Sofia), May 1, 1934, and this journal published on May 6, 1934, what purported to be a second secret protocol of March 27, 1934. M. Papanastassiou has informed the writers, however, that the allegation of a second protocol "is without foundation" (letter of June 22, 1934). The fact that the secret protocol was not published immediately in spite of promises to register it with the Secretariat of the League of Nations, gave rise to many rumors concerning it. The British government advised the signatories on April 16 to publish the document, and on April 25 the British government received a copy. Its contents were summarized in the London *Times,* April 25, 1934, and in the New York *Times,* April 26, 1934.

The London *Times,* February 10, 1934, declared editorially that "A Balkan agreement which omits Bulgaria, not to mention Albania, is a contradiction in terms. . . . There will be no disposition in Jugoslavia to attach great value to a pact which neither Bulgaria nor Albania has joined, especially if it should prove hereafter to be an obstacle to an agreement with Bulgaria." The *Times* also said that Jugoslavia was not apparently enthusiastic about the Pact, and that the provision forbidding signatories to take political action against a nonsignatory without mutual consultation was definitely inserted at the wish of Jugoslavia to enable her to use a restraining influence in Bulgaria's behalf. In reply to the British statement, M. Jevtich declared that the Pact met all the British requirements, that it was not directed against anyone, and that everything was done to bring Bulgaria in, but "unfortunately she did not wish to come in, and we could not force her to join." *Manchester Guardian Weekly,* February 16, 1934. For comment see *Christian Science Monitor,* February 10, 1934; Vera M. Dean, "Toward a New Balance of Power," *Foreign Policy Reports* (May 9, 1934); William Miller, "The Balkan Pact," *Contemporary Review* (May, 1934), 532–39; Dimitry Stanciov, "The New Atmosphere in the Balkans," *ibid.* (March, 1934), 287–95.

20 These statements are in LB, V, 93–98; *Le Méssager d'Athènes*, February 11, 1934; *L'Echo de Belgrade*, February 14, 1934; *La Bulgarie*, February 10, 12, 1934.

21 *L'Indépendance Roumaine*, February 13, 1934.

22 *La Bulgarie*, March 4, 1934.

23 For complete reports of the discussions in the Greek Chamber and Senate, with all available documentary materials, see *Méssager d'Athènes*, February 10, 14; March 4–6, 10, 12–16; April 4, 1934. See also LB, V (March-April, 1934), 281–91. Premier P. E. Tsaldaris of Greece gave a statement, "Balkans Embark on Ship of Peace," in the *Christian Science Monitor*, April 25, 1934.

24 The text of M. Jevtich's address is in *L'Europe de l'Est et du Sud-Est* (March-April, 1934), 91–106. The text of the Austro-Hungarian-Italian pacts of March 17, 1934, are in the New York *Times*, March 18, 1934. See also Dr. Beneš's statement of March 21, 1934, before the Czechoslovak Chamber, in the *Central European Observer* (March 23, 1934). Note also the speech of M. Jevtich, March 28, 1934, in *L'Echo de Belgrade*. For Mussolini's remarks of March 18, 1934, see the *Manchester Guardian Weekly*, March 23, 1934. See also A. Mousset, "L'Europe danubienne au lendemain des accords de Rome," *L'Esprit International* (July, 1934), 416–32.

25 The full text of M. Titulescu's address and the debates in the Rumanian Chamber of April 4, 1934, are in *L'Heure Actuelle*, No. 1 (May 10, 1934): *Les dossiers politiques*, "L'attitude de la Roumanie vis-à-vis de la campagne pro-revisionniste," Séance du Parlement roumain du 4 avril 1934.

26 The statement of Mushanov is in *La Bulgarie*, February 2, 1934. For King Boris' visit to Paris and his conversations with Barthou, see *ibid.*, February 24–28, 1934.

27 The full text of the address of Mushanov is in *La Bulgarie*, April 2–4, 1934. In the debate which followed, there was some opposition to his principles. Professor Ghenov, of the Radical Party, said: "The Balkan Pact is in open contradiction with the pact as conceived by the Balkan Conferences. The Pact speaks neither of the friendly settlement of eventual conflicts nor of minorities. The aim is the maintenance of present frontiers. ... The Balkan Pact does not exhaust the possibilities of a Balkan *entente*." M. Dimitrov, of the Agrarian Party, declared that the Pact had checked the "*rapprochement* between Jugoslavia and Bulgaria," and recommended the Stambuliski policy. M. Pastukhov, Social-Democrat, said: "... revisionism is in retreat. The policy of Bulgaria must be one of peace and understanding with her neighbors. ... An opposition to *rapprochement* and the policy of understanding might have disastrous effects. ... Independently of the Pact, Bulgaria must be inspired by a policy that one must not modify any frontier by force." See also Mushanov's reply and the editorial comment in *La Bulgarie*, March 31, 1934. For Jugoslav comment see *L'Echo de Belgrade*, April 4, 1934, and the Greek position in *Méssager d'Athènes*, March 31, 1934. *Le Temps*, April 2, 1934, has some interesting comment.

[28] LB, V, 109–11.

[29] The *procès-verbaux* are in LB, V, 297–312.

[30] The vote was seven to six. The following questions were placed on the agenda of the Fifth Conference: I. Statutes of the Conference and the consular convention. II. The problem of the Four-Power Balkan Pact. III. Coördination of Balkan industrial policy, collaboration in agricultural credit, statutes of a Balkan agricultural chamber, Balkan veterinary convention. IV. Social insurance, sanitary convention, rural hygiene, white slave traffic. V. Coördination of resolutions on communications, Balkan public works program. VI. Development of the Balkan educational week. The draft statutes of the Balkan Parliamentary and Social Union may be found in the Appendix to the present work, Document XI.

[31] For the Albanian position concerning the Conference and the Pact see the letter of M. Konitza to M. Papanastassiou, March 16, 1934, and the statement of Dr. Nush Bushati in the Albanian journal, *Besa; La Bulgarie*, April 11, 23, 1934. The Albanians were particularly incensed because the failure to invite their participation in the Pact was based on the Italian "protectorate" over the country dating from November, 1922, which they had never recognized. But in July, M. Konitza declared that the Balkan Conferences had done remarkable work and that "Albania is a Balkan country and has every interest in having direct relations with her neighbors, especially with Jugoslavia. For some time the relations between these two countries have become sincerely friendly and I can say that they will surely become very cordial." See LB, V, 277–78; VI (July, 1934), 120. Also X. Lefcoparidis, *A travers l'Albanie* (Athens, 1934; reprinted from LB, VI, 13–43).

[32] *La Bulgarie*, April 3–4, 10–14, 18–21, 1934; *L'Echo de Belgrade*, April 28, 1934.

[33] The manifesto is in *La Bulgarie*, May 19, 1934; the declaration of Batalov, *ibid.*, May 30, 1934. See also the *Central European Observer*, May 18, June 1, 1934. King Alexander of Jugoslavia declared in May: "Bulgaria and Albania still remain outside the Pact. We desire nothing more ardently than that these two states should adhere to this Pact, which will give the Balkans to the Balkan peoples, free from all outside influence and interference." See *Manchester Guardian Weekly*, May 18, 1934, and May 25, June 1, 1934; *Christian Science Monitor*, May 22, 1934.

[34] The text of the German-Polish Agreement, January 26, 1934, is in *Ost-Europa* (March, 1934), 375–86. See also the *Central European Observer*, April 20, May 4, 1934. For an excellent account of Polish policy see C. Smogorzewski, "La Pologne entre l'Est et l'Ouest," *L'Esprit International*, No. 31 (July, 1934), 351–76.

[35] London *Times*, June 21, 1934, and *L'Heure Actuelle*, Nos. 2–3 (June-July, 1934), 7–9. The Little Entente exchanges of June 9 with Soviet Russia are on pp. 45–47.

[36] The texts of the Barthou, Titulescu, and other addresses of June 20 in the Rumanian parliament are in *L'Heure Actuelle*, No. 2 (June-July, 1934): *Les dossiers politiques*. It was on this occasion that Barthou declared: "Any-

one who touches your soil will meet not only with your opposition but with that of France, which is with you heart and soul."

[37] For text of addresses see *L'Echo de Belgrade,* July 27, 1934. The *Central European Observer* of June 29, 1934, declared that "the conclusion of the Balkan Pact has extended this opportunity of peaceful collaboration also to the Balkans. From Prague to Ankara there thus spreads a system of treaties which guarantee peace in that part of Europe, as the French minister of foreign affairs, M. Barthou, emphasized at Bucharest."

[38] London *Times,* June 2, 1934; *L'Esprit International,* No. 31 (July, 1934), 463–64.

[39] London *Times,* June 26, 1934. The full text of the report is in *L'Esprit International,* No. 32 (October, 1934), 586–89.

[40] The interview with Jules Sauerwein, the French journalist, was published in the New York *Times,* June 30, 1934, and in the *Economic Review of the Soviet Union* (September, 1934), 157–58; see also pp. 158–61. Authors' italics.

[41] Text in *International Conciliation,* No. 302 (September, 1934), 239–66.

[42] *Manchester Guardian Weekly,* July 6, 1934.

[43] The Debates in the House of Commons are in the London *Times,* July 14, 1934.

[44] The Italian statement read: "The attitude of Italy as a signatory to the Pact of Locarno is similar to that of the United Kingdom. On the clear understanding that the Eastern Pact of Mutual Guarantee does not imply any fresh engagements on her part, Italy regards with sympathy proposals which are made on a basis of absolute reciprocity between all the countries concerned. This is particularly the case when such proposals offer fresh possibilities in the field of a limitation or reduction of armaments and as regards implicit recognition of equality of rights."

[45] The text of the statement of Mr. Baldwin and the debates are in the London *Times,* July 31, 1934.

[46] See especially the address of M. Kimon Georgiev, the Bulgarian premier, on July 12, in *La Bulgarie,* July 13–14, 1934.

[47] New York *Times,* September 3, 1934; *Central European Observer* (October 5, 1934), 338–39. The text of the Baltic Pact is in *L'Esprit International,* No. 32 (October, 1934), 606–7. For the background of the Baltic Pact see M. W. Graham, "Security in the Baltic States," *Foreign Policy Reports* (February 17, 1932). The Polish position at the time was explained also by the fact that Poland was incensed over the possible deportation of some 600,000 Polish workers in France and over the fact that French capital was avoiding Poland. Moreover, Poland was attempting to "universalize" the minorities treaties or to get rid of them. See the *Manchester Guardian Weekly,* August 17, 1934; New York *Times,* September 11, 17, 1934. See also Dr. Eduard Beneš, *Vers un regroupement des forces en Europe?* (Prague, 1934), the address before the Chechoslovak Chamber, November 6, 1934.

[48] New York *Times,* September 11, 17, 1934.

[49] The text of the *communiqués* of the Little Entente and the Balkan Entente are in *L'Heure Actuelle*, No. 5 (September, 1934), 3–4. At Geneva, too, M. Maximos and M. Batalov began to prepare the ground for a settlement of Greco-Bulgarian difficulties. Commenting on the desire for collaboration with the Balkan Entente, *La Bulgarie*, September 18, declared: "Bulgaria is in fact the country which has perhaps more interest than any other in realizing the desires indicated in the *communiqué* of the Permanent Council of the Balkan Entente. It makes, of course, no secret of its sincere and loyal desire to work for the improvement of Balkan relations."

[50] For a discussion of the Soviet entry into the League see the New York *Times*, September 13, 18, 19, 1934. For the Litvinov address, in part, see *ibid.*, September 19. See also the *Central European Observer*, September 21, 1934, for the address of M. Beneš as president of the Council, and *ibid.*, October 5, 1934. See also H. N. Howard, "The Re-orientation of Soviet Foreign Policy," *World Unity* (September, 1934), 348–64. The full text of notes and Litvinov's acceptance of League membership are in the *Economic Review of the Soviet Union* (October, 1934), 192–97. For complete materials of this session of the Council of the League of Nations see League of Nations, *Official Journal*, 15th Year, No. 11 (Part I) (November, 1934).

[51] New York *Times*, September 26, 28, 1934.

[52] For fully documented accounts, with *communiqués* and addresses, of the royal visits to Sofia, see *La Bulgarie*, September 25-October 2, 1934; *L'Echo de Belgrade*, September 26, October 3, 1934. *Politika* (Belgrade) declared on September 27 that though in the past relations between Jugoslavia and Bulgaria had been bad, it expected much happier relations as a result of the visit. *Vreme*, of the same date, said that "the moment of understanding has come and it begins by a magnificent and splendid act." The railway communications involved in the discussions were on the Vidin-Negotin and Kumanovo-Guechevo lines. While there were no spectacular results such as a Bulgarian adherence to the Balkan Pact, M. Batalov remarked on October 1 that "the understanding, cordiality, and friendship on both sides have created a valuable psychological state which is more important than all the written pacts which might have been signed." The policy of understanding and friendship was "the single way by which Balkan peace can be preserved." The sentiment was reciprocated by the Jugoslav government. The *Central European Observer*, October 5, 1934, declared that while such questions as those of Macedonia and Bulgaria's access to the sea would have to be solved, "the old volcanic Balkans which continuously threatened Europe with convulsions has disappeared and ... the foundations of a new Balkans have been laid."

[53] New York *Times*, October 7, 1934.

[54] New York *Times*, October 10–13. There is an excellent account of the possible significance of the assassination at the hands of Macedonian terrorists in Dr. Shepard Stone's article, "Again Balkan Drama Stirs Europe," New York *Times*, October 14, 1934.

Chapter VII

AFTER THE BALKAN CONFERENCES: CONCLUSION

THE FOUR-POWER BALKAN PACT continued to be a serious problem within the circles of the Balkan Conference. The subject was on the agenda of the Universal Congress of Peace which met in Locarno in the first week of September, 1934. M. Papanastassiou presented a report on that topic to the Congress.[1*] After briefly tracing the history of the Balkan Conferences, he examined the principles of the Four-Power Balkan Pact of February 9, 1934, and its relation to the Conference movement. He did not conceal his disappointment at the *lacunae* in the new pact, pointing out that it was merely a treaty of mutual guarantee based on the territorial *status quo,* that the signatories did not take into consideration the principles of the draft political pact of the Balkan Conferences, that neither Albania nor Bulgaria was an adherent, and that there was no provision for that broader collaboration in the economic, social, and cultural realms which the Conference thought so essential to any real work toward Balkan friendship. Nevertheless, M. Papanastassiou believed that "despite its limited content, the Pact of the Balkan Entente constitutes an important step toward the consolidation of peace, particularly in the Balkans. For the first time four Balkan states . . . have agreed to collaborate to preserve peace and to guarantee the Balkan frontiers." The signing of the Four-Power Balkan Pact was, therefore, an event of the first magnitude in Balkan history. Moreover, the conclusion of this Balkan agreement had made the tasks of the Conferences more important than ever. M. Papanastassiou proposed that the Congress "express its joy at the signature of the Pact of the Balkan Entente and approve the enlargement of the Pact by the adherence of . . . Albania and Bulgaria [and] by the acceptance of the propositions of the Balkan Conference on political *rapprochement,* economic coöperation . . . , and on questions con-

* Superior figures refer to notes which will be found at the end of this chapter.

[156]

cerning communications, social policy, hygiene, and intellectual *rapprochement.*" He also asked that the Congress recognize "the usefulness of the Balkan Conference, a usefulness which has grown larger since the signature of the Pact of the Balkan Entente," and express the hope that the Conference would "continue its activity and that the governments would support it."

M. Sakazov, who represented the Bulgarian delegation at the Universal Congress of Peace, opposed M. Papanastassiou's suggestions, complaining particularly about the position of the minorities and the other shortcomings of the Four-Power Pact. In the end, the Papanastassiou resolution was amended, and the final resolution which was accepted declared merely that the conclusion of the Pact was "an important political document," which ought to be amended in order to facilitate the entry of Albania and Bulgaria into the Balkan Entente, and which ought to take note of the resolutions of the Balkan Conferences, including those for the protection of the minorities.[2]

THE FUTURE OF THE BALKAN CONFERENCES
AND THE BALKAN PACT

Within a few weeks, on October 1, the Fifth Balkan Conference was scheduled to meet at Istanbul, the new permanent headquarters of the organization. It will be recalled that, like the Fourth Conference, it was originally to have met in Belgrade. As in 1933, however, the Jugoslav government declined to be the host. Moreover, the Jugoslav group intimated that it would not attend the meeting. There were two reasons for this attitude. In the first place, the Jugoslav delegation was in fundamental disagreement with the Hellenic group over the question of the reorganization of the Balkan Conference. And in the second place, many in the Jugoslav delegation felt that the making of the Four-Power Balkan Pact had rendered any further Conferences unnecessary. The foreign ministers of the new Balkan Entente, moreover, appear to have advised adjournment.[3] The result was that the fifth meeting of the Balkan Conference was postponed indefinitely, though it was announced that the next meeting would be held in April, and then in October, 1935. The Greek revolt early in 1935 and the crisis in European politics during the year prevented the calling of another Conference.[4]

Whether the Balkan Conferences have been adjourned only temporarily, or whether the Conferences have finished their task, it is a fitting moment to summarize the significant and important accomplishments of these gatherings. The fact that the Balkan Conferences were organized is itself a tribute to the men who participated in them and to their ideals of confederation and union. But the achievements of the Balkan Conferences mark the movement as one of major importance. The elaboration of the draft of a political pact at the Conference of Bucharest in 1932 was a worthy accomplishment, for it was based on the general principles of outlawry of war, arbitration, and mutual assistance, and provided definitely for the adjustment of the problem of minorities within the framework of existing treaties. It is along these lines, it would seem, that a mutually acceptable political pact for the region may be drawn up. The adoption at Bucharest of the draft convention on the status of Balkan citizens is another notable achievement. This convention would provide for greater freedom of movement among the Balkan peoples and lead toward those social, economic, and cultural contacts which give a broad popular foundation for political agreement. One of the tasks of the Balkan Labor Office would be to supervise the execution of the principles embodied in the Conference pact on the status of Balkan citizens. Another important measure was the adoption of the project for a partial Balkan Customs Union at the Salonica meeting in 1933, which provided the economic groundwork for political union and which was designed to promote the interchange of Balkan commodities and the protection of Balkan products on the world market.

The adoption of these political, social, and economic pacts alone would justify the existence and the labors of the Balkan Conferences, but there is much more to their credit. The program of intellectual coöperation which was initiated by the Conferences will be influential, not only within the circles of the movement itself, but within the broader field of the cultural relations of the Balkan peoples.[5] In the long run the program of developing intellectual relations through the universities and educational institutions, and through church and press, should have a profound effect upon all the Balkan nations. Collaboration in a broad development of social policy ought also to have its influence in the achievement of greater uniformity in social and economic legislation, in wiping out child labor and regulating the conditions of female labor, in the elimination of the white slave traffic, and in the development of a thoroughgoing program of rural hygiene throughout the peninsula. It is worth noting that the Conferences promoted a thoroughly scientific system of sanitary and veterinary treaties. The adoption of a comprehensive program of economic collaboration which calls for a Balkan system of agricultural coöperatives, a system of agricultural credit, and the establishment of a Balkan Chamber of Agriculture is also fundamental. No more complete plans for the development and improvement of communications in the Balkans have ever been presented.

It is true that many of these provisions exist only on paper, but the list of those which have been put into execution is impressive. The Balkan Chamber of Commerce and Industry, the statutes of which were adopted in 1931, came into existence officially in December, 1932, and publishes a monthly *Bulletin*. A Balkan Coöperative Office was established by the Fourth Conference, though it has not yet begun to function. The Third Conference approved the establishment of a Balkan Chamber of Agriculture which was to begin functioning after the Conference of Istanbul in 1935. The only official inter-Balkan organization which can be traced to the Balkan Conferences is the Oriental Tobacco Office (*Office pour la protection des tabacs d'Orient*), which was recommended by the Second Conference and established in September, 1933, by Bulgaria, Greece, and Turkey. A Balkan Medical Union, composed of all physicians in the peninsula, was approved at Bucharest and held its first meeting in Belgrade in September, 1933.[6] A Balkan Historical Institute was also approved at the Conference in Bucharest, but it has not begun to function, chiefly because the Turkish delegation felt that present facilities at Istanbul, which was to be the headquarters of the organization, were sufficient. One should not forget the creation of the Association of the Balkan

Press, organized after the First Balkan Conference, in December, 1930. Though it has not functioned well, it does represent important beginnings. Another significant institution is the Permanent Commission of Balkan Jurists, which has been studying the problem of legal unification, and which held three important meetings in June and October, 1932, and in November, 1933. The Balkan Tourist Federation, founded in 1931, represents an interesting attempt at collaboration in the tourist business and in the realm of communications. Following the Third Conference a Maritime Section was established in the Balkan Chamber of Commerce and Industry, at Istanbul, for the purpose of studying maritime communications among the Balkan states. Finally, the project for a Balkan Postal Union, adopted by the Second Conference, should be remembered. It has now (1936) been accepted by both Greece and Turkey. For a period of only four years these are not negligible achievements.[7]

But these accomplishments do not exhaust the possibilities, for they do not take into account the more or less intangible influences which may be traced directly or indirectly to the work of the Balkan Conferences. Although the recent political pact of February 9, 1934, was brought into being primarily because of the necessities of the moment arising from objective conditions both inside and outside the peninsula, there is little question that the Balkan Conferences, no matter what their shortcomings, played their part in preparing the psychological and spiritual background for the signing of that important treaty, faulty though it may be. Diplomatic representatives of the Balkan governments were present in the capacity of observers at all the meetings of the Conference. At each Conference the political heads of the state in whose capital the Conference was meeting gave addresses of welcome and sincere encouragement. This was true in Greece and Turkey, and in Rumania. Moreover, each Conference invited the heads of the Balkan states to serve as honorary presidents of the organization. It is also true that the different Balkan governments had much to do with the determination of the delegates and the national groups in the Balkan Conferences.

The influence of the Conference may thus be seen in the promo-

BOGOLJUB JEVTICH
Minister of Foreign Affairs of Jugoslavia

tion of better official relations among the Balkan countries. Following the Second Conference at Istanbul, Turkey and Albania resumed diplomatic relations. Shortly before the meeting of the Salonica Conference there began that series of official visits among the Balkan statesmen which contributed much to the *détente* in the region, led to the pact of February 9, and laid the foundations for a possible *rapprochement* between Jugoslavia and Bulgaria. It is true that the Four-Power Balkan Pact does not fulfill the desires of the Balkan Conference as sketched in the draft political agreement adopted at Bucharest in 1932, since it is purely a pact based on mutual guarantees of the frontiers of the Balkan signatories. But it does constitute a beginning which may be fruitful in the future. This will be true if Bulgaria and Albania adhere to the Pact and if it is broadened to include economic, social, and cultural, as well as political, collaboration. There should, of course, be more definite provisions for the protection of the cultural rights of the minority populations if Bulgaria and Albania are to be brought within the fold. Boundary lines between nations can be rendered less important—and this seems particularly so in the Balkans—only when these fundamental rights are guaranteed and when the minorities cease to be among the disaffected elements. Ultimately, if not now, the sacred and individual character of one's "nationality" will have to be recognized, as is now true of one's religion, thus separating the concept of "nationality" from that of "citizenship."[8]

EUROPEAN POLITICS AND THE BALKANS

But the problems involved, as has been indicated repeatedly, are not purely Balkan; for distinct though they are, Balkan politics cannot be separated from the currents of European politics. For centuries the Balkans have been a center of rivalry and conflict among the Great Powers—Austria-Hungary and Russia, Germany, Italy, and France, as well as Great Britain. Before the war neither Austria-Hungary nor Russia desired any kind of Balkan union which could not be dominated from either Vienna or St. Petersburg. This is analogous, in a way, to the position of the United States with reference to Latin America and especially the region of the Caribbean. Today Austria-Hungary is gone, but Italy has taken the place of the Dual Monarchy in the Balkan region. The fascist state does not look with favor on a strong Balkan confederation, and, for that matter, neither does Nazi Germany. Italy hopes to retain her hold on both Albania and Bulgaria. But if a genuine Balkan union is to be created, this hold, as well as that of any other Great Power in this region, may have to be relaxed. To make real progress the Balkan region needs to be freed from foreign interference, even though, in turn, the Balkan states should be careful of the interests of the Great Powers and treat them all alike. For, in the long run, the fate of the Balkan Peninsula is tied up with that of Europe and the world as a whole. If the present trend toward the development of regional security in Europe should lead to a genuine pacification of the old continent, then it may be reasonably certain that the same may take place within the Balkan region. But this presupposes in both Europe and the Balkans that the regional security movement will not be directed merely against a particular state or group of states. That is only to say that in neither event should the development of regional security—as represented in the proposed Eastern Locarno or in the actual Balkan Pact—be merely another name for the old system of alliances and alignments. If the movement is definitely within the universal system of the League of Nations and if it provides for those readjustments which naturally come with the changes of time and circumstances, then it may bring peace and security in its wake.

THE BALKANS FOR THE BALKAN PEOPLES

Recent indications point to a genuine *rapprochement* between Jugoslavia and Bulgaria, culminating in the visit of King Alexander to Bulgaria in the latter part of September, 1934. It is certain that the officials of the two governments discussed the adherence of Bulgaria to the Four-Power Balkan Pact, the Habsburg question, and relations with Soviet Russia. Although, as we have seen, Bulgaria did not adhere to the Pact in its present form, there could be no doubt that progress toward a policy of friendship was in process of development. The suppression of the Internal Macedonian Revolutionary Organization (IMRO) is an earnest of the Bulgarian government's intentions. There have been indications of an improvement in Albanian-Jugoslav relations, though Italy has taken steps to prevent these two Balkan neighbors from becoming "too close."[9]

It does not appear that the assassination of King Alexander will curtail or delay the development of closer collaboration and friendship in the Balkan Peninsula. That tragedy, however, does throw light on a host of historical problems which one day must be solved if Balkan unity is to be achieved. Some provision for autonomous development within Jugoslavia appears to be a necessity. This again, however, leads us into the policy of Italy—for there can be no devolution within Jugoslavia as long as there is a possibility of a threat from across the Adriatic, or from a Hungary allied to Italy, which refuses to recognize any autonomy to the large number of Slovene Jugoslavs within its borders.

The events following the assassination of King Alexander indicated a striking manifestation of unity within Jugoslavia and a fundamental desire to preserve the peace of Europe. Both the Little Entente and the Balkan Entente took their stand beside Jugoslavia and demanded an investigation of the circumstances which led to the assassination. When in December, 1934, the Council of the League of Nations met to consider the question, these two groups of states in Central and Balkan Europe, with the support of France, Great Britain, and Soviet Russia, obtained a moral satisfaction in the final resolution of the Council that Hungary investigate the charges that she had been harboring terroristic organizations with designs against Jugoslavia. It is noteworthy that Bulgaria preserved not merely a correct, but indeed a very cordial attitude during the entire crisis—an evidence of the new *rapprochement* which had taken place in Bulgar-Jugoslav relations.[10]

There was evidence that the agreements signed on January 7, 1935, between France and Italy would prepare the way for a fundamental coöperation between the states of Central and Balkan Europe and Italy, and serve in particular to promote more correct relations between Italy and Jugoslavia. At any rate, following the conversations in January, 1935, between M. Laval and Signor

Mussolini, France and Italy agreed to recommend to the neighboring and succession states of the old Habsburg Empire the conclusion of a convention and a self-denying ordinance not to interfere in each other's internal affairs. Moreover, the independence of Austria was once more affirmed, with provision for a regional collective guarantee. The fundamental significance of the Franco-Italian agreements lay not only in the fact that Paris and Rome were beginning to coöperate in the face of a possible common danger, but also in the fact that apparently the Rome government was moving from the revisionist to the *status quo* group on the continent of Europe. These agreements also adjusted Italo-French differences in Africa and laid the foundations for Mussolini's adventure of conquest in Ethiopia.[11] The Franco-Italian position was endorsed by the Councils of the Little Entente and the Balkan Entente some days later.[12]

Following the Franco-Italian accords and the settlement of the Saar issue between France and Germany through the plebiscite of January 13, 1935, it was possible for France once more to approach London to complete the *rapprochement* which had been effected in the summer of 1934. The conferences, which were held in London, February 1–3, resulted in a general series of agreements. The British government welcomed the *rapprochement* between Italy and France and the prospective coöperation of the powers concerned in Central Europe. The two governments felt that the progress achieved could be continued "by means of direct and effective coöperation with Germany." The general settlement "would make provision for the organization of security in Europe" particularly by means of the conclusion of pacts freely negotiated between all interested parties and insuring mutual assistance in Eastern Europe and the system foreshadowed in the Rome *procès-verbal* for Central Europe. For Western Europe it was proposed that an air nonaggression pact, in which Germany, France, Great Britain, and Belgium would be included, should be made.[13]

The question was now in the hands of Germany. On February 15, the German government announced its readiness to accept the air pact for Western Europe, under conditions of equality. It was prepared to examine the other proposals. But no mention was made about the Eastern Locarno, the Danubian region, or Germany's return to the League of Nations.[14] Some observers viewed the German reply as a clever attempt to separate France from England, and Western Europe from Soviet Russia.[15]

The next steps followed in quick succession, for the situation was growing more tense than it had been since the end of the World War. On March 16, the French government announced an extension of military service, and on the same day Germany abolished the armament clauses of the Versailles treaty and decreed universal military service. The protests of Italy, France, and England against this measure went unanswered—Germany had attained "equality."[16] Late in March came the series of "exploratory" conferences between Sir John Simon and Anthony Eden and the German, Russian, and Polish governments, which served to isolate Germany and to draw Great Britain and Russia together.

Following these maneuvers, representatives of the Italian, French, and British governments met at Stresa from April 11 to April 14. Would the meeting at Stresa bring unity or division? When the meetings closed, it was apparent that Germany had not broken the unity of the Powers. Although the Stresa meeting formulated no definitely constructive measures, it did provide some substantial gains for the peace of Europe. The Powers agreed to support the French protest to the League against Germany's rearmament. They repeated their position on Austrian independence, and recommended the calling of a Danubian conference to be held in Rome in June. They agreed to examine the request of Austria, Hungary, and Bulgaria, in collaboration with the Little Entente. They decided to continue their examination of regional pacts—Germany herself, while the conference was in session, announced her willingness to participate in a mutual nonaggression pact. Finally, the three Powers declared the object of their policy to be the maintenance of peace within the framework of the League of Nations, and they agreed in opposing any unilateral denunciation of treaties likely to endanger the peace of Europe.[17]

A few days later, the League Council denounced Germany's abrogation of Part V of the Versailles treaty. Even Poland voted for the resolution. On May 2, France and Russia signed a mutual assistance treaty within the framework of the League. This was followed by a similar treaty between Czechoslovakia and the Soviet Union. Meanwhile, the Little Entente and the Balkan Entente were preparing a concerted policy for the Danubian and Balkan region.[18]

But the Stresa front did not endure. On June 18, 1935, England signed a naval agreement with Germany, and by the summer Italy was definitely preparing the war of conquest in Ethiopia which began in October with the Italian invasion of that country.[19]

Meanwhile, the Council of the Balkan Entente, based on the Four-Power Balkan Pact of February 9, 1934, had, as we have seen, begun to function seriously. It held an important meeting at Ankara, Turkey, from October 20 to November 2, 1934, in which a plan of action was outlined. In a formal *communiqué* issued at the close of the session, the Council declared that

peace will not only not be threatened in the Balkans, but if it is threatened elsewhere, the Balkan Entente will remain master of the situation, in virtue of the coördination of the action of the Balkan Entente with other peaceful factors.

The Council also expressed its satisfaction "with the constant progress" in the relations between the members of the Balkan Entente and Bulgaria and Albania. In consonance with certain of the proposals of the Balkan Conference, the Council decided to appoint a committee to study the question of legal unification among the members of the Balkan Entente. Two of the most significant steps taken at Ankara were embodied in the Statute of Organization of the Balkan Entente and the Statute of the Advisory Economic Council.[20] The first of these provided for a Permanent Council, composed of the four foreign ministers, which would meet at least twice a year in regular session for the discussion of their mutual problems. A Secretariat was also to be established. The second statute created an Advisory Economic Council, to be composed of four national sections. Following the basic principles laid down by the Balkan Conferences, the Advisory Economic Council was to consider such problems as general commercial policy, agricultural questions, industrial problems, financial questions, and matters of communications. Not the least important suggestion was one for the creation of a Balkan Bank—a proposal which had been made repeatedly in the Balkan Conferences. It is also interesting to note that the Economic Council was to meet at least twice a year.

At the closing session of the Council many significant comments were made by the foreign ministers present.[21] Referring to the prospect of Balkan unity, M. Titulescu declared: "No longer will the intrigues and rivalries of the great powers be able to pit one of us against the other and thus plunge this part of the world into a war which means a greater conflagration than that of 1914." This would depend, of course, on the ability of the Balkan Entente to conciliate both Albania and Bulgaria. Three days later, on November 5, M. Titulescu arrived in Sofia. He told the Bulgarian press:[22]

The four states signatories of the Balkan Entente consider that Bulgaria must be treated by them with the same benevolent friendship as though she had signed the Balkan Pact. This is the most eloquent witness of the high appreciation in which the peaceful work of Bulgaria is everywhere held. It is also the best proof that the fear that the Balkan Entente was directed against Bulgaria was without foundation.

The Advisory Economic Council of the Balkan Entente held its first session from January 3 to January 9, 1935, at Athens, and at the conclusion of its meeting it prepared a protocol which was to be submitted in May to the Permanent Council. This protocol covered agreements on economic questions, communications, tourist traffic, a Balkan bank, the collaboration of economic institutions, and the problem of internal economic organization.[23] Was the Balkan Entente preparing to follow along the broader road toward understanding which the Balkan Conferences had pointed out?

In a significant editorial, *La Bulgarie* (January 15, 1935), the semiofficial organ of Sofia, cordially received the proposals of the Advisory Economic Council:

The recent labors of the Balkan Economic Council are worthy of the highest interest and could not, consequently, leave indifferent those who wish to contribute in every way to the prosperity and the economic well-being of the Balkans. Though not among the Powers adhering to the Balkan Entente, Bulgaria is not at all opposed to the method of collaboration and the spirit of understanding which are today at the basis of international life, or to any constructive effort.

Nor was the Bulgarian attitude changed, apparently, by the recent alterations in the government. Remaining as foreign minister in the Zlatev government, M. Batalov announced that the new government would "follow the same path as the preceding cabinet—the path leading to a solid and durable peace in the Balkans, to relations of good neighborhood and friendship with neighboring countries, and to economic and commercial relations with states near and far." The cabinet of M. Toshev announced in April that the foreign policy would remain unchanged—that policy emphasized, "above all, very friendly and sincere relations with our neighbors."[24] Neither did the resignation of M. Jevtich and the coming to power of M. Stojadinovich in Jugoslavia, nor the later changes in the Bulgarian government (November, 1935), foreshadow any fundamental alterations in foreign policy. This, likewise, was seemingly true of the monarchist revival in Greece, in November, 1935, under George II.[25]

Meanwhile, a notable example of the effectiveness of the Balkan Entente was seen in the Venizelist revolt in Greece in March, 1935. The revolt was reduced to an affair of internal Greek politics, instead of serving as the beginning of a Balkan, if not a general European, war. It remains to be seen what effect the crisis which has been brought about in the relations of Italy and Ethiopia and the League of Nations will have on the Balkan Entente. Suffice it to say, the Balkan Entente has been acting essentially as a unit, in spite of the obvious economic difficulties involved, in support of the system of collective security, under the League of Nations. In this connection it is apparent, however, that England's stand in the Near East is in line with what has been indicated elsewhere in this study.[26]

As we have seen, the Fifth Balkan Conference did not meet either in the spring or in the fall of 1935. But even if the Balkan Conferences have been permanently adjourned, their labors have been thoroughly worth while. There is a feeling among Balkan leaders that these meetings should go on. The task was not completed with the signature of the Four-Power Balkan Pact of 1934. Future Conferences, in new and reorganized form, in accordance with the proposed amendments to the statutes, may fill a very real need in broadening and deepening the provisions of the recent political pact. Without the influence of the Conferences the new Balkan Entente may be in danger of becoming an organ of the four states alone; under the influence of the Conferences there may be a prospect for genuine coöperation among all the states of the peninsula, including Bulgaria and Albania. Moreover, the kind of groundwork done in the Balkan Conferences may well have a future elsewhere in the Near East in leading other neighboring states to take similar action in these directions. Within recent years and months there have been conversations concerning a Middle Eastern Pact in which Turkey, Iraq, Iran, Afghanistan, and Saudi Arabia have been involved. Perhaps an independent Egypt might come into such an arrangement.

Only when the Balkans are really for the Balkan peoples—when the Near East is for the Near Eastern peoples—may there be serious hope for peace and security within that troubled region. Through some kind of confederation or union, based on principles similar to those laid down by the Balkan Conferences, the Balkan and Near Eastern peoples may eventually come into their own. Perhaps, also, through some kind of Mediterranean agreement, the pressure might be lifted from the vicinity of the Adriatic and the strategic waters of the Straits. Freed from foreign domination and interference, the Balkan peoples, within a confederation of their own making, may go forward into the rich heritage that is theirs. It has been the challenging service of the Balkan Conferences to point the way.

NOTES TO CHAPTER VII

[1] A. Papanastassiou, *Les Conférences balkaniques et le Pacte balkanique: Rapport soumis aux XXXᵉ Congrès universel de la paix* (Athens, 1934).

[2] See *La Bulgarie*, September 13, 1934; *Zora* (Sofia), September 12, 1934; IV CB, 5–10.

[3] *L'Echo de Belgrade*, September 26, 1934; LB, VI, Nos. 8–9 (August-September, 1934), 353.

[4] See especially the memoranda in LB, VI, Nos. 8–9, 10–11 (August-September, October-November, 1934), 369–420, 642–661, and the list in the appendix. A letter of January 1, 1935, from Dr. Boris Petkov, secretary of the Bulgarian group, however, advises the authors that the Bulgarians do not expect much of the Balkan Conferences since the signing of the Four-Power Balkan Pact.

[5] See the summary in Stevan Petrovich, *L'Union et la Conférence balkanique* (Paris, 1934), 247–51. These included the following meetings in Balkan Weeks: (1) In 1931: In Albania, meeting of municipal representatives; in Greece (April), merchants, bankers, and industrialists; in Bulgaria (May), agricultural organizations; in Turkey (April), tourist and student organizations; in Jugoslavia (May) congress of women's organizations. (2) In 1932: At Athens (May), representatives of sanitary and medical institutions; at Istanbul (May), representatives of commerce and industry; at Belgrade (June), meeting of the Legal Commission; at Sofia (July), university congress. (3) In 1933: At Athens (April), meeting of the Balkan Maritime Committee; at Sofia (June), meeting of the Commission on Communications, Tourist Traffic, and Aviation; at Istanbul (May), meeting of the commercial and industrial delegates; at Belgrade (September), meeting of the Balkan Medical Union; at Bucharest (March), meeting of the council of the Balkan Conferences. The first Congress of Balkan Mathematicians was held in Athens in September, 1934.

[6] The minutes of the Balkan Medical Union are in LB, V, Nos. 5–6 (May-June, 1934), 537–650. See also *ibid.*, VII, Nos. 1–7 (January-July 1935), 108–14.

[7] There is an excellent summary in Petrovich, pp. 227–69. For the third session of the Legal Commission see LB, VI, No. 12 (December, 1934), 786–796.

[8] See especially R. W. Seton-Watson, "The Problem of Revision and the Slavonic World," *Slavonic Review*, IX (March, 1931), 509–24; XII (July, 1935), 24–35. See also his work on *Treaty Revision and the Hungarian Frontiers* (London, 1934).

[9] Following the withdrawal of the Italian fleet on July 1 from Albanian waters it was announced that Rome was to make a new loan to Albania for military purposes and that Italy was to send 10,000 colonists to the Mushakia Valley.

[10] An excellent account of the significance of King Alexander may be found in Hamilton Fish Armstrong's "After the Assassination of King Alexander," *Foreign Affairs*, XIII, No. 2 (January, 1935), 204–25. The *communiqué* of

the Little Entente and the Balkan Entente is in LB, VI, Nos. 10–11 (October-November 1934), 625–26. For the December, 1934, meeting of the Council of the League of Nations, see League of Nations. *Official Journal.* 15th Year, No. 12 (Pt. II) (December, 1934). *Minutes of the Eighty-third (Extraordinary) Session of the Council* (December 5–11, 1934). Turkey was a member of the Council.

11 See the *Manchester Guardian Weekly,* January 4, 11, 1935. The official *communiqué* is in the latter issue. See also the New York *Times,* January 8–13, 1935.

12 See *L'Echo de Belgrade,* January 16, 23, 1935; the *Central European Observer,* January 25, 1935; New York *Times,* January 12, 1935; London *Times,* January 12, 1935. The semiofficial Belgrade journal, *Politika,* declared on December 23, 1934: "It is not a question of a particular conflict between Italy and Jugoslavia, or still less of a fear of the latter for its independence. It is a question of the general lines of the policy of Mussolini bearing on the ... European situation. ... The Jugoslav government asks nothing of Rome more than that which is in the interest of peace on our continent. ... The probability of establishing a more direct collaboration between Paris and Rome is small. First Mussolini must renounce the direction of the revisionist movement. ... Though there is little probability of a more or less important change in Italian policy, Jugoslavia greets the attempt of an understanding between Paris and Rome, for nothing must be neglected which can contribute, in one way or another, to European stability."

13 For the text see the New York *Times,* February 4, 1935. See also Frederick T. Birchall's article in the New York *Times,* February 10, 1935.

14 For the text see the New York *Times,* February 16, 1935. In general see also *International Conciliation,* No. 310 (May, 1935).

15 By notes exchanged at Geneva on December 5, 1934, France and Soviet Russia were pledged "not to enter into negotiations which might be aimed at concluding multilateral or bilateral agreements, capable of jeopardizing the preparation for and conclusion of the Eastern Regional Pact. ..." See the *Economic Review of the Soviet Union,* X, No. 1 (January, 1935). See also Litvinov's statement to the Czechoslovak press delegation in Moscow on January 3, 1935, *ibid.,* X, No. 2 (1935), 56–57.

16 See *International Conciliation,* No. 310 (May, 1935), for pertinent texts.

17 The text of the Stresa *communiqué* is in the New York *Times,* April 15, 1935.

18 For statements, documents, and the resolution of the Council, see League of Nations, *Official Journal,* 16th Year, No. 5 (May, 1935), *Minutes of the Eighty-fifth (Extraordinary) Session of the Council* (April 15–17, 1935). At this meeting the Turkish foreign minister once more pressed for removing the military restrictions with reference to the Straits. He was opposed by the British, Italian, and French delegates, but supported by M. Litvinov. The text of the Franco-Soviet pact of mutual assistance is in the New York *Times,* May 3, 1935. On May 21, Hitler made a seemingly conciliatory address before the Nazi Reichstag, declaring Germany's readiness to stand by the Locarno agreements, to enter an air pact for Western Europe and bi-

172   *Balkan Conferences and Balkan Entente*

lateral nonaggression treaties, and to participate in endeavors to limit armaments. He was vague, however, with reference to collective security. See the New York *Times*, May 22, 1935, for text.

[19] See the New York *Times*, June 19, 1935, for text. In general also see *International Conciliation*, Nos. 314 and 315 (November, December, 1935) ; Walter Duranty, "Europe—War or Peace?" (New York, 1935), World Affairs Pamphlets, No. 7.

[20] For the texts of these two documents see Documents XV and XVI in the Appendix to the present work. The Balkan Entente also voted adherence to the Argentine Anti-War Pact, of October 10, 1933. See Norman J. Padelford, *Peace in the Balkans*, pp. 115 ff.

[21] See *L'Indépendance Roumaine*, November 1–4, 1934, for pertinent documents.

[22] *La Bulgarie*, November 7, 1934.

[23] *L'Echo de Belgrade*, January 10, 1935. The meeting in May, 1935, fully endorsed the Athens program. See LB, VII, Nos. 1–7 (January-July, 1935), 146–52, and C. Petrov, "Considérations sur certains des buts de la Banque balkanique," *Bulletin de CCII*, Nos. 22–23 (June, July, 1935), 23–28, 29–33.

[24] *La Bulgarie*, January 23, 28, March 23, 1935.

[25] See LB, VII, Nos. 1–7 (January-July, 1935), 115–37; *La Bulgarie*, November 25, 26, 1935; the *Central European Observer*, October 4, November 1, 15, 1935. See also G. E. R. Gedye, "Slowly Peace Advances in the Balkans," *New York Times Magazine*, May 5, 1935.

[26] Note particularly the attempt of England to align Turkey, Greece, Rumania, Jugoslavia, and Czechoslovakia—all members of the Little Entente and the Balkan Entente—for action in the Mediterranean against Italy. See the New York *Times*, December 21, 22, 1935. The policy of Czechoslovakia is well explained in Dr. Eduard Beneš's address before the Foreign Affairs Committee of the Czechoslovak Parliament on November 5, 1935: *The Struggle for Collective Security in Europe and the Italo-Abyssinian War* (Prague, Orbis, 1935).

APPENDIX

RESOLUTION NO. 2 ADOPTED BY THE TWENTY-SEVENTH UNIVERSAL CONGRESS OF PEACE HELD AT ATHENS, OCTOBER 6–10, 1929

The necessity for more limited federations within the framework of a universal federation having been recognized, the Conference considers that a union among the Balkan peoples is most opportune, and that for this purpose special Balkan Conferences should be organized annually.

The Congress notes with satisfaction the agreement reached in the Balkan Commission among the representatives of the Balkan States and asks the International Bureau of Peace to take the initiative in convening the First Balkan Conference, in collaboration with the international parliamentary organizations and, if possible, under the auspices of the League of Nations, and in constituting, if necessary, a provisional bureau for this purpose.

The Congress thinks that it would be desirable for the representatives of the above-mentioned organizations and the International Bureau of Peace, as well as of any other organizations whose collaboration might be solicited, to participate in the conference.

Considering that a systematic effort toward *rapprochement* of the Balkan peoples would be useful, the Congress expresses the wish that the League of Nations create an Institute of Balkan Cooperation similar to the Institute of Intellectual Coöperation.

[Translated and reprinted from *XXVIIe Congrès universel de la paix. Tenu à Athènes du 6 au 10 octobre 1929. Documents officiels* (Bureau International de la Paix, Geneva, 1930), 220–21. See also the English translation, *ibid.*, 237.]

DOCUMENT II

CIRCULAR INVITATION OF THE
INTERNATIONAL BUREAU OF PEACE
TO THE MINISTERS OF FOREIGN AFFAIRS
OF THE BALKAN STATES

Geneva, May 12, 1930.

Mr. Minister,

In the course of the Twenty-seventh Universal Congress of
Peace which was held at Athens, October 6–10, 1929, under the
presidency of M. Papanastassiou, former President of the Council, there was formed within the commission organized for the purpose of investigating the question of the "Federation of Peoples,"
a subcommission composed almost exclusively of representatives
of the Balkan countries, to which were assigned the tasks of studying the most appropriate ways and means of arriving at *rapprochement* among the different Balkan states and of submitting,
if possible, pertinent propositions to the Congress. This subcommission set to work immediately with a zeal and ardor which
greatly pleased the delegates of the other countries. At the third
plenary session of the Congress, it brought in the following draft
of a resolution, which was adopted by acclamation [here follows
Resolution No. 2 cited above]. . . .

The International Bureau of Peace accepted willingly the mission assigned to it, and it is in execution of this mission with which
it is honored, that it addresses to you, Mr. Minister, the present
memorandum.

On the aim to be attained we can be brief. To bring together the
peoples who, by reason of their location, economic condition, cultural aspirations, and history, have special interests and affinities,
is to act for the good of the peoples whom we wish to direct toward
collaboration and is within the spirit of the League of Nations. On
this point it appears that there can be no fear of difference of
opinion.

Concerning the means to be employed, the Congress of Athens
envisaged a conference which would be composed of represent-

atives of political circles, the world of industry and commerce, agricultural and labor circles, the great peace associations, the universities, the intellectual circles, and the press of each country. Such a conference, though unofficial, independent, and in no manner obligating the governments, could not, however, either materially or morally, get along without the support of the latter, which are to be represented by "observers," who will be in communication with their governments concerning the deliberations, suggestions, and intentions of the Conference.

The participation of the governments will be a guarantee of the nature of the work to be pursued, and will constitute, moreover, in the eyes of the interested peoples, a tangible proof of their desire to march hand in hand in the noble effort toward making solutions of justice and right prevail.

Program of the Conference.—To examine all questions of a special interest to the Balkan states, the solution of which would be of a nature to bring them together; to study the ways and means by which the different groups in the interested countries could be led to work toward indispensable and fruitful understandings; and to promote a clearer understanding of the necessities of today and the possibilities of tomorrow. In truth, we believe that since the Conference is primarily an organ acting only on its own responsibility and placed under the general control of universal public opinion, its program should have no other limits than those suggested by its concern for the common welfare and the wisdom and equity of the solutions which it will outline.

Composition of the Conference.—We think that the Conference should be composed of a number of delegates sufficient to permit representation of the circles enumerated above and easy establishment of the indispensable personal contacts, without, however, constituting too unwieldy a body. It has been suggested that the number of delegates for each country be fixed at a maximum of thirty. The directing committee of the International Bureau of Peace favors this figure, it being understood that each country is to have an equal number of votes, so that whatever be the number of its delegates, even though less than that specified, the principle of equality may be safeguarded.

Choice of the delegates.—We believe that it would be well at first to appeal to people who play an effective rôle in the political life of the different Balkan countries, which permits them to have views on the needs and aspirations of the interested populations. Consequently, it would be desirable for the great social organizations to be represented.

Moreover, we expect to invite, in the capacity of benevolent observers, one or two representatives of the League of Nations, the International Labor Office, the International Chamber of Commerce, the Inter-Parliamentary Union, and the International Parliamentary Union of Commerce, under the express reservation of not being obligated, either in fact or in law, by the resolutions adopted or the suggestions proposed.

The seat of the first Conference.—Since the Balkan Conference is to meet in turn in all the Balkan capitals, the choice of the city in which it will meet for the first time has no great importance. The directing committee of the International Bureau of Peace has decided that the first Conference shall be held at Athens because the historic setting of this city is especially appropriate for such a first Balkan meeting, and because it was in this city, at the time of the last Congress of Peace, that the idea was developed. Consequently, there exists already a committee, organized at the time of the Twenty-seventh Congress of Peace, which will willingly undertake the preparatory labors and the material organization of the Conference.

Date of the Conference.—The directing committee thought that the beginning of October, and more precisely the fifth of that month, would be the most suitable time for assembling the persons called to take part in the Conference. In September public attention will still be absorbed by the debates of the League of Nations. This body meets on September 10 and normally sits for three weeks. It would be undesirable for the Balkan Conference to be overshadowed and not obtain the attention to which it is entitled. . . .

We hope that we may count on your assistance and that your government will not refuse to be benevolently interested in and to promote an experiment which, the first of its kind, will have at least the merit of crystallizing, in the eyes of Europe and the world, the true sentiments which animate the peoples and governments of the Balkans. There are legends to which we must put an end. The Balkans will cease to be the neuralgic point of Europe only when, having understood that their interests will never be better protected than by themselves, they look only to themselves for remedies to the maladies from which they have suffered in the past.

We have reasons for believing that the idea of a Balkan Conference will be received with great favor in your country, but we wished, before any other *démarche,* to communicate with you and to ask you to give us the benevolent support of your government. Indeed, the success of our enterprise will depend upon the attitude and the sacrifices of the different Balkan governments; it is their collaboration which will assure the authority which you yourself certainly wish to confer on it.

Permit us finally, Mr. Minister, to ask you to be good enough to offer your assistance in the formation of a local committee among your people which will consider the adequate participation of your country in the Conference, and which might send a representative to the general committee of organization of the Conference at Athens.

We express to you in advance our very great gratitude and ask you to accept the assurance of our most distinguished consideration.

For the International Bureau of Peace:

The Secretary-General: H. GOLAY

The President: H. LAFONTAINE

[Translated and reprinted from *Première Conférence balkanique. Athènes, 5–12 octobre 1930. Documents officiels* (Athens, 1931), pp. 17–21.]

DOCUMENT III

THE STATUTES OF THE BALKAN CONFERENCE

The First Balkan Conference assembled at Athens from October 5 to October 12, 1930, has decided to create a permanent organization under the title of the "Balkan Conference." It will be governed by the present statutes.

THE AIM OF THE CONFERENCE

Article 1.—The Balkan Conference will aim to contribute to the *rapprochement* and collaboration of the peoples of the Balkans in their economic, social, intellectual, and political relations, in order to direct this *rapprochement* ultimately toward the union of the Balkan states (Albania, Bulgaria, Greece, Jugoslavia, Rumania, and Turkey).

SEAT OF THE CONFERENCE

Article 2.—The Balkan Conference will meet in turn in each Balkan country.

ORGANS OF THE CONFERENCE

Article 3.—The organs of the Conference are: a) The General Assembly; b) The Council; c) The Bureau [of the Presidency] and the Secretariat; d) The National Groups.

THE NATIONAL GROUPS OF THE CONFERENCE

Article 4.—1) The delegates present at the First Balkan Conference, as well as those who take part in the successive Conferences, form the national groups of the Balkan Conference in their countries. These groups will seek to coöperate with organizations which pursue the same ideal or in general the ideal of peace, as well as with representatives of the political world (parliamentary or not) and with the organs of local administration. They will seek also to coöperate with the representatives of the press and of commercial, industrial, agricultural, labor, intellectual, and women's organizations.

2) The chiefs of the delegations of each Assembly of the Conference are the presidents of the respective national groups until the new session of the Assembly. It is to these that the Bureau [of the Presidency] will make all communications.

3) Each group has the right to elect a vice-president.

4) The national groups must be in contact with their own governments as well as with the diplomatic representatives of the other Balkan governments in their countries.

THE GENERAL ASSEMBLY

Article 5.—1) The General Assembly of the Conference meets regularly each year in October on the date fixed by the Council.

2) Three months before this date each national group will reach an understanding with the government of its country in order to form a committee of organization, which will name the delegates to the Assembly as well as the chief of the delegation.

3) Each delegation will include only thirty delegates, aside from experts and secretaries. Primarily the delegates will be chosen from among the representatives of the political and administrative world, municipalities, universities, and other intellectual centers, the press, and peace, professional, and women's organizations.

4) The representatives of the Balkan governments at the seat of the Assembly have the right to follow its work in the capacity of observers and to take part in the debates.

5) The League of Nations and the International Labor Office will always be invited to send observers to the Assembly.

Article 6.—The Assembly is convoked by the call of the Secretariat, which is also charged with communicating to the national groups as well as to the Balkan governments the agenda and the reports and other documents which are submitted to it.

Article 7.—1) The president of the Council of the Conference performs the functions of president of the Assembly until the constitution of his office, which is composed of a president and five vice-presidents.

2) On the proposal of the Council, the Assembly proceeds to the election of its president by absolute majority of the votes cast. If after the first ballot no candidate has obtained a majority, a second

ballot will be taken on the candidates who have obtained the greatest number of votes.

3) Each chief of delegation, if he is not elected president, is in full right vice-president of the Assembly.

4) The office [of the presidency] is assisted by six secretaries designated by the respective delegations. The secretary chosen by the delegation of the country in which the Assembly is meeting assumes the functions of the secretary-general.

5) The functions of the president of the Assembly and of the secretary-general terminate on January 31, on which date they are transmitted to the president and secretary of the delegation of the country in which the next session of the Assembly will meet.

Article 8.—1) The following six commissions function within the framework of the Conference: a) Commission on Organization; b) Commission on Political Relations; c) Commission on Intellectual Coöperation; d) Commission on Economic Relations; e) Commission on Communications; f) Commission on Hygiene and Social Policy.

2) By the decision of the Council the Assembly may form other commissions.

3) Each delegation designates among its delegates and experts at least two members for each commission.

4) The Council of the Conference may call together any commission whatever, even in the interval between the sessions of the Assembly.

Article 9.—1) The debates in the Assembly and in the commissions are in French. The delegates who wish to use their own language will have their addresses translated into French.

2) The plenary sessions of the Assembly are public.

Article 10.—1) The quorum in the plenary session and in the commissions is fixed at two-fifths of the total number of the votes of all the delegations.

2) Resolutions are adopted by absolute majority of the votes cast. Nevertheless, a proposition cannot be considered as accepted if it has not obtained a majority above three-fifths of the quorum.

3) In the event of the total absence of a delegation, the decisions of the Assembly are adjourned for a single session.

Article 11.—1) Each delegate has one vote. If the number of delegates of a country is below thirty, the chief of the delegation of that country has the right to designate those who may have more than one vote, three being the maximum. If, on the contrary, the number of the delegates of a country is more than thirty, the chief of the delegation must designate those who may exercise the right to vote.

2) No delegation has more than thirty votes in all.

Article 12.—1) In the commissions each delegation has a maximum of five votes.

2) In the event of the total absence of a delegation, the decisions of the commission are adjourned for a single session.

Article 13.—The order of business as well as the internal order of the Assembly and its commissions is regulated by a special statute.

Article 14.—Before adjourning, the Assembly designates, on the motion of the Council, the place of the next session.

THE COUNCIL OF THE CONFERENCE

Article 15.—1) The Council of the Conference is composed of the chiefs and two members of each delegation.

2) The president of the Conference assumes the functions of president of the Council until the January 31 following the Assembly. After this date these functions are transmitted to the president of the national group of the country in which the next Assembly will meet.

3) The chiefs of the delegations are *ex officio* the vice-presidents of the Council.

4) The other members of the Council are designated by each delegation before the closure of the session of the Assembly, in the same manner as the two additional members.

5) The Council is renewed every year.

Article 16.—The Council is the supreme executive organ of the Assembly. It represents the Conference in the interval between the Assemblies. It presents annually an account of its labors to the General Assembly. It approves the budget and controls the administration. It fixes the precise date and agenda of the next Assembly.

Article 17.—The Council meets on the invitation of its president or on the request of seven members.

The Council regulates its own internal organization.

Article 18.—The president has executive charge of the decisions of the Council. He names the functionaries. He directs the labors of the Secretariat and supervises its activities.

Article 19.—The government observers and the diplomatic representatives of the Balkan states in the country in which the Assembly is meeting may function as a consultative committee which the president of the Council consults on questions concerning the work of the Conference.

Article 20.—In circumstances of urgency, the Bureau [of the Presidency] convoked by the president may adopt a resolution instead of the Council.

THE SECRETARIAT

Article 21.—1) The Secretariat is composed of the Secretary-General and five other members designated in a ratio of one to each delegation. It is charged with the correspondence and the publication of the minutes of the Assembly, the service of the archives, and the annual preparation of the budget of the Conference. As soon as possible, it will publish a periodical bulletin in French in which all the national groups will be invited to collaborate.

2) The Secretariat will be divided into sections according to the different activities of the Conference. The sections may be transformed into institutes; if this is done the Council will formulate their rules.

Article 22.—The Secretariat is installed at the seat of the Council.

THE FINANCES OF THE CONFERENCE

Article 23.—1) The annual quotas of the national groups will be determined in proportion to the budget of expenses fixed by the Assembly.

2) The Council of the Conference will meet as soon as possible

for the purpose of fixing the budget and quotas for this year especially.

3) The service of accounts of the Conference is performed by the Secretariat. All expenses must be approved by the president, who will choose a treasurer from among the secretaries.

FINAL PROVISIONS

Article 24.—The correspondence of the Conference will be in French.

Article 25.—Each delegation is obligated to do everything possible in its own country for the realization of the resolutions and the ideals of the Conference.

The delegations will submit to the Assembly an annual report on the results of their efforts.

Article 26.—The emblem of the Balkan Conference consists of a parallelogram, 20 by 13, striped in white, blue, green, yellow, red, and white colors, decorated in the center by a white sphere circled by six yellow stars. The two white stripes are twenty per cent larger than the four others, which are of equal size.

[Translated and reprinted from *Première Conférence balkanique. Athènes, 5–12 octobre 1930. Documents officiels* (Athens, 1931), pp. 375–80.]

DOCUMENT IV

GENERAL RESOLUTION ON THE BALKAN UNION
ADOPTED BY THE
FIRST BALKAN CONFERENCE,
OCTOBER, 1930

The First Balkan Conference, taking into consideration the decision of the Twenty-Seventh Universal Congress of Peace that the union of the Balkan peoples is indispensable for the purpose of the consolidation of peace, the reënforcement of the work of the League of Nations, and the progress of the cultural and economic interests of the Balkan peoples,

Interpreting the wishes of these peoples and considering their will to maintain their national existence and political independence,

Approves enthusiastically the idea of the Balkan union, on which the firm bases for the prosperity of the Balkan peoples will be laid, and,

Declares that their union must have the character of a grouping of independent nationalities, bearing no reflection on the sovereignty of the participating states, having no tendency to stifle the existing ethnic entities, but only consolidating peace among them, and by a free and more direct relationship, a closer *entente*, a more systematic collaboration, multiplying their common elements of civilization and harmonizing their forces for the good of all without discrimination; moreover, it must be within the framework and spirit of the League of Nations.

For the purpose of the success of this noble ideal, so beneficial to the Balkan peoples, it urges them, and especially their leaders, to forget old differences in order that, inspired by humanitarian sentiments and feelings of solidarity, they may work systematically toward a union which will constitute an important step in their history and the point of departure for an entirely new state of things in the Balkans, auguring well for the future.

The Council of the Conference will address a questionnaire concerning the precise form and details of the organization of the Balkan Union, to all the national delegations, which are invited to reply before the Second Balkan Conference.

RESOLUTION ON POLITICAL RAPPROCHEMENT (OCTOBER, 1930)

The First Balkan Conference, aware of the necessity of assuring, as soon as possible, an era of peace among the Balkan nations,

Noting the sincere desire for security and mutual protection which animates the said nations,

Considering that for this purpose it is important to obliterate all the differences which stand in the way of a moral *détente* and political *rapprochement* among the Balkan nations, and

Believing that in order to arrive at such a result it is indispensable to give to the Balkan nations complementary guarantees of security within the framework of existing treaties and to assure the loyal execution of all the other obligations which arise from the said treaties, including those concerning the minorities:

Expresses the following wishes:

1) That the ministers of foreign affairs of the Balkan states meet regularly each year in one of the cities of these states, for the purpose of exchanging their views on Balkan affairs and on the means of assuring solidarity among their countries;

2) That the Balkan Conference proceed to the study of a pact among the Balkan nations on the basis of the following principles: a) the outlawry of war; b) the settlement by pacific means of every difference, of whatever nature, which might arise among the Balkan nations; c) mutual assistance in the event of violation of the engagements not to make war, and decides,

That the Council of the Conference appoint a special committee for the examination of a preliminary draft of a Balkan pact and for the study of all the difficulties which stand in the way of a moral *détente* and political *rapprochement* among the Balkan peoples. This committee will present to the next Conference a report on all the questions contained in the present resolution.

[Translated and reprinted from *Première Conférence balkanique. Athènes, 5–12 octobre 1930. Documents officiels* (Athens, 1931), pp. 364–65.]

DOCUMENT V

THE BALKAN POSTAL CONVENTION

[Adopted by the Second Balkan Conference (October, 1931)]

Article 1.—The countries among which the present convention is concluded form, under the designation of the Balkan Postal Union, a single postal territory for the reciprocal exchange of correspondence. The Balkan Postal Union proposes the organization and perfection of the different Balkan postal services, such as letters, registered mail, small packages, parcel post, money orders, subscriptions to journals and periodicals, and postal savings accounts.

All questions not included in the clauses of the present convention are regulated by the Universal Postal Convention, its rules of execution and final protocols.

Article 2.—The contracting parties adopt the following rates for the correspondence exchanged in their reciprocal relations:

	Francs gold
Letters	
To 20 grams	0.20
Beyond that, by 20 grams	0.12
Postal cards	
Simple	0.12
With paid return	0.24
Business papers, by 50 grams	0.03
Minimum rate	0.15
Printed matter, by 50 grams	0.03
Samples, by 50 grams	0.03
Minimum rate	0.06
Journals and periodicals sent directly by editors to subscribers, by 50 grams	0.02
Books and music papers	0.02
Registration	0.20
Receipt	0.20

The respective administrations will determine the equivalents of the foregoing rates according to their monetary valuation, without, however, exceeding a margin of 10 per cent more or less.

Article 3.—The contracting parties agree to issue and use regularly in their postal relations a postal stamp representing the rate of an ordinary letter and bearing the inscription in French: "Union Postale Interbalkanique."

Article 4.—The administrations of the contracting parties will, in agreement with the respective railway administrations, take the measures necessary for the continued and direct circulation of mail cars among their countries.

This provision remains advisory for the interested countries.

[Translated and reprinted from *Les Balkans*, Nos. 13–14 (October-November, 1931), 139–40.]

DOCUMENT VI

THE STATUTES OF THE
BALKAN CHAMBER OF COMMERCE AND INDUSTRY

[Adopted by the Second Balkan Conference, Istanbul, October, 1931]

Article 1.—The name of the organization is: The Balkan Chamber of Commerce and Industry.

The objects of the Balkan Chamber of Commerce and Industry are:

1) To facilitate and encourage by every possible means the strengthening of economic relations among the countries of the Balkan Peninsula.

2) To exercise a continuous influence for the improvement of conditions of commerce and industry in the different Balkan countries.

3) To solve different problems of an economic nature existing or arising among the signatory states, such as an *entente* among producers of similar products, overproduction, stabilization of prices, monetary structure, customs understanding, land and sea communications, facilities for travel, frontier traffic, monetary unification, etc.

4) To organize Balkan fairs and expositions. To create commercial museums in the principal centers of commerce in each signatory state.

5) To work for a *rapprochement* among the countries and an understanding among the statesmen and [economic] organizations of the signatories.

6) To strive for the creation of a Balkan conscience among the peoples of the peninsula in order to form a direct collaboration which will constitute the most effective guarantee of the consolidation of peace.

7) To settle by arbitration every difference arising among the commercial and industrial concerns of the Balkan countries.

The Balkan Chamber of Commerce and Industry is a federation of the principal economic forces of the signatories united within each country into a national committee, constituting a section of the national group for the Balkan Conference of each country.

Article 2.—1) the members of the Balkan Chamber of Commerce and Industry are: the commercial, industrial, financial, and maritime institutions and individual and other enterprises of Albania, Bulgaria, Greece, Jugoslavia, Rumania, and Turkey.

2) There are active, associate, and individual members.

3) The active members are the Chambers of Commerce and Industry, the industrial and commercial federations, and the dependent economic institutions of the states.

4) The associate members are all the other commercial, industrial, maritime, and financial organizations such as the different unions, syndicates, and corporations.

5) The individual members are individuals, corporations, establishments, firms, and financial, industrial, and commercial concerns in the territories of the countries above named, provided they are registered in the national Chambers of Commerce and Industry in their respective regions.

6) The individual members regularly enrolled with the Chamber have the right to be present at the congresses. They may speak, but may not have the right to vote.

7) In general all members are admitted on the proposal of the national committees in their countries.

Article 3.—1) The Council is composed of twenty-four members, four from each country affiliated with the Balkan Chamber of Commerce and Industry.

2) The members of the Council of the Balkan Chamber of Commerce and Industry are elected by the respective national committees of each country.

3) The term of the members of the Council is three years. Their election must be reported immediately by the national committees to the secretary-general.

4) The members of the Council, with the approval of the national committee, may be represented by third parties provided with proxies by the national committees.

5) The Council will direct the affairs of the Balkan Chamber of Commerce and Industry, will pursue energetically the ends it

proposes, and will use every means to assure the realization of the initial program of the Balkan Chamber of Commerce and Industry and of every project voted by the congress.

6) The seat of the Council will be the same as that of the Balkan Chamber of Commerce and Industry, namely, Istanbul or Salonica. The Council will be convoked twice a year. No meeting may be called without at least thirty days' notice.

7) The Council will transmit annually to the members, through the intermediary of the national committees, a report on the measures taken concerning the affairs of the Balkan Chamber of Commerce and Industry. It will submit to each congress a list of the members of the Balkan Chamber of Commerce and Industry, a financial statement and a report on the general labors and results obtained.

8) The quorum of the Council consists of a majority of the members, provided each country is represented by at least one member, either personally or by proxy.

Article 4.—1) The executive committee includes six members, one from each country affiliated with the Balkan Chamber of Commerce and Industry. These members will be elected by the Council. They will be members of the Council and their term will be three years, the same as that of the Council.

2) The executive committee will be the bureau of the Chamber. It will be composed of: a) one president, b) two vice-presidents, c) one secretary-general, d) one legal adviser, e) one treasurer. The president will be elected each time from a different country. The two vice-presidents also will be elected each time from a different country.

3) The executive committee will direct all the general affairs of the Balkan Chamber of Commerce and Industry. Its acts will be subject to the approval of the Council, before which it will have to render an account.

4) Four members will constitute a quorum of the executive committee.

5) The members of the executive committee, with the approval of the national committee, may be represented by third parties provided with proxies by the national committees.

Article 5.—1) The members of the Balkan Chamber of Commerce and Industry will meet once a year in congress. This congress will meet in turn in the capital or principal city of each signatory. The date and place of each congress are fixed by the preceding congress. The first congress will meet at Istanbul, the date to be determined by the Council. The notification of the congress will be given at least three months in advance. The agenda will be communicated to all members at the same time.

2) The agenda will be determined by the Council. For the preparation of the labors of each congress there will be a program committee appointed for two years. This committee will be selected by the Council.

3) Every active or associate member of the Balkan Chamber of Commerce and Industry has the right to be represented by delegates at all sessions in accordance with the stipulations of paragraph 6 below. Each delegate has one vote.

4) A quorum will be obtained when the registered delegates of active or associate members represent at least four of the Balkan countries, and when the number of active and associate members make at least a third of the active or associate members affiliated with the Balkan Chamber of Commerce and Industry.

5) In the event that the quorum stipulated in the preceding paragraph cannot be obtained at the first meeting, the congress will meet eight days later regardless of the number of participants.

6) Each active or associate member has the right to one delegate to the congress. Each delegate may represent by proxy, as provided by the national committee of his country, a maximum of three members, having the right to the number of votes of the active and associate members he represents (three).

7) The individual members may send delegates to the congress. These delegates may speak, but may not have the right to vote. Persons of recognized competence in economics may be invited to participate with the same rights as individual members.

8) The governments of the Balkan countries may be invited to send a maximum of two delegates to the congress. The delegates of the governments may speak, but may not have the right to vote. Any question of a political nature is excluded completely from

the deliberations of the different organs of the Balkan Chamber of Commerce and Industry.

9) The congress will make no decision on subjects which are not included in the agenda. However, by a vote of two-thirds of the delegates present, exclusive of the representatives, it may discuss a subject which is not included in the agenda, but which is consonant with the general aims of the Balkan Chamber of Commerce and Industry. By a similar vote, it may send such subjects to the Council for inscription on the agenda of the next congress.

10) Resolutions are adopted by majority vote. A member who has been present at the session, but who has to refrain from voting at the moment, is always allowed a written vote before leaving the place of voting.

11) The president of the Balkan Chamber of Commerce and Industry will preside over the congresses.

12) The minutes of all the sessions of the Council, the executive committee, and the congresses will be deposited with the secretary-general. All the decisions will be transmitted to the executive committee in order that it may carry them out.

13) As soon as possible after the close of the congress the secretary-general will transmit to each member a résumé of the debates.

14) The national committees will try to draw the attention of the competent public authority to all subjects on which the Balkan Chamber of Commerce and Industry has made decisions, and will make every effort to adopt in their countries the measures necessary for realizing as rapidly as possible unity of action in the countries affiliated with the Balkan Chamber of Commerce and Industry.

15) Periodically each national committee will submit a report of its progress to the secretary-general of the Balkan Chamber of Commerce and Industry.

Article 6.—1) The headquarters of the Balkan Chamber of Commerce and Industry will be at Istanbul.

2) The Secretariat-General will include:

a) The secretary-general elected by the Council. The secretary-general will be responsible to the executive committee, which in turn will be responsible to the Council.

b) Six commissioners, in the capacity of chiefs of sections, one to be named by each national committee, who will represent the national point of view of each of the six Balkan countries. They will have equal remuneration and prerogatives. The six commissioners, under the presidency of the secretary-general, will constitute the Council of Service, whose internal administrative functions will be determined by rules ratified by the Council.

3) The other employees necessary for the functioning of the Balkan Chamber of Commerce and Industry will be chosen from specialists residing in Istanbul regardless of nationality.

4) Under the direction of the secretary-general the Secretariat will have charge of the following:

a) It will centralize information on: economic and social conditions, facts relative to agricultural, mineral, and industrial production, the needs of each Balkan country and the possibilities of satisfying them in the Balkans, the probable needs in the future and the possibilites of production.

b) It will study systematically the different Balkan products of every nature and will facilitate their marketing abroad in a spirit of understanding and collaboration.

c) It will study the question of the future customs union, as well as every question capable of stimulating and facilitating inter- and extra-Balkan commerce.

d) It will be an organ of liaison and will suggest all regulations or appropriate legislative measures for facilitating and developing economic relations.

e) It will place at the disposition of the members and official institutions the reports and conclusions which may be published in accordance with the present articles.

f) It will clarify public opinion by publishing the facts relative to business and economic conditions.

Article 7.—1) In each Balkan country affiliated with the Balkan Chamber of Commerce and Industry there will be established a secretariat with the national committee.

2) The rôle of the national committee is to maintain constant relations with the Secretariat-General and coöperate with it.

3) The national committee in each Balkan country will formu-

late the statutes and rules for the creation, functioning, and resources of its secretariat.

Article 8.—1) Each national committee of the Balkan countries having a right to four members on the Council pays to the Balkan Chamber of Commerce and Industry a quota of 5,000 francs gold annually.

2) The quota of each individual member is fixed at £1 annually.

3) The national committee of each country may add to the quota of each member a proportional contribution to cover the costs of its own functions.

4) The national committees may receive subventions from their governments.

Article 9.—1) The Balkan Chamber of Commerce and Industry will constitute a court of conciliation and arbitration the aim of which will be to settle all commercial differences which may arise between commercial, industrial, and financial or other concerns of the Balkan countries.

2) The Balkan Chamber of Commerce and Industry will formulate within six months after its establishment a special set of regulations for conciliation and arbitration to be submitted to the national committees of the signatory states. The national committees will return these regulations with their remarks and objections within a period of at least two months after their submission. The final regulations will be submitted to the approval of the congress.

Article 10.—1) Any active [group] or associate or individual member whose affiliation with its national committee ceases for any reason whatever is, *ipso facto*, dropped from the list of members of the Balkan Chamber of Commerce and Industry.

2) Any active [group] or individual member may resign from membership in the Balkan Chamber of Commerce and Industry. This resignation must be transmitted by the national committee, and the resigning member must pay the quota for the current year.

[This document is based on the Greek draft in *Les Balkans*, No. 12 (September, 1931), 65–69, the Turkish draft, *ibid.*, Nos. 13–14 (October-November, 1931), 44, and the modifications adopted in the final resolution of the Second Balkan Conference, *ibid.*, Nos. 13–14, pp. 138–39. The Third Balkan Conference at Bucharest made a slight change, which has been embodied in the document above. See *Les Balkans*, III, Nos. 1–2 (October-November, 1932), 181–82.]

DOCUMENT VII

A HELLENIC RESPONSE TO THE QUESTIONNAIRE ON THE BALKAN UNION

[Presented in the name of the special committee of the Hellenic Group to the Second Balkan Conference, by M. A. Svolos, Professor of Constitutional Law in the University of Athens. This was the only response which was given to the questionnaire prepared by M. Papanastassiou for the Council of the Balkan Conference, January 30–February 1, 1931.]

This response is only a sketch of the constitutional bases and the legal form of a Balkan Union. Left vague purposely on certain points, it serves only to make concrete for the first time the idea of the Balkan Union in order to make it better understood by the Balkan peoples. Thus a point of departure is established for a more detailed study of the problems of organization which arise from this idea.

For the purpose of presenting a practical project, it is necessary, in our opinion, to take note of the existing social, political, and constitutional realities of the Balkan states. The form of the union should not be pushed beyond the limits which these conditions necessarily impose on us. Nevertheless, the transformation of the social conditions, which is being accelerated among the Balkan peoples, will doubtless facilitate the future formation of a more closely knit economic union which will surely be the ideal of the political and economic confederation of the Balkan peoples and their laboring masses. We are, however, unanimous in admitting that the definite form of the union will be achieved only by a gradual process.

I. The Balkan Union will take the form of a confederation of sovereign and independent states, constituted by treaty.

The sovereignty of the member states will be limited only by the powers reserved to the competence of the Union.

II. The Union will be of unlimited duration.

The participating states may withdraw freely after previous denunciation, but on the condition that they will, however, remain bound by a Balkan pact of nonaggression, pacific solution of disputes, and guarantee. The denunciation on the part of one or several member states will not affect the validity of the Union for the others.

III. The business of the Union will be confided to 1) a popular Assembly, 2) a Council of the Governments, and 3) a federal Administration.

IV. The popular Assembly will be the supreme and constituent power of the Union. It will be composed of representatives of the peoples of the member states, elected for a sufficiently long period according to an organic law of the Union. This law will be based on the following principles : 1) Each people will have in the Assembly a number of votes proportionate to its population; the number of votes of the largest state shall not, however, exceed threefold the number of votes of the smallest state. The number of representatives of each people may not be less than ten. 2) A number of the representatives will be chosen by the legislative body of each country, and the rest will be elected by the members of the municipal and communal councils and the universities. A special representation will be assured in the Assembly to the most representative agricultural, labor, commercial, and industrial organizations of each country.

V. The decision of the Assembly will be expressed by an absolute majority of the votes. In the constitution of the Union certain matters for which a greater majority will be demanded may be designated. For the modification of the treaty on the constitution of the Union, unanimity will be necessary.

VI. The federal legislative power will belong to the popular Assembly and the Council of the Governments.

The Assembly will vote on its own initiative or on that of the Council : 1) laws having obligatory force in the territory of the participating states, and 2) recommendations which would have force only if they were adopted by the legislative power of each country.

The Assembly may order popular referenda on questions of

general importance. It may also make suggestions to the Council on any question of general importance; if this is done, the Council will be obliged to respond by a considered opinion or to submit the proposition to the interested governments with its opinion.

VII. The laws voted by the Assembly will be submitted to the sanction of the Council, which may, before making use of its right of veto, return them to the Assembly with its considered opinion.

VIII. The Council of the Governments will be composed of delegates of the governments of the member states.

All the states will have the same number of votes in the Council. The president of the popular Assembly will be present and will have a consultative opinion in the deliberations of the Council.

The Council will be presided over, in turn, by one of the delegates of each member state.

IX. The Council of the Governments will be in contact with the Assembly but will not depend on it. It will name an executive committee which will meet in circumstances of urgency. It will call the Assembly into ordinary session at least once each year, and into extraordinary session every time it is requested to do so by a third of the members of the Assembly. It will sanction the laws voted by the Assembly and will promulgate them in the official journal of the Union.

Moreover, the Council will attempt to coördinate the policy of the member states in the entire domain which remains in their competence.

X. There will be 1) a chief Balkan administration of highways and communications, posts, telegraphs, and telephones; 2) a chief Balkan administration of hygiene, labor, and social policy; 3) a permanent committee for the minorities and their questions; 4) a general secretariat of the Council, to which will be attached the statistical services of foreign commerce and agriculture.

These administrative organizations, the personnel of which will be recruited among the nationals of all the member states, will be subject to the Council or the executive committee which will nominate the functionaries.

XI. The chief institutions will have jurisdiction over the following: 1) the conclusion of treaties of commerce; 2) the preparation and constitution of a customs union among the member states unless the union is stipulated in the creation of the Balkan Union; 3) the constitution of a union of posts, telegraphs, and telephones, in the event that the union is not stipulated in the treaty of the Balkan Union; 4) the institution of a chief administration of ways and communications (railways, ports, navigation, etc.); 5) the establishment of a monetary system; 6) the establishment of common measures of public hygiene for the protection of labor, social policy, and agricultural products; 7) the unification of certain branches of private law; 8) the establishment of common principles in the domain of public instruction and the creation of a Balkan institute of studies and intellectual coöperation; 9) disarmament; and 10) the declaration of war and the conclusion of peace.

XII. The member states will not have the right to enter into treaties of alliance with other states. They will have the right to conclude other treaties, on the condition that these will not be directed against the security of the Union or of a member state, that they will not be contrary to the stipulations of the constitution of the Union, and that they will not restrict the independence of the signatory member state.

The territorial modifications among the member states may be discussed by the chief institutions of the Union, but may be determined only with the consent of the interested parties of the Union.

XIII. A federal tribunal will be organized, which will have jurisdiction over: 1) the statement of conclusions, at the request of the Council or member state, on the conformity of the laws of a member state with the federal laws, or of measures taken by a member state under these same laws; 2) the solution of judicial disputes among member states; 3) the examination or impeachment of high administrative functionaries of the Union for derelictions in service.

The tribunal may be presided over by a jurist designated by the Hague Court of Justice.

XIV. An aggressive war by the Union is absolutely excluded. 1) The member states will bind themselves never to make war under any pretext whatsoever or to settle their disputes by force of arms, but to submit them to the Council, which will endeavor to mediate. If the Council does not succeed in solving the dispute it will be taken to the Assembly, which may send its solution to a tribunal to which the contending parties will submit without appeal. 2) The member states engage to defend not only the Union but also every member state in the event of attack. For this purpose they will bind themselves to offer mutual assistance against the aggressor, whether it be a member state or a foreign state. Mutual assistance and common defense against the aggressor will be assured by coöperation of the military forces and by financial aid. 3) They will bind themselves to teach at least one Balkan language in their schools.

XV. The obligations of the member states arising from the *Covenant* of the League of Nations will remain in force.

The Union may decide that the member states will have a common representation in any international organization (Assembly and Council of the League of Nations, etc.) or in foreign states, by extraordinary or permanent delegations designated by the Council.

XVI. Any recommendation voted by the Assembly must be submitted by the government of each state to the approval of the competent authorities, who will be free to accept it or not.

XVII. The following personal rights will be assured to the nationals of the member states in the territory of the Union: 1) equality of treatment with the nationals of each state; 2) admission and freedom of circulation; 3) freedom of religion, language, and nationality; 4) freedom of the press; 5) the right of domicile, for the purpose of pursuing a trade, and in general the freedom of economic activity. The exercise of the above-named rights will be regulated by the laws of the Union.

XVIII. The financial organization of the Union will be based on 1) an additional levy of a very light tax, imposed by law of the Union, and 2) fixed quotas formulated by the Council for each member state.

XIX. The headquarters of the Union will be at Salonica or Istanbul. Its official language will be French.

[Translated and reprinted from *Les Balkans*, Nos. 13–14 (October-November, 1931), 67–69.]

DOCUMENT VIII

THE DRAFT BALKAN PACT OF THE BALKAN CONFERENCE

[The draft Balkan Pact was adopted at the third plenary session of the Third Balkan Conference, at Bucharest, October 26, 1932. It is based on an original draft submitted to the Second Balkan Conference by Professor J. Spiropoulos of the University of Athens. At a meeting of the Special Committee on the Balkan Pact in Istanbul, in February, 1932, the original draft had been modified in order to provide for the protection of minorities. At the Fourth Balkan Conference, at Salonica, November 5–11, 1933, the pact was once more approved by representatives from Albania, Greece, Jugoslavia, Rumania, and Turkey. The Bulgarian group approved, with a statement of reservations. The draft of M. Spiropoulos is in *Les Balkans,* No. 12 (September, 1931), 35–44; that of the Special Committee in *Les Balkans,* No. 24 (September, 1932), 699–703.]

POLITICAL RAPPROCHEMENT: THE BALKAN PACT

The Third Balkan Conference, recognizing the solidarity which unites the Balkan peoples and the necessity of assuring the general peace, security among their states, and their political *rapprochement,*

Animated by the desires of putting completely into force the application of the system provided in the *Covenant* of the League of Nations for the pacific settlement of differences among the Balkan states, of giving complementary guarantees of security within the framework of existing treaties, and of assuring the execution of the clauses contained in the said treaties, including those concerning the protection of minorities,

Sincerely recommends consideration of the following draft of a Balkan Pact to the respective governments:

CHAPTER I.—NONAGGRESSION—FRIENDSHIP

Article 1.—Each of the high contracting parties agrees to make no attack or invasion, and not to resort to war against another contracting party, but to submit to processes of pacific settlement, in the manner stipulated in the present pact, all questions of whatever nature which have not been settled by ordinary diplomatic procedure.

The provisions of the preceding paragraph do not affect: 1) the exercise of the right of legitimate defense; 2) an action in application of Article 16 of the *Covenant* of the League of Nations; and 3) an action following a decision of the Assembly or the Council of the League of Nations, or in application of Article 15, line 7, of the *Covenant* of the League of Nations, provided that in the last-named circumstance, this action is directed against an aggressor state.

Article 2.—The contracting parties agree to take all the necessary measures for the strict application of the obligations arising from the existing treaties and for the cultivation of a spirit of understanding and friendship among their populations.

CHAPTER II.—PEACEFUL SETTLEMENT OF CONFLICTS

Section I.—Concerning Conciliation

Article 3.—Differences of every nature between two or more contracting parties, which have not been settled by diplomatic means, with the exception of: a) those relative to the territorial *status* of the contracting parties, and b) those which international law leaves to the exclusive competence of states, will be taken before a Permanent Commission of Conciliation to be constituted within six months after the present convention becomes effective.

Article 4.—The Permanent Commission of Conciliation will be composed of representatives of the contracting powers. Each contracting party will have only two representatives and only one vote; it may replace the representatives named by it at any time.

Any vacancies which may occur on account of death, resignation, or any other reason will be filled within the briefest period.

Article 5.—The functions of president of the Commission will be performed, in turn and in the alphabetical order of the contracting parties, by one of the representatives of each member state of the Commission. The term of the presidency is fixed at one year.

Article 6.—The Commission will take cognizance of the dispute through a request addressed to the president by one of the parties in dispute.

The request, after having stated summarily the object of the litigation, will contain the invitation to the Commission to proceed to all proper measures leading to conciliation.

Article 7.—The Commission will meet in the place designated by its president. This place must be on the territory of one of the contracting parties unless the Commission unanimously decides otherwise.

Article 8.—The deliberations of the Commission of Conciliation will be public only by decision of the Commission with the consent of the parties in dispute.

Article 9.—The Commission of Conciliation will determine its own procedure, which must always involve the hearing of all the parties. In the matter of the inquest, the Commission, if it does not unanimously decide otherwise, will conform to the stipulations of Title III of the Hague Convention, of October 18, 1907, for the Pacific Settlement of International Conflicts.

Article 10.—The parties in dispute will be represented with the Commission of Conciliation by agents who will serve as intermediaries between them and the Commission; they may, moreover, be assisted by counsel and experts named by them for this purpose and may ask the hearing of all persons whose testimony may appear useful to them.

Article 11.—The Commission, on its side, will have the right to ask oral explanations of the agents, counsel, and experts of the two parties, as well as of all persons it might judge useful to have appear with the consent of their government.

Article 12.—The decisions of the Commission will be made by majority of the votes of the members present at the session.

In the event of a tie, the president has the deciding vote. This rule does not apply when the Commission is to pronounce on the arrangement to be proposed in accordance with Article 15, paragraph 1.

Article 13.—The parties agree to facilitate the work of the Commission of Conciliation and in particular to provide it as fully as possible with all documents and useful information, as well as to assist it in proceeding on their territory and according to their legislation to the summoning and hearing of witnesses or experts, and to furnish transportation.

Article 14.—The general costs of the Commission will be borne equally by the contracting parties.

Article 15.—The Commission of Conciliation will elucidate the questions in litigation, collect all useful information for this purpose by means of inquiry or otherwise, and attempt to conciliate the parties. The Commission, after examination of the dispute, will explain to the parties the terms of the arrangement which it considers suitable.

At the end of its work the Commission will prepare a *procès-verbal* stating whether the parties have agreed, and if so, the conditions of the agreement, or whether the parties could not be conciliated. The *procès-verbal* will not mention whether the decisions of the Commission have been reached unanimously or by majority.

Unless the parties in dispute agree otherwise, the work of the Commission must be terminated within a period of six months, beginning with the day when the Commission assumes jurisdiction.

Article 16.—The *procès-verbal* of the Commission will be made known immediately to the parties in dispute. The parties will decide on publication.

Section II.—Judicial or Arbitral Settlement

Article 17.—If an understanding has not been reached within a month following the date of the communication of the result of the deliberations of the Commission to the parties, the dispute will be submitted for judgment to the Permanent Court of International Justice on the request of one party, unless the parties reach an agreement to have recourse to an arbitral tribunal.

Article 18.—If the parties in dispute reach an agreement to have recourse to an arbitral tribunal, they will formulate a *compromis.*

In default of an agreement between the parties in dispute on the *compromis,* or in default of the designation of arbitrators or of the functioning of the arbitral tribunal for any reason whatsoever, either party will have the right, after a previous notice of three months, to take the dispute to the Permanent Court of International Justice.

CHAPTER III.—MUTUAL ASSISTANCE

Article 19.—If one of the high contracting parties believes that a violation of the obligation of nonaggression of the first article of the present pact has been committed or is being committed, it will submit the question immediately to the Council of the League of Nations.

When the Council of the League of Nations has declared by a four-fifths majority, excluding the votes of the parties in dispute, that a violation has been committed, it will give an immediate opinion to the signatory powers of the present pact, and each is obligated to offer its assistance to the power against which the criminal act has been directed.

Article 20.—In the event of a flagrant violation by one of the high contracting parties of the obligation of nonaggression of Article 1 of the present pact, each of the other contracting parties agrees to offer its immediate assistance to the party against which such a violation or contravention has been directed, as soon as the said Power has taken note that this violation constitutes an unprovoked act of aggression and that as a consequence immediate action is necessary, whether because of the violation of the frontier or the beginning of hostilities. Nevertheless, the Council of the League of Nations, having taken cognizance of the question in accordance with the first paragraph of the preceding article, will make known the result of its deliberations. The high contracting parties agree in such circumstances to act in accordance with the recommendations of the Council which have received four-fifths of the votes, excluding the representatives of the powers engaged in hostilities.

CHAPTER IV.—PROTECTION OF MINORITIES

Article 21.—In order to render more effective the protection of minorities, the contracting parties, on the basis of the respective clauses of the treaties concerning minorities, which will remain in force, assume the following obligations :

Article 22.—Each contracting party will create an Office of Minorities to which petitions on the application of the treaties concerning minorities may be addressed.

Article 23.—The contracting parties will create a Balkan Commission of Minorities, which will be composed of six members, one designated by each contracting party, and which will meet annually in turn in each of the signatory states.

Article 24.—The Commission will formulate its own regulations.

On the request of the Commission the Offices of Minorities will submit to it the petitions addressed to them, and will communicate the *démarches* made as well as the results obtained. After the examination of each case the Commission will deliver its decision.

Article 25.—a) The contracting states agree to conform to any recommendation unanimously adopted by the Commission.

b) In the event of difference of view in the Commission, that body will transmit the *dossier* to the Secretariat of the League of Nations if the petitioner, making use of the right provided in the minorities treaties, addresses likewise a petition to the Secretariat of the League of Nations.

Article 26.—Petitions concerning the protection of minorities must give expression to the free will of the interested populations. The minorities must conduct themselves loyally toward the state on whose territory they live and abstain from any action directed against the state.

The contracting parties agree to take the measures necessary for preventing any kind of action likely to disturb the peace and good relations among the Balkan peoples.

CHAPTER V.—GENERAL STIPULATIONS

Article 27.—The differences for the solution of which a special procedure is provided in other conventions in force among the contracting parties will be settled in accordance with the stipulations of those conventions.

The present pact does not infringe on existing agreements which establish a procedure of conciliation, arbitration, and judicial settlement for the contracting parties, nor on engagements assuring the solution of the differences. Nevertheless, if these agreements provide only a procedure of conciliation, the provisions of the present pact relative to judicial or arbitral settlement will be applied when this procedure has been exhausted.

Article 28.—If the Commission of Conciliation is informed by one of the contracting parties of a difference which the other party in dispute, relying on existing conventions between the parties, has submitted to the Permanent Court of International Justice or to an arbitral tribunal, the Commission will suspend examination of the dispute until the court or the tribunal has decided its competence in the conflict. The same procedure will apply if the court or the tribunal has been informed by one of the parties in dispute in the course of conciliation.

Article 29.—If there is a difference which, in accordance with the internal legislation of one of the parties in dispute, raises the competence of its judicial or administrative authorities, this party may suggest that the difference be submitted within a reasonable period to the several procedures provided by the present pact, before a definitive decision has been rendered by the competent authority.

The party which in this circumstance wishes to have recourse to the procedures provided by the present pact must notify the other party of its intention within a period of one year beginning with the decision indicated above.

Article 30.—If the judicial or arbitral opinion declares that a decision reached or measure ordered by an authority of one of the parties in dispute is entirely or partly in opposition to international law, and if the constitutional law of the said party does not permit or only imperfectly permits the elimination of the consequences of this measure, it is agreed that the judicial or arbitral decision must accord to the injured party an equitable satisfaction.

Article 31.—In every case in which the difference is the object of an arbitral or judicial procedure, particularly if the question which divides the parties results from acts already effected or on the point of being so, the Permanent Court of International Justice, in accordance with Article 41 of its statute, or the arbitral tribunal, will indicate in the briefest possible period what provisional measures must be taken. The parties in dispute will be obliged to conform thereto.

If the Commission of Conciliation takes cognizance of the dispute, it can recommend to the parties the provisional measures which it deems useful.

The contracting parties agree to abstain from any measure likely to be prejudicial to the execution of the judicial or arbitral decision or to the arrangements proposed by the Commission of Conciliation, and in general not to commit any act whatsoever likely to aggravate or extend the difference.

Article 32.—The present pact will be applicable between the contracting parties even though a third power has an interest in the case.

In the procedure of conciliation the parties in dispute may, by common agreement, invite a third power.

In the judicial or arbitral procedure, if a third power considers that it has a juridical interest in the dispute, it may address a request for intervention to the Permanent Court of International Justice or to the arbitral tribunal.

Article 33.—When there is a question of the interpretation of a convention in which states other than the contracting parties have participated, the registrar of the Permanent Court of International Justice or the arbitral tribunal will advise [these states] without delay.

Each [of these states] will have the right of intervening; if it exercises this right, it is bound by the interpretation contained in the opinion.

Article 34.—Differences relative to the interpretation or application of the present pact, with the exception of those mentioned in Article 3, line a, will be submitted to the Permanent Court of International Justice.

Article 35.—In the event of a dispute arising among more than two contracting parties, the statute of the Permanent Court of International Justice for judicial procedure will be applied.

Article 36.—No stipulation of the present pact can be interpreted as restraining the League of Nations from taking appropriate measures at any time for safeguarding the peace of the world.

208 *Balkan Conferences and Balkan Entente*

No stipulation of the present pact can be interpreted as violating the obligations arising from the *Covenant* of the League of Nations for contracting parties of the present convention who are also members of the League of Nations.

Article 37.—The present pact will enter into force on the ninetieth day following receipt by the Secretary-General of the League of Nations of the ratification of at least four contracting parties.

Article 38.—The present pact will be ratified and the ratifications will be deposited at ———. It will be registered with the Secretariat of the League of Nations.

Article 39.—The following conventions are abrogated by the present pact: [different conventions of arbitration, conciliation, etc., existing among the Balkan states, which, by consequence of the signature of the present pact, become superfluous, are here cited].

In faith of which the plenipotentiaries above mentioned have signed the present pact.

Done at ——— the ——— in six copies.

[Translated and reprinted from *IIIᵉ Conférence balkanique. Bucarest, 22–29 octobre 1932. Documents officiels* (Bucharest, 1933), pp. 347–56. See also *Les Balkans*, III, Nos. 1–2 (October-November, 1932), 172–79.]

THE CONVENTION ON THE
PERSONAL STATUS OF BALKAN CITIZENS

[Adopted by the Third Balkan Conference at Bucharest (October, 1932)]

Article 1.—Citizens of each of the high contracting parties will be admitted freely into the territory of any other contracting party without passport formalities and will enjoy therein, in accordance with its laws and regulations, the same freedom of movement, sojourn, establishment, and association as nationals. They will have the right of free exit from the territory unless prevented by a competent authority in accordance with the legislation of the country and international law. It is understood, however, that these provisions do not infringe on the recognized rights of the contracting parties to regulate movements of population by law in accordance with the advice of the Balkan Labor Office, which will define what is meant by movements of population (*migrations*).

Article 2.—1) In the territories of each of the high contracting parties and under the restrictions of their laws and regulations, citizens of the other high contracting parties admitted to settlement therein, conforming to Article 1 of the present convention, will be placed on a footing of complete equality in law and in fact with the nationals, concerning:

a) The exercise of any commercial, financial, industrial, or any other economic activity, no distinction being made among autonomous establishments, branches, affiliated businesses, or agencies of enterprises situated on the territory of the said high contracting parties;

b) The exercise of professions which the law of the said high contracting parties permits freely to their nationals, or with respect to professions possessing rights or special guarantees, the exercise of these professions, under the reservation of the granting of the same rights or guarantees, or guarantees the equivalent of which would be recognized under the condition of reciprocity by the interested high contracting party.

2) The provisions of the preceding paragraph do not apply to the exercise of the following professions, occupations, industries, and enterprises on the territory of each of the high contracting parties:

a) The functions, work, or employment (of a judicial, administrative, military, or other nature) which imply a devolution of the power of the state or a mission given by the state, or functionaries chosen either by the state or by administrations of the state, whether of a territorial, general, or local character;

b) Professions such as those of lawyer, solicitor, notary, stockbroker, as well as professions or employment which, as regulated by national legislation, imply a particular responsibility on account of the public interest;

c) Industries or enterprises which are operated as a state monopoly;

d) State enterprises;

e) Peddling and transportation;

f) Fishing in the territorial and external waters and exploitation of the riches of the said waters, exercise of the coastwise trade, pilot service, and service of the ports;

g) Service on ships and airplanes under the national flag.

Article 3.—Citizens of one of the high contracting parties domiciled on the territory of another high contracting party or who, without being domiciled there, pursue their business there, are free to name, according to their choice, for the direction of their businesses or the regulation of their affairs, persons whom they judge fit and capable, as well as a limited number of administrative or technical assistants necessary for the effective operation of their enterprises, if they are unavailable in the national labor market, without being subject to prescriptions incompatible with the provisions of the present convention. In applying their laws and regulations for the protection of the national labor market, the high contracting parties agree to permit the choice of citizens of the other high contracting parties for the employments provided above.

Article 4.—Citizens of each of the high contracting parties will enjoy in the territory of the other high contracting parties legal and judicial protection of their persons, goods, rights, and interests equally with nationals. Consequently, they will have free access to the tribunals as plaintiffs and defendants. They will have the right to appear before the competent administrative authorities and to have recourse to their intervention for the safeguard of their rights or interests in all cases in which nationals have that right. The citizens of the high contracting parties will have the right to choose attorneys, solicitors, notaries, and other persons authorized by the national laws of the country, for the defense of their interests in all courts and all jurisdictions or before administrative authorities.

They will enjoy under the same conditions as nationals the right to appear in court as plaintiffs and to appear before the competent administrative authorities in order to safeguard their rights or interests, in accordance with the existing laws in the said territory. These laws are to be applied to nationals and foreigners alike. The citizens of the high contracting parties will have the right to choose attorneys, solicitors, notaries, and other persons authorized by the national laws of the country, for the defense of their interests before the courts and administrative authorities. The question of the execution of the judgments or arbitral sentences rendered on the territory of one of the high contracting parties and demanded of another high contracting party is determined by the internal legislation of each party or by agreements which have been concluded for that purpose.

Article 5.—1) Citizens of each of the high contracting parties will be treated on a basis of equality with nationals in the matter of patrimonial rights, the right to acquire, possess, or confirm the possession of movable or immovable goods, as well as that of disposal, without any modification or restriction of any kind, except under a contrary constitutional provision concerning the acquisition of rural property.

2) Each of the high contracting parties recognizes the freedom of the citizens of the other high contracting parties to export, under the same conditions as nationals, movable objects belonging to them, as well as the proceeds from the sale of both movable and immovable goods. The regulation relative to foreign bequests

resulting from this exportation may not vary according to the nationality of the exporter.

3) The provisions of the present article constitute no obstacle to the right reserved by the contracting parties to exclude and admit only on condition of a previous authorization, for reasons of security or national defense, the right of foreigners to possess and use immovable goods or enterprises.

4) In exceptional circumstances arising particularly from a monetary crisis, if the measures concerning the principle of equality affirmed in line 1 of the present article do not suffice to safeguard the interests [of the state], foreigners will be forbidden to acquire movable or immovable properties in cases in which this acquisition tends toward or threatens a monopoly of the vital economic resources of the country.

Article 6.—1) Nationals of each of the high contracting parties will be exempt from any judicial or administrative function on the territory of the other high contracting parties.

2) They will also be exempt from any obligatory service relating to the national defense or militia and from all personal military service, in time of peace as in time of war, on the territory of the other high contracting parties. Likewise, they will be exempt from any payments in money or kind which may be imposed.

3) Citizens of each of the high contracting parties domiciled on the territory of another must, however, submit to the charges pertaining to the ownership of landed and immovable property, such as forced security and other payments or special military requisitions, to which all citizens of the country must submit by virtue of legal provisions as possessors or owners of immovable or landed property. Under no circumstances may one of the high contracting parties make a charge which is not demanded also of its nationals.

4) Citizens of one of the high contracting parties on the territory of another, may not have either their landed or movable property expropriated, or be deprived even temporarily of the enjoyment of their property except with respect to a legally recognized public utility and then only after legal procedure.

5) Each of the high contracting parties must grant to the citizens of the other high contracting parties a treatment equal to that

given its own nationals in matters of indemnities for payments, requisitions, expropriations, or temporary privations provided in Sections 3 and 4 above, and in any event must assure a just indemnity corresponding to the real value of the expropriated property.

Article 7.—Citizens of each of the high contracting parties will enjoy equally with nationals the same treatment and protection from the fiscal authorities and jurisdictions on the territory of the other high contracting parties in matters of imposts and taxes of all kinds and any other fiscal charge without regard to the account under which they are collected and in the matter of their persons as well as property, rights, and interests, including their business, industries, and professions.

No discrimination in the determination of the rate of any imposts and taxes on commerce and industry may be established on account of the foreign origin of the merchandise used or placed on sale.

Article 8.—Each of the high contracting parties agrees not to submit the permanent industrial, commercial, or agricultural establishments of the other high contracting parties on its soil, having their principal offices on another territory, to imposts or taxes higher than the imposts or taxes paid under similar conditions by its own citizens.

The contracting parties will regulate the manner of application of the present article either by adaptation of their internal legislation or by means of bilateral or multilateral agreements.

Article 9.—1) For the purposes of the present convention, stock companies and other commercial, industrial, or financial companies, including insurance companies, navigation, transportation, and other communication companies, regularly constituted in accordance with the legislation of the party, and having their headquarters therein, will be considered as companies of one of the high contracting parties.

The companies of each of the high contracting parties will be recognized by the other parties as regularly constituted.

2) The activity of the companies of one of the high contracting parties so far as it is exercised on the territory of another party will be subject to the laws and regulations of the latter.

3) The high contracting parties which permit the activity of foreign companies on their territory, this activity being manifested by the existence of permanent establishments or in any other manner, are forbidden to hinder by a license tax the activity or establishment of the companies engaged in an activity generally permitted to the companies of all other countries in similar circumstances.

They agree particularly not to impose conditions on a foreign company to which its activity had not been subjected previously, except with respect to new measures applicable under the same conditions to national companies.

4) The companies of each of the high contracting parties on the territory of the other parties, whether permanent establishments or not, will enjoy a treatment similar to that provided for citizens under the same conditions; however, foreign companies may not claim more favorable treatment than that given to national companies under the same conditions.

5) The high contracting parties agree not to infringe acquired rights unnecessarily and not to revoke in consequence a license once given except in the event of an infraction of the laws and regulations of the country.

6) Under the reservation of Article 5, Section 1, the companies of each of the high contracting parties may, in accordance with the laws and regulations of the high contracting party on whose territory they are admitted, acquire, possess, or lease movable or immovable property and exercise their rights or conduct their industries and business; they will have free and easy access to the courts and other administrative authorities and will enjoy in general, so far as is applicable to them, the rights granted by Articles 5 and 6 to the citizens of the high contracting parties.

The companies will always enjoy after their admission the same rights which are or will be accorded in these matters to companies of the same nature of the most favored nation.

Nevertheless, the most-favored-nation clause will not permit one of the high contracting parties to demand for its companies a more favorable treatment than that which it would grant to the companies of the other party.

7) The treatment and protection which will be granted to the companies of each of the high contracting parties, defined in Article 1, will be analogous in all points to that provided for the citizens of each of the high contracting parties in Articles 1 and 8.

Article 10.—1) The high contracting parties agree not to bear any ill will toward the citizens of one or more high contracting parties in the eventual exercise of the rights which will be reserved for them by the provisions of the present convention.

2) Though the present convention assures the benefit of the régime applicable to its nationals to the citizens of the high contracting parties on the territory of one high contracting party, the said high contracting party is forbidden to institute this régime in such a manner that it implies conditions the application of which would lead to the exclusion pure and simple of the citizens of the other high contracting parties, or would lead to a differential régime to the detriment of the said citizens.

Article 11.—The high contracting parties agree not to infringe on the guarantees of equality for national and foreign enterprises, such as are provided in the preceding articles, either by means of exemption from imposts or taxes or by differential regulations relative to production and trade or the price régime.

Article 12.—1) If a high contracting party, after the signature of the present convention and within its limits, makes any restrictions whatsoever on the previously authorized activity of the citizens or companies of the other high contracting parties, it must, as much as possible, respect the acquired patrimonial rights.

2) In a general way the high contracting parties agree to make only such use of the reservations provided by the present convention as will bear the least possible prejudice to international commerce.

Article 13.—The high contracting parties agree that all differences arising among them on the interpretation or application of the present convention will, unless settled by direct negotiations, be submitted on the request of one of the parties in dispute, to the Permanent Court of International Justice, unless, by application of an existing convention or by common agreement, they have proceeded to settlement of the difference by arbitration or otherwise.

Article 14.—The application of each of the provisions of the present convention to the citizens and companies of one of the contracting parties rests upon the express condition of perfect reciprocity in regard to the citizens and companies of the other party.

Article 15.—It is agreed that this convention makes an integral part of the project of the Balkan Pact and the economic convention for the creation of a partial customs union, under the condition that the acceptance of this project can in no circumstance be interpreted as implying *ipso jure* the extension to the citizens of other states of rights granted to Balkan citizens.

The effective application of this convention is to take place only after the acceptance and the simultaneous application of the foregoing conventions.

Article 16.—The present convention is subject to ratification.

[Translated and reprinted from *IIIe Conférence balkanique. Bucarest, 22–29 octobre 1932* (Bucharest, 1932), pp. 363–70. See also *Les Balkans*, III, Nos. 1–2 (October-November, 1932), 182–88.]

DOCUMENT X

THE DRAFT OF A
REGIONAL ECONOMIC UNDERSTANDING

[Adopted at the Fourth Balkan Conference, Salonica, November, 1933]

PREAMBLE—OBJECT OF THE AGREEMENT

The governments of the Balkan states, motivated by the desire:

1) To develop in the largest possible degree the exchange of products and services among the national markets of the Balkan countries; and

2) To coöperate for the most effective protection of their principal products in the extra-Balkan markets;

Agree to conclude, within the period of one year, a regional economic understanding as the first step toward a Balkan customs union, on the following bases:

BILATERAL AND GENERAL MOST-FAVORED-NATION TREATMENT

Article 1.—The contracting parties mutually grant most-favored-nation treatment for the exchange of products coming from their respective countries.

PREFERENTIAL INTRA-BALKAN TREATMENT

Article 2.—1. Given the special intra-Balkan character of this regional understanding, the signatory states agree to insert a formal "Balkan Clause" in derogation of the most-favored-nation clause in their commercial treaties with extra-Balkan states.

2. The signatory states mutually grant, also, special treatment and preferential rights, that is, lower duties in their minimum respective tariffs, for articles which are particularly necessary in their national economies.

3. The nature and number of these articles, and the percentage of reduction to be granted on the minimum tariff in which they are taxed, as well as the quantity on which the preferential tariff is to be applied in each importing state, are to be regulated in accordance with the provisions of Article 3.

APPLICATION OF INTRA-BALKAN PREFERENTIAL TREATMENT

Article 3.—1. The intra-Balkan preferential treatment will be applied to the exports of one Balkan country to another up to the point of competition of a preferential contingent, the mounting total and composition of which will be determined after an understanding among the interested governments and after consultation with the Permanent Commission.

2. These understandings may be submitted to periodic revision in accordance with the needs and on the request of the interested parties.

3. For agricultural products, the revision must, when necessary, be made as soon as possible after the results of the respective harvests are known at the end of each season.

PREROGATIVES OF INTRA-BALKAN PREFERENCE

Article 4.—In order that the imports and exports between two of the signatory states be regulated by restrictions or special conditions, these measures are agreed upon, so far as they concern the preferential treatment provided in Article 3, after consultation with the Permanent Commission and at the same time as the establishment of the preferential contingent.

THE RÉGIME OF COMMERCIAL RELATIONS OUTSIDE PREFERENTIAL TREATMENT

Article 5.—Commercial relations among the signatory states, outside of matters treated in the present agreement, are under an entirely autonomous régime, provided there is no bilateral treaty of commerce between the states.

SPECIAL RÉGIME FOR MERCHANDISE UNDER MONOPOLY OR RÉGIE

Article 6.—The respective administrations will reach an understanding directly among themselves and with the interested governments concerning commercial exchanges dealing with products or merchandise in general which are under a state monopoly or special laws instituting a monopoly for imports or exports.

UNIFICATION OF NOMENCLATURE AND CUSTOMS FORMALITIES

Article 7.—For the purpose of facilitating the uniform application of the principles of this regional understanding, a special subcommission of experts within the Permanent Commission will be charged to prepare, within a period of one year following the entry into force of the understanding, projects for the unification of the nomenclature of the customs tariffs of the signatory states and for classification of merchandise concerning transportation costs, a draft of customs regulations and formalities, and methods of evaluation for statistics of international commerce.

COMMON COMMERCIAL POLICY

Article 8.—1. The signatory states, in their commercial policy toward extra-Balkan states, will combine their efforts for the most effective protection and defense of their foreign exports, in order to assure the largest possible outlet of the principal products of the Balkan countries.

2. With this in view, the signatory states, before concluding a commercial agreement with an extra-Balkan state, will proceed each time, after a mutual exchange of views, within the framework of the Permanent Commission.

3. Moreover, the signatory states will consider in common the practical measures to be adopted for the purpose of a concerted action for the protection of the principal products common to all or to some of the interested parties.

4. The Balkan states agree also to offer mutual assistance to facilitate the export of their products abroad by assuring them free and direct transit under the best conditions, on the basis of equality of treatment.

CHAMBER OF COMPENSATIONS FOR INTERNATIONAL EXCHANGES

Article 9.—1. The signatory states agree to create within the Permanent Commission, a Chamber of Compensations for the International Commerce of the Balkan Countries. This is to facilitate, especially during the transition period, the exchange of their products and the regulation of payments and transfers arising from commercial exchanges on the basis of intra-Balkan preferential treatment, and to permit the realization, in the largest degree possible, of all combinations (bilateral, tripartite, or multilateral) of international exchanges of merchandise or of particular favors, in the spirit of the present agreement, and especially of Article 8.

2. The drafts for the organization of this Chamber, the means for its functioning, etc., will be elaborated and proposed to the interested governments by the Permanent Commission.

THE PERMANENT COMMISSION

Article 10.—1. A Permanent Commission of the International Commerce of the Balkan Countries is instituted for the purpose of assembling the necessary documents and of advising concerning the means of encouraging the foreign commerce of the Balkan countries, and especially their mutual trade.

2. The Permanent Commission, acting on its own initiative, on the proposal of the national groups of the Balkan Conference, or on the request of one of the governments of the signatory states, is charged to examine questions concerning the commercial relations of the Balkan countries, especially as to the application of preferential treatment, as well as to the coördination of their commercial policies, and to draw up advisory opinions on these questions, and to formulate concrete proposals to be submitted to the interested governments.

3. The principal task of the Permanent Commission will be to advise as to the means of eliminating the obstacles to intra-Balkan commerce and to advance the economic *rapprochement* of the Balkan countries. In this sense the Permanent Commission will submit to the interested governments propositions and projects of treaties to be concluded or other measures to be adopted in favor of the development of national economies and commercial relations of the signatory states.

COMPOSITION AND FUNCTIONING OF THE PERMANENT COMMISSION

Article 11.—1. The Permanent Commission of the International Commerce of the Balkan Countries is composed of three delegates of each signatory state, the presidency being filled annually in turn by the first delegate of each of the signatory parties.

2. The Commission will draw up its own statutes and regulations for its work and services.

DURATION OF THE UNDERSTANDING—PROVISION FOR DENUNCIATION

Article 12.—1. The regional understanding to be concluded will enter into force three months after the exchange of the instruments of ratification, and will have an unlimited duration.

2. The signatory states may denounce this understanding only after a minimum period of two years and after a previous notice of twelve months.

[Translated and reprinted from *Les Balkans,* IV, Nos. 14–15 (November-December, 1933), 1088–91.]

DOCUMENT XI

DRAFT STATUTES OF THE
BALKAN PARLIAMENTARY AND SOCIAL UNION

[Prepared by M. Alexander Papanastassiou, of the Greek Delegation of the Balkan Conference, following the decisions of the Council of the Balkan Conference, March 31–April 3, 1934.]

AIM AND HEADQUARTERS OF THE UNION

Article 1.—In the spirit of the recommendations of the League of Nations in favor of regional unions, and in order to give effect to the wishes and aspirations of the Balkan peoples, there is constituted, under the name of The Balkan Parliamentary and Social Union, an organism, the purpose of which is the *rapprochement* and collaboration of the Balkan peoples in the political, economic, intellectual, and social domains, for the purpose of the establishment of the Union of the Balkan Nations (Albania, Bulgaria, Greece, Jugoslavia, Rumania, and Turkey).

Article 2.—The headquarters of the Union is Istanbul.

ORGANS OF THE CONFERENCE

Article 3.—The organs of the Union are: a) the General Assembly, that is, the Balkan Conference; b) the Council; c) the Bureau [office of the Presidency]; d) the Secretariat; e) the National Groups.

THE NATIONAL GROUPS OF THE UNION

Article 4.—1) A Group of the Union is formed in each Balkan state.

2) The deputies and senators of each country are admitted on their request as members of the respective National Groups.

3) Physical and legal persons [individuals and associations] who adhere to the idea of the Balkan Union and who contribute to its realization may become members of the National Groups.

4) Persons who have taken part in a Balkan Conference as delegates of their countries are considered *ipso jure* as members of the respective Groups.

5) The Groups will seek to become associated with representatives of the political, intellectual, commercial, industrial, agricultural, labor, women's, peace, and press circles.

6) Persons, institutions, or organizations whose activity or program is contrary to the principles of the Balkan Union are not accepted as members or collaborators.

7) The Groups function according to their statutes.

8) The Groups must conform to the resolutions or recommendations of the Conference and the Council.

9) The Groups must be in contact with their own governments as well as with the representatives of the other Balkan governments in their countries.

THE BALKAN CONFERENCE

Article 5.—1) The Balkan Conference, supreme organ of the Union, meets regularly each year in the autumn, on the date and in the place determined by the Council. Three months before this date each National Group will communicate to the government of its country the list of the delegates to the Conference.

2) Each delegation will include only thirty delegates, aside from experts and secretaries. Primarily the delegates will be chosen from among parliamentary and administrative circles, and from among the representatives of municipalities, universities, professional, peace, and women's organizations, the press, and other intellectual, economic, and social institutions or groups.

3) The number of parliamentary delegates must, if possible, not be less than half the total of the members of each delegation.

4) The representatives of the Balkan governments in the country in which the Conference is meeting, as well as a special representative of the government of that country, have the right to follow the work of the Conference in the capacity of observers and to take part in the debates. The members of the government in which the Conference is meeting have the same right.

5) The League of Nations and the International Labor Office will always be invited to send observers to the Conference. The Bureau of International Peace, the Carnegie Endowment for In-

ternational Peace, and the international parliamentary organizations will also be invited to be represented at the Conference.

Article 6.—The Conference is convoked by the president, who communicates to the National Groups and the Balkan governments the agenda and the reports or other documents which are submitted to him for this purpose.

Article 7.—1) The president of the Council of the Union performs the duties of president of the Conference until the election of that officer.

2) On the proposal of the Council, the Conference elects its president from among the chiefs of the delegations by absolute majority of the votes cast. The president of the Conference is also president of the Union. If after the first ballot no candidate has obtained a majority, a second ballot will be taken on the candidates who have obtained the greatest number of votes.

3) The other chiefs of delegations are in full right vice-presidents of the Conference.

4) The president and the vice-presidents of the Conference form the Bureau [of the Presidency]. If necessity requires, the Bureau may make decisions in place of the Council.

5) The Bureau is assisted by the six general secretaries of the National Groups. One of these secretaries, chosen by the president, assumes the functions of secretary-general of the Conference and the Bureau.

6) The functions of the president terminate on January 31, on which date they are transmitted to another chief of the group designated by the Council, who will assume the functions of the president of the Union and the Council until the election of the president as provided in paragraph 1) of the present article.

7) The transmission of the said functions may be postponed, if necessary, by decision of the Council for a period not exceeding two months.

Article 8.—1) The following commissions function within the framework of the Conference: a) The Legal and Organization Commission; b) The Political Commission; c) The Commission on Economic Relations; d) The Commission on Intellectual Coöperation; e) The Commission on Social Policy and Hygiene; f) The Commission on Communications and Public Works.

2) The Conference, on the proposal of the Council, may create other commissions and subcommissions.

3) Each delegation designates at least two members for each commission from among its delegates and experts.

4) The Council may call together any commission whatever, even in the interval between the sessions of the Conference.

Article 9.—1) The official language of the Union is French. Delegates who wish to use their national language in the debates will have their addresses translated into French.

2) The plenary sessions of the Conference are public. The commissions may admit the public to their sessions also.

Article 10.—1) The quorum in the plenary session and in the commissions is fixed at three-fifths of the total number of the votes of all the delegations.

2) Resolutions are adopted by absolute majority of the votes cast.

3) In the event of the total absence of a delegation, the decisions of the Conference are adjourned for one session.

Article 11.—Each delegate has one vote. If the number of delegates of a country is below thirty, the chief of the delegation of that country has the right to designate those who may have more than one vote, three being the maximum. If, on the contrary, the number of the delegates of a country is more than thirty, the chief of the delegation must designate those who may exercise the right to vote. No delegation has more than thirty votes in all.

Article 12.—1) In the commissions each delegation has a maximum of five votes.

2) In the event of the total absence of a delegation, the decisions of the commission are postponed for one session.

Article 13.—The order of business of the plenary sessions and commissions of the Conference is regulated by a special statute.

Article 14.—Before adjourning, the Conference, on the motion of the Council, designates the place of the next session, or remands it to the Council, which must decide the matter not later than its January session (Article 15).

THE COUNCIL OF THE UNION

Article 15.—1) The Council of the Union is composed of three members of each group. The president of the Union presides over it.

2) The Council will meet at the end of January to attend to the transmission of the presidency (Article 8) and the determination of the agenda of the next Conference. The date of this session of the Council may be postponed until the end of April.

Article 16.—The Council is the executive organ of the Union. It represents the Union in the interval between the Conferences. It presents annually an account of its labors to the Conference. It approves the budget and controls its administration. It determines the precise date and agenda of the next Conference.

Article 17.—The Council meets on the invitation of its president or on the request of seven members.

In exceptional circumstances when members of the Council cannot meet and when there are urgent questions to be settled, the Council may arrive at decisions by correspondence.

The Council regulates its own internal organization.

Article 18.—The president has executive charge of the decisions of the Council. He names the functionaries. He directs the labors of the Secretariat and supervises its activities.

Article 19.—The government observers and diplomatic representatives of the Balkan States in the country in which the Assembly is meeting may function as an advisory committee which the president of the Council consults on questions concerning the work of the Conference.

THE SECRETARIAT

Article 20.—1) The Secretariat is composed of the secretary-general and five other members designated in a ratio of one to each delegation. It is charged with the correspondence, the publication of the minutes of the Conference, the service of the archives, and the annual preparation of the budget of the Union. It will publish as soon as possible a periodical bulletin in French in which all the National Groups will be invited to collaborate.

2) The Secretariat will be divided into sections according to

the different activities of the Union. The sections may be transformed into institutes; in such case the Council will fix their rules.

THE FINANCES OF THE UNION

Article 21.—1) The annual quotas of the National Groups will be determined in proportion to the budget of expenses fixed by the Conference.

2) The service of accounts of the Union is performed by the Secretariat. All expenses must be approved by the president.

FINAL PROVISIONS

Article 22.—All the National Groups are obligated to do everything possible in their own countries for the realization of the resolutions and the ideals of the Conference. For this purpose they must among other things communicate to the parliaments, through those who are deputies or senators, the resolutions of the Conference and ask that they be taken into consideration.

The groups will submit to the Conference an annual report on the results of their labors.

Article 23.—The emblem of the Union consists of a parallelogram 20 by 13, striped in white, blue, green, yellow, red, and white colors, and decorated in the center by a white sphere circled by six yellow stars. The two white stripes are twenty per cent larger than the four others, which are of equal size.

[Translated and reprinted from *Les Balkans*, VI, Nos. 8–9 (August-September, 1934), 381–89.]

THE PACT OF THE SOVIET UNION
WITH THE LITTLE ENTENTE
[CZECHOSLOVAKIA, JUGOSLAVIA, AND RUMANIA]
AND TURKEY.
LONDON, JULY 4, 1933

[The following pact, signed at London on July 4, 1933, differs from that signed on July 3, only in Article 4, which provides for ratification and adherence. Signatories of the pact of July 3 were: the U. S. S. R., Poland, Esthonia, Latvia, Rumania, Turkey, Persia, and Afghanistan. A similar separate treaty was signed with Lithuania. The Central Executive Commttee of the U. S. S. R. ratified the treaties on September 16, 1933.]

The Central Executive Committee of the Union of Socialist Soviet Republics, His Majesty the King of Rumania, His Excellency the President of Czechoslovakia, His Excellency the President of the Turkish Republic, and His Majesty the King of Jugoslavia,

Desirous of strengthening the peace existing between their countries,

Believing that the Briand-Kellogg Pact, of which they are signatories, forbids all aggression,

Deeming it necessary in the interests of general security to define as precisely as possible the conception of aggression, in order to eliminate every pretext for its justification,

Declaring that every state has an equal right to independence, security, defense of its territories, and the free development of its institutions,

Inspired by the desire, in the interest of universal peace, to assure to all nations the inviolability of the territory of their countries,

Considering it useful in the interest of universal peace, to put into force among them, precise rules for the definition of aggression, pending the universal recognition of these rules,

Have decided for this purpose to conclude the present convention and have duly accredited: [Here follow the names of the representatives signing the convention].

Who have agreed upon the following provisions:

Article 1.—Each of the high contracting parties undertakes to recognize in its relations with each of the other parties, beginning with the day this convention enters into effect, the definition of aggressor outlined in the report of the Security Committee of May 24, 1933 [the Politis Report], at the Disarmament Conference, based upon the proposal of the Soviet delegation.

Article 2.—Therefore, the aggressor in an international conflict, under the reservation of existing agreements among the parties in conflict, will be considered the state which is the first to commit any of the following acts:

1) Declaration of war against another state;

2) Invasion by armed forces, even without a declaration of war, of the territory of another state;

3) An attack by land, naval, or air forces, even without a declaration of war, upon the territory, naval vessels, or aircraft of another state;

4) Naval blockade of the coasts or ports of another state;

5) Support to armed bands formed on the territory of a state and invading the territory of another state, or refusal, in spite of the demand of the invaded state, to take all possible measures on its own territory to deprive the said bands of any aid or protection.

Article 3.—No consideration of a political, military, economic, or any other nature may serve as an excuse or justification for aggression as specified in Article 2. [For example see Appendix, below.]

Article 4.—The present convention is open to the adherence of all other nations. Adherence will confer the same rights and impose the same obligations as with respect to the original signatories. Notification of adherence will be made to the government of the Soviet Union, which will immediately notify the other participants.

[The signatures follow.]

APPENDIX TO ARTICLE 3 ON THE DEFINITION OF AGGRESSION

The high contracting parties signatory to the convention defining aggression, desirous, while retaining the complete inviolability of the absolute meaning of the rule formulated in Article 3 of the said convention, of giving certain indications permitting the determination of an aggressor, declare that none of the circumstances mentioned below may be used to justify any act of aggression in the sense of Article 2 of the said convention:

The internal position of any state, as, for example: its political, economic, or social structure; alleged shortcomings of its administration; disorder following upon strikes, revolutionary or counterrevolutionary movements, and civil war;

The international conduct of any state, as, for example: infringement or a threat of infringement upon the material or moral rights of a foreign state or its citizens; rupture of diplomatic or economic relations; measures of economic or financial boycott; conflicts in the sphere of economic, financial, or other obligations in connection with foreign governments; border incidents which do not fall under any of the categories of aggression indicated in Article 2.

At the same time the high contracting parties unanimously recognize that the present convention must in no circumstances serve to justify infringements of international law which might fall under the obligations included in the foregoing list.

[This translation is based on the documents in *Les Balkans*, IV, No. 10 (July, 1933), 305–06, and the *Soviet Union Review*, XI, Nos. 7–8 (July-August, 1933), 169–70.]

DOCUMENT XIII

THE GRECO-TURKISH PACT OF SEPTEMBER 14, 1933

Article 1.—Greece and Turkey mutually guarantee the inviolability of their common frontiers.

Article 2.—The high contracting parties agree that in all international questions in which they are interested, a preliminary consultation conforms to the general direction of their policy of understanding and collaboration and to their respective and common interests.

Article 3.—In all international conferences of limited representation, Greece and Turkey are disposed to consider that the delegate of one of them will have the mission of defending the common and special interests of the two parties, and they agree to unite their efforts to assure this common representation either to each in turn, or, in particular questions of special interests, to the country most concerned.

Article 4.—The present pact is concluded for a period of ten years.

If it is not denounced by one of the high contracting parties one year prior to the date of its expiration, it will remain in force for a new period of ten years.

Article 5.—The present pact will be ratified and the ratifications will be exchanged at Athens as soon as possible.

It will enter into force beginning with the last ratification, which will be communicated by note to the other contracting party.

[Translated and reprinted from *Les Balkans*, IV, Nos. 12–13 (September-October, 1933), 624–25.]

DOCUMENT XIV

THE FOUR-POWER BALKAN PACT
[GREECE, JUGOSLAVIA, RUMANIA, AND TURKEY].
ATHENS, FEBRUARY 9, 1934

The President of the Republic of Greece,
His Majesty the King of Rumania,
The President of the Republic of Turkey,
His Majesty the King of Jugoslavia,

United in the desire to contribute toward the permanence of peace in the Balkans, animated by the spirit of mutual understanding and conciliation which inspired the development of the Pact of Paris and the decisions relative thereto by the Assembly of the League of Nations, firmly determined to assure respect for contractual agreements already existing and the maintenance of present territorial boundaries in the Balkans, have decided to conclude a Balkan Pact, and for that purpose have designated as their respective plenipotentiaries:

His Excellency M. Demetrius Maximos, Greek Minister of Foreign Affairs,

His Excellency M. Nicolae Titulescu, Rumanian Minister of Foreign Affairs,

His Excellency M. Tevfik Rushdi Bey, Turkish Minister of Foreign Affairs,

His Excellency M. Bogoljub Jevtich, Jugoslav Minister of Foreign Affairs.

These plenipotentiaries, having exchanged credentials in due form, have concluded the following agreement:

Article 1.—Greece, Rumania, Turkey, and Jugoslavia mutually guarantee the security of all their Balkan frontiers.

Article 2.—The high contracting parties obligate themselves to agree upon measures to be taken in case of eventualities capable of affecting their interests as defined in this agreement. They pledge themselves not to undertake any political action as regards any other Balkan country not a signatory to the present agreement without previous mutual conference and not to assume any political obligation toward any other Balkan country without the consent of the other contracting parties.

Article 3.—This agreement will enter into full force and effect from the date of its signature by all the contracting powers and will be ratified as quickly as possible. It will be open to all Balkan countries, whose adherence will be looked upon favorably by the contracting parties, and will take effect when the other signatory countries shall have expressed their agreement.

In witness whereof the aforesaid plenipotentiaries have signed this treaty.

Done at Athens, February 9, 1934, in four copies, one of which has been delivered to each of the high contracting parties.

> B. JEVTICH
> D. MAXIMOS
> N. TITULESCU
> T. RUSHDI BEY

[The English text is in the New York *Times*, February 18, 1934; the French text in *Les Balkans*, V, Nos. 1–2 (January-February, 1934), 92–93.]

DOCUMENT XV

THE STATUTE OF ORGANIZATION
OF THE BALKAN ENTENTE

[Ankara, October 30-November 2, 1934]

The states signatory of the Balkan Pact, desirous of maintaining and organizing peace, having a firm will to intensify economic relations among all states without distinction and among the signatories of the Balkan Entente in particular,

Determined to give to the relations of friendship and alliance which exist among the four states of the Balkan Entente an organic and permanent basis,

Convinced of the necessity of realizing this stability by the constitution of a directing organ of their common policy,

Have resolved to confirm the practice of their common work realized since the signature of the Pact of the Balkan Entente and to agree in the future as follows:

Article 1.—A Permanent Council of the states of the Balkan Entente, composed of the Ministers of Foreign Affairs of the respective countries, is constituted as the directing organ of the common policy of the group of four states. The decisions of the Council will be adopted in unanimity.

Article 2.—The Permanent Council, outside of regular diplomatic relations, will meet at least twice a year. The annual meetings will take place in turn in each of the four states.

If necessary, extraordinary meetings of the Permanent Council may be called by the president at Geneva or elsewhere.

Article 3.—The president of the Permanent Council is the Minister of Foreign Affairs of Greece for the period of a year from February 9, 1934, the date of the signature of the Pact of the Balkan Entente, at Athens. On February 9, 1935, the presidency of the Permanent Council will pass in full right to the Minister of Foreign Affairs of Rumania, on February 9, 1936, to the Minister of Foreign Affairs of Turkey, and on February 9, 1937, to the Minister of Foreign Affairs of Jugoslavia. The rotation will continue in the same manner by alphabetical order [in the French language], Greece, Rumania, Turkey, and Jugoslavia, and for the period of a year following February 9. The president takes the initiative in fixing the date and designating the place of the meeting, determines the agenda, and prepares the decisions to be adopted.

Article 4.—In all the questions which are discussed as well as in all the decisions which are adopted, whether concerning the mutual relations of the states of the Balkan Entente or their relations with others, the principle of the absolute equality of the four states of the Balkan Entente is rigorously respected.

Article 5.—An advisory Economic Council of the states of the Balkan Entente for the progressive coördination of the economic interests of the four states is constituted. It will be composed of specialists and experts on economic, commercial, and financial matters and will function as an auxiliary organ of the Permanent Council.

Article 6.—The Permanent Council has the right to establish other permanent or temporary organs, commissions, or committees, whether for a special question or groups of limited questions, for the purpose of studying them and preparing their solutions for the Permanent Council. All these organs will have an advisory and auxiliary character.

Article 7.—A Secretariat of the Permanent Council is created. Its headquarters is established always for one year in the capital of the president of the Permanent Council.

[Translated and reprinted from *Bulletin de la Chambre de Commerce et d'Industrie d'Istanbul* (November, 1934), 103. See also *L'Indépendance Roumaine,* November 4, 1934, and *Les Balkans,* VI, Nos. 10–11 (October-November, 1934), 628–29.]

DOCUMENT XVI

THE STATUTE OF THE ADVISORY ECONOMIC COUNCIL OF THE BALKAN ENTENTE

[Ankara, October 30-November 2, 1934]

Article 1.—The Economic Council of the Balkan Entente is composed of four national sections: Hellenic, Rumanian, Turkish, and Jugoslav.

Article 2.—Each section will be composed of five delegates, namely: a) for general commercial policy; b) for agricultural questions; c) for industrial questions; d) for financial questions, questions of credit, and central banks of issue; e) for questions of communications.

Article 3.—In each section experts and specialists having knowledge of practical economic life may be named to assist the delegates in the examination of the economic activity of the four countries.

The sections may also be divided into committees to consider special questions or a group of special questions.

Article 4.—Each section prepares its studies and its concrete propositions in its national meetings.

The four sections meet regularly at least twice a year in the capitals of each country, in turn, to coördinate their particular labors in the sections and to prepare their common propositions, which are then presented to the Permanent Council for decision.

Article 5.—The detailed program of the studies of the Economic Council, as well as its internal regulation, will be the subject of a later decision of the Permanent Council. For the moment, the Permanent Council decides that, within the five months to come, the Economic Council in Athens and in Ankara will present, on the occasion of the meeting of the Balkan Entente which is to take place in Bucharest on May 10, 1935, a report on the following questions:

a) Intensification of the economic and commercial relations among the signatories of the Balkan Entente;

b) Development of the means of inter-Balkan communications, especially those which, utilizing the Danube and the Black Sea, will permit the facilitation of [commercial] exchanges of the Balkan states and of Central Europe with Asia, as well as the other means of maritime communication;

c) Possibility of creating a Balkan Bank;

d) General tourist traffic.

[Translated and reprinted from *Bulletin de la Chambre de Commerce et d'Industrie d'Istanbul* (November, 1934), 103–04. See also *L'Indépendance Roumaine*, November 4, 1934, and *Les Balkans*, VI, Nos. 10–11 (October-November, 1934), 629–30.]

BIBLIOGRAPHY

INTRODUCTION

THE PREPARATION of a bibliography on the problem of Balkan union or confederation is a difficult and complicated task. Strange though it may seem, the problem does not appear to have been widely studied, even in the Balkan region itself. Such works as have been written are usually unobjective or biased, in behalf of the Great Powers interested in the region, or in behalf of a particular Balkan state. Few documentary sources for a background of the present movement toward confederation are available. It is not until we reach the period of the Balkan Conferences themselves that the materials become relatively abundant and available. The authors therefore believe that a selected bibliography of the readily accessible works will be of use to students of Balkan and Near Eastern problems.

With reference to works on the subject of Balkan union, it has been thought best to divide the materials into three general sections: (I) *Bibliographical Guides;* (II) *Sources:* (A) Current Periodicals and Newspapers; (B) General Documentary Bibliography; (C) Special Documentary Bibliography on the Balkan Conferences: (1) The Documentary Publications; (2) The First Balkan Conference; (3) The Second Balkan Conference; (4) The Third Balkan Conference; (5) The Fourth Balkan Conference; (6) The Fifth Balkan Conference; (III) *Secondary Accounts of Balkan Problems:* (A) Selected Books on Balkan Problems; (B) Books Dealing Especially with the Problem of Confederation and the Balkan Conferences; (C) Magazine Articles on Balkan Problems.

BIBLIOGRAPHICAL GUIDES

There are several excellent bibliographies which are of value to students of the Near Eastern question. One of these is William Henry Allison and others, *A Guide to Historical Literature* (New York, Macmillan, 1931). A special section (Section T), prepared by Professors Albert H. Lybyer and Robert J. Kerner, relates to Southeastern Europe and Southwestern Asia: The Balkans and the Near East since the Rise of the Ottoman Turks. Moreover, Professor Kerner has given particular attention to the Balkan scene in his *Slavic Europe: A*

Selected Bibliography in the Western European Languages, Comprising History, Languages, and Literatures (Cambridge, Harvard University Press, 1918). Dr. J. G. Kersopoulos has prepared a bibliography of materials in the French language on each of the Balkan nations, beginning with Albania and Bulgaria, which is appearing serially in *Les Balkans*, V–VI–VII (1934–35). Another good bibliographical source is that of W. L. Langer and H. F. Armstrong, *Foreign Affairs Bibliography* (New York, Harpers, 1933), which contains sections on the Balkans and the Near East. M. Léon Savadjian is publishing annual volumes dealing exclusively with Balkan problems: *Bibliographie balkanique* (Paris, France). Four volumes have already appeared: 1920–30, 1931–32, 1933, 1934.

SOURCES

CURRENT NEWSPAPERS AND PERIODICALS

A large number of newspapers and periodicals has been of use in making a study of the Balkan Conferences and the Four-Power Balkan Pact, as well as of the more recent developments in the European political system. The newspapers outside the Balkan peninsula which have been of particular value are the New York *Times*, the London *Times*, the Manchester *Guardian* (Weekly Edition), the *Christian Science Monitor*, and *Le Temps* (Paris).

The authors have used a representative number of newspapers and periodicals from Central Europe and the Balkan region. Most of these give an official or semiofficial view and contain valuable statements of policy. *La Bulgarie: quotidien politique, littéraire et économique* (Sofia, Bulgaria) has been used rather extensively because of its value in tracing the development of Bulgarian policy. *L'Echo de Belgrade: journal yougoslave hebdomadaire* (Belgrade, Jugoslavia) frequently publishes official materials. *L'Europe Centrale: revue de documentation politique, économique, littéraire et artistique* (Prague, Czechoslovakia) reflects the official Czech view and frequently publishes articles on the Balkans. Another Czech periodical, the *Central European Observer* (Prague), has published several official statements on foreign policy by Dr. Beneš, the foreign minister, and contains valuable news items. *Le Journal d'Orient* (Galata, Istanbul, Turkey, daily) published the *procès-verbaux* of the Second Balkan Conference, which met in Istanbul in October, 1931. *La Macédoine: journal politique* (Geneva, Switzerland; Sofia, Bulgaria), published by the Macedonian Revolutionary Organization, was suppressed after the *coup d'état* of May 19, 1934. It was useful because it reflected the extreme Macedonian view. *Le Méssager d'Athènes* (Athens, Greece, daily) is another semiofficial paper which contains official statements of policy. Frequently it has been possible to follow the debates in the Greek Parliament through this journal. *L'Indépendance Roumaine* (Bucharest, Rumania, daily) performs a similar service for Rumania. The Ministry of Foreign Affairs in Paris publishes an excellent summary of the Turkish press in its *Bulletin périodique de la Presse turque*.

Two sources of a somewhat different kind have been indispensable for current economic materials, studies of Balkan trade and commerce, and statistics. The first of these is: Chambre de Commerce et d'Industrie Interbalkanique,

Bulletin mensuel (Istanbul, Turkey), which appears monthly. The second is: Chambre de Commerce et d'Industrie d'Istanbul, *Bulletin mensuel* (Istanbul, Turkey), the first issue of which appeared in January, 1885. Both of these publications publish the texts of economic, and even political, treaties among the Balkan states.

GENERAL DOCUMENTARY BIBLIOGRAPHY

A relatively plentiful source of documentary materials has been available. The following selected citations will indicate the more generally useful materials in following the trends of European politics.

Beneš, Eduard. "The Problem of Central Europe," *International Conciliation*, No. 300 (May, 1934), 159–72. Statement before the Foreign Affairs Committee of the Czechoslovak Parliament, March 21, 1934. Reprinted from the *Central European Observer*, XII (March 23, 1934).

——— *Une nouvelle phase de la lutte pour l'équilibre européen. Exposé du Ministre des Affaires Étrangères fait devant la Chambre des Députés et le Sénat le 2 juillet 1934* (Prague, Orbis, 1934), 62 pp. An English edition may be found in *International Conciliation*, No. 302 (September, 134), 239–66.

——— *Vers un regroupement des forces en Europe? Exposé du Ministre des Affaires Étrangères fait devant la Chambre des Députés et le Sénat le 6 novembre 1934* (Prague, Orbis, 1934), 33 pp.

——— *Le sens politique de la tragédie de Marseille. Discours tenu devant le Conseil de la Société des Nations à Genève le 7 et le 10 décembre 1934* (Prague, Orbis, 1934), 47 pp.

Briand, Aristide. "Memorandum on the Organization of a Régime of European Federal Union, May 17, 1930," *International Conciliation, Special Bulletin* (June, 1930).

——— "European Federal Union. Replies of Twenty-Six Governments of Europe," *International Conciliation*, No. 265 (December, 1930).

Communication du gouvernement yougoslave au Conseil de la Société des Nations relative aux responsibilités encourues par les autorités hongroises dans l'action terroriste dirigée contre la Yougoslavie. Genève, 28 novembre 1934. (Belgrade, 1934) 31 pp.

"Conclusions adoptées par le Comité de Sécurité, 25 juin 1934," *L'Esprit International*, No. 32 (October, 1934), 586–89. Full text of the Politis Report.

"Deutsch-polnisches Abkommen von 26. Januar 1934," *Ost-Europa*, VI (March, 1934), 375–89.

Les dossiers politiques de l'Heure Actuelle (Bucharest, Rumania):

"L'attitude de la Roumanie vis-à-vis de la campagne pro-revisionniste. Séance du Parlement Roumain du 4 avril 1934." No. 1 (May 10, 1934), 37 pp.

"France et Roumanie. Visite de S. E. M. Louis Barthou, Ministre des Affaires Étrangères de la République Française, à Bucarest, 20–23 juin 1934." No. 2 (June-July, 1934), 50 pp. Debates in the Rumanian Parliament, June 20, 1934, at which M. Barthou spoke.

"Le texte du 'Pacte balkanique' signé le 9 février 1934 à Athènes.—Le texte du 'Traité turco-roumain' signé le 17 octobre 1934 à Ankara." No. 5 (September, 1934), 16–17, 18–23.

"Sommaire: Les responsabilités dans le double crime de Marseille. Le différend yougoslavo-hongrois devant le Conseil de la Société des Nations. Le memorandum yougoslave.—Le mémoire hongrois.—Les exposés de M. Jevtich et Echhart.—Les discours prononcés par MM. Laval, Beneš et Nicolae Titulescu.—La résolution votée le 10 decembre 1934 par le Conseil de la Société des Nations." Supplément exceptionnel (December, 134), 39 pp.

Jevtich, B. "La politique étrangère de la Yougoslavie," *L'Europe de l'Est et du Sud-Est*, Nos. 3–4 (March-April, 1934), 91–106. The address of March 12, 1934, before the Chamber of Deputies.

League of Nations. *Records of the Conference for the Reduction and Limitation of Armaments. Series A. Verbatim Records of Plenary Meetings.* Volume I. February 2nd–July 23rd, 1932. IX. Disarmament. 1932.IX.60. (Geneva, 1932), 201 pp.

———— *Series B. Minutes of the General Commission.* Volume I. February 9th–July 23rd, 1932. IX. Disarmament. 1932.IX.64 (Geneva, 1932), 205 pp.

———— *Series B. Minutes of the General Commission.* Volume II. December 14th, 1932–June 29th, 1933. IX. Disarmament. 1933.IX.10 (Geneva, 1933), 643 pp.

———— *Official Journal. Special Supplement No. 102. Records of the Special Session of the Assembly.* II. July, 1932 (Geneva, 1933).

———— *Official Journal. Minutes of the Eighty-third (Extraordinary Session) of the Council.* December 5th to December 11th, 1934 (Geneva, 1935).

"Les lettres échangées entre MM. Nicolae Titulescu et Litvinov, le 9 juin 1934 à Genève, décidant et réglant la réprise de relations normales entre l'Union des Républiques Socialistes Soviétiques et la Roumanie." *L'Heure Actuelle*, Nos. 2–3 (June-July, 1934), 45–47.

Papanastassiou, Alexander. *Les Conférences balkaniques et le Pacte balkanique: Rapport soumis aux XXXe Congrès Universel de la Paix* (Athens, 1934), 28 pp.

"Peace in Europe." Debate in the British House of Commons, July 13, 1934. *International Conciliation*, No. 302 (September, 1934), 267–97.

"Le protocole entre le groupe albanais et le groupe bulgare au sujet de minorités. 9 janvier 1932." *Les Balkans*, Nos. 17–18 (February-March, 1932), 327–28.

"Le statut de l'organisation de l'Entente Balkanique. Le Statut du Conseil Economique consultatif de l'Entente Balkanique." *Bulletin de la Chambre de Commerce et d'Industrie d'Istanbul* (November, 1934), 103–04; *Les Balkans*, VI, Nos. 10–11 (October-November, 1934), 628–30; *L'Indépendance Roumaine*, November 4, 1934.

Titulescu, Nicolae. "La politique étrangère de la Roumanie," *L'Europe de l'Est et du Sud-Est*, Nos. 3–4 (March-April, 1934), 67–90. The discourse of April 4, 1934.

———— *Le Différend yougoslavo-hongrois devant le Conseil de la Société des Nations. Le discours de M. N. Titulescu, Ministre des Affaires Étrangères de Roumanie, Président du Conseil permanent de la Petite Entente. Séance du 10 décembre 1934* (Bucharest, 1934), 16 pp.

Tibal, André. *La crise des États agricoles européenne et l'Action internationale: Documents recueillis et commentées* (Paris, Carnegie, 1931), 436 pp. All the Balkan and Danubian conferences on agricultural questions.

"Traité de Collaboration entre les États baltes. Lithuanie, Esthonie, Lettonie," Geneva, September 12, 1934. *L'Esprit International*, No. 32 (October, 1934), 606–07.

The Union of Socialist Soviet Republics:
Soviet nonaggression pacts: Finland and Soviet Russia, January 21, 1932; Poland and the U. S. S. R., January 25, 1932; Latvia and the U. S. S. R., February 5, 1932. *Soviet Union Review*, X, No. 3 (March, 1932), 57–60.

Litvinov, M. M. Address before the General Commission of the Disarmament Conference at Geneva, February 6, 1933. *Soviet Union Review*, XI, No. 3 (March, 1933), 55–60; League of Nations. *Records of the Conference for the Reduction and Limitation of Armaments*. Series B, II, 234–39.

——— Speech of June 14 at the London Conference, 1933. *Soviet Union Review*, XI, Nos. 7–8 (June-August 1933), 146–49.

——— Litvinov's plan for war prevention, address of May 29, 1934, at Geneva. *Soviet Union Review*, XII, No. 7 (July, 1934), 154–58.

——— "The Proposed Eastern European Pact," *Economic Review of the Soviet Union*, IX, No. 9 (September, 1934), 157–61. The interview with Jules Sauerwein, June 29, 1934.

——— Litvinov's speech at the League Assembly, September 18, 1934. *Economic Review of the Soviet Union*, IX, No. 10 (October, 1934), 193–97.

The Conventions of July 3, 4, 5, 1933, London. *Soviet Union Review*, XI, Nos. 7–8 (July-August, 1933), 164–66. Conventions with the members of the Little Entente, Turkey, Lithuania, Afghanistan, Esthonia, etc.

The renewal of the political pacts of nonaggression with Poland, Esthonia, Lithuania, Latvia, and Finland. *Soviet Union Review*, XII, Nos. 5–6 (May-June, 1934), 117–20.

Soviet diplomatic relations with the Little Entente (Czechoslovakia and Rumania), June 9, 1934. *Soviet Union Review*, XII, No. 7 (July, 1934), 163–64.

Special Documentary Bibliography on the Balkan Conferences

THE DOCUMENTARY PUBLICATIONS

The documentary materials for a study of the Balkan Conferences, on which the present investigation has been based, are now readily accessible. The first of these is: *XXVIIᵉ Congrès universel de la paix. Tenu à Athènes du 6 au 10 octobre 1929. Documents officiels* (Athens, 1931), 274 pp. It contains the minutes and resolutions of the meetings which initiated the Balkan Conferences. *Les Balkans*, a monthly review published under the auspices of the Balkan Conferences and with the support of the *Centre Européen de la Dotation Carnegie pour la paix international*, contains all the official documents of the Balkan Conferences and numerous articles on Balkan and Near Eastern affairs. The editor of this journal is M. X. Lefcoparidis. It is published at Athens, Greece; the beginning date of Volume I is October, 1930. The Dotation Carnegie has also published separate volumes on each Balkan Conference. There are two volumes covering the First Balkan Conference at Athens, October, 1930. These are: *Première Conférence balkanique. Athènes, 5–12 octobre 1930. Documents officiels. Première partie* [(Athens, 1931), 222 pp.] and *Première Conférence balkanique. Athènes, 5–12 octobre 1930. Documents officiels* (Athens, 1931), 435 pp. The first volume contains only the documents and memoranda pertaining to the Conference. The second contains the complete materials, including the *procès-verbaux.* The sources for the Second Balkan Conference were published in *IIᵉ Conférence balkanique. Istanbul-Ankara, 19–26 octobre 1931. Documents officiels. Première partie* (Istanbul, 1932), 310 pp. This volume, however, does not include the minutes of the Conference. The documents of the Third Balkan Conference may be found in *IIIᵉ Conférence balkanique. Bucarest, 22–29 octobre 1932. Documents officiels* (Bucharest, 1933), 372 pp. The minutes, however, were not published, and even some of the important documents are missing. The materials for the Fourth Conference are available in *IVᵉ Conférence balkanique. Salonique, 5–12 novembre 1933. Documents officiels* (Athens, 1934), 267 pp. Only the memoranda are published in this volume.

The National Groups of the Balkan Conferences, on some occasions, published separate issues of their own memoranda which were submitted to the Conference. The Greek group, for example, published a complete set for the First Conference. Likewise, the Jugoslav group published a volume of its reports: *Prva balkanska konferencija. Rad jugoslovenske nacionalne grupe* (Belgrade, 1931), 139 pp. The Greek and Turkish groups published sets for the Second Conference. The Bulgarian group printed collections for both the Second and the Fourth Conferences. The Jugoslav delegation mimeographed a complete set of memoranda for the Third Conference, and the Rumanian delegation published a complete file.

Moreover, the Balkan governments have been of assistance in making available the materials of the Balkan Conferences. The Greek and Turkish governments have published copies of the *Résolutions de la Iᵉ Conférence balkanique.* The Turkish government also published another small volume: *IIᵉ Conférence balkanique. Résolutions et vœux de la Deuxième Conférence balkanique* (Istanbul, 1931). The Rumanian government published: *Journal de la IIIᵉ Conférence balkanique, 22–29 octobre 1932* (Bucharest, 1932), the official journal of the Third Conference.

Many of the memoranda and the minutes of the Balkan Conferences were published in newspapers. The minutes of the First Balkan Conference at Athens were published in *Le Méssager d'Athènes,* October 5–13, 1930. *Le Journal d'Orient,* October 20–29, 1931 (Istanbul) and *L'Indépendance Roumaine* (Bucharest), October 21–30, 1932, performed similar services for the Second and Third Balkan Conferences.

The authors have thought it best to indicate the memoranda submitted to the various Balkan Conferences in order to portray the fundamental character of the studies which have been made in the political, economic, social, and intellectual domains, and to show at a glance the major interests of each national delegation. For purposes of brevity a key has been used, as in the footnotes. *Les Balkans* has been cited as LB. The volumes of documents, such as *Première Conférence balkanique. . . . Documents officiels,* have been cited as I CB, II CB, III CB, and so on. It is hoped that this complete citation of the memoranda and documents will be useful to students of the movement.

THE FIRST BALKAN CONFERENCE (ATHENS, 1930)

THE PRELIMINARY DOCUMENTS

Circulaire invitation du Bureau International de la Paix aux Ministres des Affaires Étrangères des États balkaniques. I CB, 17–21.

La Conférence balkanique devant le Parlement hellénique, 9 juin 1930. I CB, 22–27.

Échange de dépêches entre le Président du Parlement hellénique et les Présidents des Conseils et des Chambres balkaniques. I CB, 28–30.

Lettre de M. Spyros Mercouris, Maire d'Athènes et Président de l'Union des villes grecques, adressée aux Municipalités des autres États balkaniques. I CB, 31.

Règlement provisoire des travaux de la Première Conférence balkanique. I CB, 32–38.

Programme des Séances et réceptions. I CB, 39–40.

L'Ordre du jour de la Conférence. I CB, 41.

THE POLITICAL MEMORANDA

The Greek Delegation—

Maccas, Leon. Les mesures précises à proposer en vue de faciliter le rapprochement des États balkaniques. I CB, 71–89.

Papanastassiou, A. Les principes essentiels devant servir de base à l'Union balkanique. I CB, 45–56.

Spiropoulos, Jean. Des mesures propres à favoriser le rapprochement politique des peuples des Balkans. I CB, 87–90.

Svolos, A. Projet des statuts de la Conférence balkanique. I CB, 81–86.

The Jugoslav Delegation—

Georgevich, Tched. Le mouvement balkanique. I CB, 57–70.

THE MEMORANDA ON INTELLECTUAL PROBLEMS

The Greek Delegation—

Delmouzos, A. L'école et l'enseignement national. I CB, 97–109.

The Jugoslav Delegation—

Jonich, Velibor. L'affinité mentale des peuples balkaniques. I CB, 93–96.

Bogdanovich, Militza. La réforme de l'enseignement de l'histoire. I CB, 110–20.

The Rumanian Delegation—

Cantacuzène, G. Les fondements d'un Institut de Coopération balkanique. I CB, 125–34.

THE MEMORANDA ON ECONOMIC RELATIONS

The Greek Delegation—

Bacalbassis, A. La protection des tabacs d'Orient. I CB, 179–86.

Loverdo, Sp. La fondation d'un Institut Économique interbalkanique. I CB, 187–91.

Pesmazoglou, G. De l'union monétaire balkanique. I CB, 192–94.

Santis, D. K. De la collaboration économique des États balkaniques. I CB, 135–47.

The Jugoslav Delegation—

Georgevich, Voislav V. L'agriculture des pays balkaniques. I CB, 172–78.

Gregorich, Svetko. L'entente économique des États des Balkans, du point de vue industriel. I CB, 148–65.

Mohovich, Ivan. Problème de la collaboration économique des pays balkaniques. I CB, 166–71.

Vrbanich, Milan. De la création d'une Chambre de Commerce interbalkanique. I CB, 195–97.

THE MEMORANDA ON COMMUNICATIONS

The Greek Delegation—

Agapitos, Sp. Transports et tourisme balkaniques. I CB, 210–16.

Joannidès, F. Communications interbalkaniques par automobile et Touring Club de Grèce. I CB, 217–18.

Lachnidakis, I. K. Union postale interbalkanique. I CB, 202–05.

Lascarakis, T. Des avantages de la création d'un réseau aérien de communications interbalkaniques en collaboration avec les États limitrophes. I CB, 206–09.

Koronis, S. Moyens de communications entre pays interbalkaniques. I CB, 198–201.

THE MEMORANDA ON SOCIAL AND HYGIENE PROBLEMS

The Greek Delegation—

Calitsounakis, D. *Le règlement uniforme des questions ouvrières balkaniques.* Athens, *Le Méssager d'Athènes,* 1930.

Lambiris, I. Le statut des ressortissants balkaniques. I CB, 91–92.

Théodoropoulo, Mme Avra S. Le rôle des femmes dans le rapprochement balkanique. I CB, 121–24.

THE SECOND BALKAN CONFERENCE

Compte-rendu des travaux de la 2ᵉ Conférence balkanique (19–26 octobre 1931). LB, Nos. 13–14 (October-November, 1931), 70–142. The minutes and resolutions.

La 3ᵉ session du Conseil de la Conférence balkanique à Salonique. January 30–February 1, 1931. LB, No. 5 (February, 1931), 24–36. Minutes of the meeting.

THE POLITICAL MEMORANDA

The Bulgarian Delegation—

Mishev, D. Mémoire sur les difficultés qui s'opposent à la détente morale et du rapprochement des États balkaniques. II CB, 65–74; LB, No. 12 (September, 1931), 24–28.

Petkov, B. P. Mémoire relatif à l'application des dispositions du traité de Neuilly concernant la recherche et l'entretien des sépultures des officiers et soldats bulgares, ainsi que des internés civils des guerres de 1912–1918. II CB, 87–91; LB, No. 12 (September, 1931), 28–31.

Toshev, A. Exposé concernant la question minoritaire bulgare. II CB, 75–86.

The Greek Delegation—

Papanastassiou, A. De la stricte application des traités et des obstacles que rencontre le rapprochement politique des peuples balkaniques. II CB, 92–100; LB, No. 12 (September, 1931), 31–44.

Spiropoulos, J. Avant-projet d'un pacte balkanique. LB, No. 12 (September, 1931), 35–44.

Svolos, A. Une réponse au questionnaire sur l'Union balkanique. II CB, 101–06; LB, Nos. 13–14 (October-November, 1931), 67–69.

The Jugoslav Delegation—

Georgevich, Tched. Sur la conclusion de pactes de conciliation, de non-aggression et d'arbitrage entre les différents États balkaniques. II CB, 110–14.

Mémoire du Groupe yougoslave. Sur les conditions de rapprochement politique entre les nations balkaniques. II CB, 107–09; LB, No. 12 (September, 1931), 79–80.

Topalovich, Zhivka. Sur le pacte balkanique. II CB, 115–23; LB, Nos. 13–14 (October-November, 1931), 54–58.

The Turkish Delegation—

Association pour l'Union balkanique. *Statuts.* Istanbul, 1931.

THE MEMORANDA ON INTELLECTUAL PROBLEMS

The Albanian Delegation—

Groupe albanais. Le rapprochement intellectuel des États balkaniques. II CB, 127–28; LB, No. 12 (September, 1931), 23.

The Bulgarian Delegation—

Nicolaev, H. P. La Bulgarie et la coopération intellectuelle interbalkanique. II CB, 129–32; LB, Nos. 15–16 (December, 1931–January, 1932), 213–15.

The Greek Delegation—

Cassimatis, G. Les possibilités et les moyens d'unification du droit privé des pays balkaniques. II CB, 43–55; LB, No. 12 (September, 1931), 51–57.

Droit balkanique: Cassimatis, G. Les traits généraux des droits positifs des pays balkaniques. MM. Svolos, Castorkis, Cassimatis, Anastassiadès, le Groupe turc et le Groupe yougoslave. Rapports soumis à la commission pour l'unification du droit. LB, No. 22 (July, 1932), 469–503.

Triandaphillopoulos, C. De l'unification du droit privé des pays balkaniques. LB, No. 12 (September, 1931), 48–50.

The Rumanian Delegation—

Clarnet, Adolphe. L'Association interbalkanique de la presse. II CB, 133–36.

The Turkish Delegation—

Ahmed Samin Bey. Rapport de la Commission de l'unification du droit. II CB, 60–62; LB, Nos. 13–14 (October-November, 1931), 38–39.

Fazil Ahmed Bey. Rapport de la commission turque de rapprochement intellectuel. II CB, 137–44; LB, Nos. 13–14 (October-November, 1931), 34–37.

Rapport du Groupe turc à l'Association interbalkanique de la presse. II CB, 135–36; LB, Nos. 17–18 (February-March, 1932), 332.

THE MEMORANDA ON ECONOMIC RELATIONS

The Greek Delegation—

Groupe hellénique. Chambre de commerce et d'industrie d'Athènes. Projet de statuts de la Chambre de Commerce interbalkanique. LB, No. 12 (September, 1931), 65–69.

Groupe hellénique. Données statistiques: réunis, d'après les publications statistiques officielles des États balkaniques. LB, Nos. 15–16 (December, 1931–January, 1932), 231–46; LB, Nos. 19–20 (April-May, 1932), 389–92.

Loverdos, Sp. Rapport sommaire sur l'initiative que les Banques balkaniques peuvent exercer sur le développement du commerce et des transactions interbalkaniques. II CB, 208–09; LB, No. 12 (September, 1931), 57–58.

Sideris, A. Rapport sur les travaux de la Réunion agricole à Sofia (mai-juin, 1931), II CB, 191–94; LB, No. 12 (September, 1931), 63–65.

Simonides, B. La protection des céréales et autres produits intéressant les États balkaniques. II CB, 180–90; LB, No. 12 (September, 1931), 58–63.

The Jugoslav Delegation—

Georgevich, V. V. Le problème du blé. II CB, 195–207; LB, Nos. 15–16 (December, 1931–January, 1932), 215–21.

Groupe yougoslave. Les possibilités de la création d'un domaine économique des Balkans et l'activité économique et les échanges commerciaux des peuples Balkaniques. II CB, 159–70; LB, Nos. 17–18 (February-March, 1932), 333–38.

——— Le tabac en Yougoslavie. II CB, 174–79; LB, Nos. 15–16 (December, 1931–January, 1932), 221–23.

Markovich, Miljanka. Collaboration des Instituts financiers balkaniques. II CB, 214–26; LB, Nos. 15–16 (December, 1931–January, 1932), 223–29.

The Turkish Delegation—

Ahmed Midhat Bey. Rapport sur l'union douanière. II CB, 151–58; LB, Nos. 13–14 (October-November, 1931), 40–43.

Groupe turc. Chambre de Commerce et d'Industrie interbalkanique. LB, Nos. 13–14 (October-November, 1931), 45.

——— Création d'un Office interbalkanique des tabacs. II CB, 171–73; LB, Nos. 13–14 (October-November, 1931), 44–45.

Ibrahim Fazil Bey. Sur l'Union monétaire balkanique. II CB, 210–11; LB, Nos. 13–14 (October-November, 1931), 39–40.

THE MEMORANDA ON COMMUNICATIONS

The Greek Delegation—

Agapitos, S. P. Raccordement des chemins de fer balkaniques. II CB, 234–37; LB, No. 12 (September, 1931), 69–71.

Bouyoukas, G. P. Considérations générales au sujet de l'amélioration de la communication ferroviaire interbalkanique. II CB, 229–33; LB, Nos. 13–14 (October-November, 1931), 65–67.

Groupe hellénique. Le développement des communications télégraphiques et téléphoniques interbalkaniques. II CB, 245–46; LB, No. 12 (September, 1931), 75.

Lachnidakis, Jean. L'amélioration des relations postales interbalkaniques. II CB, 243–44; LB, No. 12 (September, 1931), 74.

Lascarakis, G. Communications aériennes interbalkaniques. II CB, 238–40; LB, No. 12 (September, 1931), 71–73.

Pentheroudakis, M. La poste aérienne balkanique. II CB, 241–42; LB, No. 12 (September, 1931), 73.

The Turkish Delegation—

Ali Rana Bey. Rapport de la commission turque des communications. II CB, 247–49; LB, Nos. 13–14 (October-November, 1931), 45–47.

THE MEMORANDA ON SOCIAL AND HYGIENE QUESTIONS

The Greek Delegation—

Kyriazidis, K. H. L'Entente sanitaire balkanique. II CB, 282–90; LB, No. 12 (September, 1931), 76–78.

Mamopoulos, P. La nationalité de la femme mariée. II CB, 299–301; LB, No. 12 (September, 1931), 50–51.

Svolos, A., and Lambiris, J. Rapport sur le projet de convention concernant le statut des ressortissants balkaniques. II CB, 253–61; LB, No. 12 (September, 1931), 44–48.

The Jugoslav Delegation—

Markovich, Z. B. Collaboration des institutions sanitaires entre les États balkaniques. II CB, 291–98; LB, Nos. 13–14 (October-November, 1931), 61–64.

Popovich, Stevan. La liberté du travail et de la circulation. II CB, 275–81; LB, Nos. 13–14 (October-November, 1931), 58–61.

Topalovich, Mme Milica. La liberté du travail et de la circulation. II CB, 272–74; LB, Nos. 15–16 (December, 1931–January, 1932), 229–30.

The Turkish Delegation—

Akil Mukhtar Bey. Rapport de la Commission turque d'hygiène et de politique sociale. II CB, 288–90; LB, Nos. 13–14 (October-November, 1931), 53–54.

THE THIRD BALKAN CONFERENCE

La Troisième Conférence balkanique. Compte-rendu des travaux. LB, III, Nos. 1–2 (October-November, 1932), 71–199. October 22–29, 1932.

Journal de la IIIᵉ Conférence balkanique, 22–29 Octobre 1932. Bucharest, Imprimeria Centrală, 1932. Official journal.

La cinquième session du Conseil de la Conférence. January 28–February 1, 1932. LB, Nos. 17–18 (February-March, 1932), 320–27. Minutes.

THE POLITICAL MEMORANDA

The Greek Delegation—

Spiropoulos, J. Rapport sur le Pacte balkanique. III CB, 13–17; LB, III, No. 3 (December, 1932), 291–94.

The Rumanian Delegation—

Stoicovici, V. V. Considérations rélatives aux problèmes inscrits à l'ordre du jour de la IIIᵉ Conférence balkanique. III CB, 115–35; LB, III, Nos. 6–7 (March-April, 1933), 606–23.

THE MEMORANDA ON INTELLECTUAL PROBLEMS

The Greek Delegation—

Amantos, M. C. Projet d'une ouvrage sur l'histoire de la civilisation des peuples balkaniques. LB, No. 24 (September, 1932), 692–93.

Bées, Nicos. A. Rapport sur l'Institut de recherches historiques. LB, No. 24 (September, 1932), 689–92.

Cassimatis, G. Sur l'unification des législations balkaniques—lettre de change, billet à l'ordre, chèque. Presenté à la Commission permanente pour l'unification du droit (deuxième session, octobre 1932). LB, No. 24 (September, 1932), 693–94.

The Jugoslav Delegation—

Groupe yougoslave. Films cinématographiques balkaniques. LB, IV, No. 11 (August, 1933), 581–83.

Popovich, G. Rapport sur la semaine juridique balkanique et sur la première session de la Commission préparatoire interbalkanique de juristes. III CB, 17–20.

Radio-Station de Belgrade. La radiodiffusion comme moyen de rapprochement des peuples balkaniques. LB, IV, No. 11 (August, 1933), 579–80.

The Rumanian Delegation—
Bucutza, Em. Les films balkaniques. III CB, 38–40; LB, IV, No. 10 (July, 1933), 383–85.
Clarnet, Adolphe. Mémoire sur les rapports de presse interbalkaniques. III CB, 47–49; LB, IV, No. 10 (July, 1933), 390–92.
Constantinescu, N. A. Rapport sur l'élaboration d'un manuel de la civilisation des peuples balkaniques. III CB, 25–34; LB, IV, No. 10 (July, 1933), 325–28.
Eftimiu, Victor. Traduction d'œuvres littéraires; traduction et représentation de pièces de théâtre balkaniques. III CB, 35–38; LB, IV, No. 10 (July, 1933), 380–82.
Giurescu, G. C. Statuts de l'Institut balkanique de recherches historiques. III CB, 21–25; LB, IV, No. 10 (July, 1933), 367–70.
Munteanu, C. L'action de la radiodiffusion pour le rapprochement des peuples balkaniques. III CB, 41–44; LB, IV, No. 10 (July, 1933), 386–89.

The Turkish Delegation—
Fazil Ahmed Bey. Le rapprochement intellectuel. III CB, 44–47.

THE MEMORANDA ON ECONOMIC RELATIONS

The Greek Delegation—
Sideris, A. D. Rapport sur la Chambre d'Agriculture interbalkanique. LB, No. 24 (September, 1932), 685–87.
Simonides, B. Vers l'Union douanière et économique des Balkans—Avant-projet d'accord préliminaire. LB, No. 24 (September, 1932), 703–05.

The Jugoslav Delegation—
Novakovich, Antoine. La collaboration des pays balkaniques au développement du crédit agricole. III CB, 88–104; LB, IV, No. 11 (August, 1931), 476–90.

The Rumanian Delegation—
Chiritzescu-Arva, M. Rapport sur la collaboration des États balkaniques dans le domaine des sciences agricoles. III CB, 69–80; LB, III, Nos. 6–7 (March-April, 1933), 585–94.
Mladenatz, Gr. Les relations inter-coopératives. III CB, 80–88; LB, III, Nos. 6–7 (March-April, 1933), 624–30.
Osiceanu, C. L'exportation des produits pétrolifères de Roumanie dans les pays balkaniques de 1922 à 1931. III CB, 108–14; LB, III, Nos. 4–5 (January-February, 1933), 469–75.
Popescu, S. J. Union douanière partielle et collaboration économique interbalkanique. III CB, 56–67; LB, III, Nos. 6–7 (March-April, 1933), 595–605.
Raducanu, I. Les pays balkaniques et la dépression économique mondiale. III CB, 51–56; LB, III, No. 3 (December, 1932), 307–11.
Teodoru, Radu. Mémoire sur le problème du sel. III CB, 104–07; LB, III, Nos. 6–7 (March-April, 1933), 582–84.
Union des Chambres d'Agriculture de Roumanie. Rapport sur la création d'une Chambre d'Agriculture interbalkanique. III CB, 68–69; LB, III, Nos. 6–7 (March-April, 1933), 572–81.

THE MEMORANDA ON COMMUNICATIONS

The Greek Delegation—

Cantacuzène-Pascani, Colonel A., and Sturdza, A. M. Communications aériennes. III CB, 169–73; LB, IV, No. 10 (July, 1933), 347–53.

Nicolau, M. Établissement d'un plan de travaux publics interbalkaniques. III CB, 166–69; LB, IV, No. 10 (July, 1933), 354–57.

Sfintzescu, T., and Filip, Simion. Rapport sur la prolongation par voie d'automobile des lignes ferroviaires afin de faciliter les communications entre les capitales balkaniques ainsi que sur le raccordement des voies ferrées et routes de ces pays. III CB, 154–59; LB, IV, No. 10 (July, 1933), 358–62.

Vasilescu, Gr. Le développement en commun des communications et transports maritimes des pays balkaniques comprenant aussi la création d'un Office maritime interbalkanique siégeant à Istanbul. III CB, 137–41; LB, IV, No. 10 (July, 1933), 363–66.

The Turkish Delegation—

Reshid Saffet Bey. Rapport sur le tourisme. III CB, 173–77; LB, IV, No. 11 (August, 1933), 473–75.

THE MEMORANDA ON SOCIAL AND HYGIENE PROBLEMS

The Greek Delegation—

Dimacopoulos, J. Conventions vétérinaires. LB, No. 24 (September, 1932), 695–96.

Scaramanga, Pierre. Avant-projet de convention sanitaire spéciale pour l'institution d'un Bureau interbalkanique d'informations sanitaires. III CB, 283–85; LB, No. 24 (September, 1932), 698–99.

Studitis, Mme Agnes. La traite des femmes en Grèce. III CB, 225–28; LB, III, No. 3 (December, 1932), 304–06.

Svolos, A. Avant-projet de statuts de l'Office balkanique du travail. III CB, 188–90.

Tsamboulas, N., and Kyriadzidis, K. Rapport sur la collaboration des États balkaniques pour la lutte contre la tuberculose. LB, No. 24 (September, 1932), 697–98.

The Jugoslav Delegation—

Atanatskovich, Mlle Milean. Les enfants et les adolescents devant la loi en Yougoslavie. III CB, 217–25; LB, IV, No. 11 (August, 1933), 545–52.

Godjevats, Mme Anna. Nationalité de la femme dans la nouvelle loi yougoslave. III CB, 253–59; LB, IV, No. 11 (August, 1933), 515–20.

———— La situation de la femme en Yougoslavie suivant le droit civil et suivant les lois speciales. III CB, 259–72; LB, IV, No. 11 (August, 1933), 603–14.

Kitcevats, Mme Vera. La législation se rapportant à la réglementation de la prostitution et à la traite des femmes et des enfants en Yougoslavie. LB, IV, No. 11 (August, 1933), 541–44.

Markovich, Dr. Z. B. Les conventions sanitaires et vétérinaires entre les États balkaniques. III CB, 278–80; LB, IV, No. 11 (August, 1933), 527–28.

Popovich, Dr. Stefan. La législation du travail et les institutions sociales en Yougoslavie. III CB, 194–204; LB, IV, No. 11 (August, 1933), 491–502.

Rougichich, Dr. Ouroch S. Aperçu sur la protection du nourrisson. III CB, 211–17; LB, IV, No. 11 (August, 1933), 529–40.

The Rumanian Delegation—

Botez, Mme Calypso. La situation juridique de la femme dans la législation roumaine. III CB, 231–38; LB, IV, Nos. 8–9 (May-June, 1933), 199–205.

Cantacuzène, Mme Alexandrine. Rapport sur la Charte de l'Enfant. III CB, 205–08; LB, IV, Nos. 8–9 (May-June, 1933), 190–95.

———— Législation de la femme mariée. III CB, 239–49; LB, IV, No. 10 (July, 1933), 311–20.

Constantinescu, Dr. G. Rapport sur la conclusion d'une convention vétérinaire balkanique. III CB, 280–83; LB, IV, No. 10 (July, 1933), 325–27.

Costin, Alexandre. La situation de la femme mariée dans la législation roumaine. III CB, 249–53; LB, IV, No. 10 (July, 1933), 221–24.

Irimescu, Dr. St. La lutte en commun contre la tuberculose. III CB, 285–302; LB, IV, No. 10 (July, 1933), 328–43.

Manicatide-Venert, Dr. E. La lutte contre la traite des femmes en Roumanie. III CB, 229–31; LB, IV, Nos. 8–9 (May-June, 1933), 196–98.

Mezincescu, Dr. D. Rapport sur la convention sanitaire interbalkanique et le statut sanitaire du Danube. III CB, 273–76; LB, IV, No. 10 (July, 1933), 344–46.

Popescu-Buzeau, Dr. M. La Confédération médicale balkanique. III CB, 276–78; LB, IV, Nos. 8–9 (May-June, 1933), 206–08.

Vladescu-Racoassa, G. Le statut personnel des ressortissants des États balkaniques. III CB, 179–86; LB, IV, Nos. 8–9 (May-June, 1933), 140–77.

———— Considérations sur les statuts d'un Office balkanique du travail. III CB, 190–92; LB, IV, Nos. 8–9 (May-June, 1933), 188–89.

The Turkish Delegation—

Nizamettin Ali Bey. Projets de statuts de l'Office balkanique du travail. III CB, 192–94; LB, IV, No. 11 (August, 1933), 467–68.

Efzayis Suat Hanim. La Charte de l'Enfant. III CB, 208–10; LB, IV, No. 11 (August, 1933), 469–70.

Musliheddin Adi Bey. Le régime des ressortissants balkaniques. III CB, 186–88; LB, IV, No. 11 (August, 1933), 464–67.

THE FOURTH BALKAN CONFERENCE

La Quatrième Conférence balkanique. Compte-rendu des travaux. LB, IV, Nos. 14–15 (November-December, 1933), 992–1111.

Le Conseil de la Conférence balkanique, 31 mars–3 avril 1934. LB, V, Nos. 3–4 (March-April, 1934), 297–312.

La Semaine Médicale balkanique de Belgrade, 11–13 septembre 1934. LB, V, Nos. 5–6 (May-June, 1934), 537–630.

THE POLITICAL MEMORANDA

The Greek Delegation—

Groupe hellénique. Projet de convention consulaire. LB, IV, Nos. 12–13 (September-October, 1933), 673–85; IV CB, 17–29.

Papanastassiou, A. Modification du statut de la Conférence. IV CB, 30–34; LB, IV, Nos. 12–13 (September-October, 1933), 686–90.

The Jugoslav Delegation—

Groupe yougoslave. Projet de modifications du statut de la Conférence. LB, IV, Nos. 12–13 (September-October, 1933), 845–48.

——— Projet de modifications du règlement de l'Assemblée. LB, IV, Nos. 12–13 (September-October, 1933), 849–51.

Novakovich, A. La modification des statuts de la Conférence. IV CB, 35–52; LB, V, Nos. 3–4 (March-April, 1934), 362–68.

THE MEMORANDA ON INTELLECTUAL PROBLEMS

The Bulgarian Delegation—

Diakov, B. Collaboration interbalkanique dans le domaine du droit pénal. LB, V, Nos. 1–2 (January-February, 1934), 155–60; IV CB, 58–63.

Dikov, L. Aperçu général sur les sources du droit civil bulgare. IV CB, 64–74; LB, V, Nos. 1–2 (January-February, 1934), 139–47.

Chichkov, P. Revue du droit commercial bulgare positif. IV CB, 53–57; LB, V, Nos. 1–2 (January-February, 1934), 148–52.

Zhabinsky, N. Le code pénal bulgare. IV CB, 73–74; LB, V, Nos. 1–2 (January-February, 1934), 153–54.

The Greek Delegation—

Lascaris, M. Les manuels d'histoire. LB, IV, Nos. 14–15 (November-December, 1934), 1130–34.

Saratsi, Dr. La semaine pédagogique. LB, IV, Nos. 12–13 (September-October, 1934), 711–17.

The Jugoslav Delegation—

Hadji-Tachkovich, Gl. La semaine pédagogique. LB, V, Nos. 3–4 (March-April, 1934), 341–44.

Popovich, V. L'enseignement des langues balkaniques. LB, V, Nos. 3–4 (March-April, 1934), 349–61.

Zhivkovich, Sv. Sport et éducation physique. LB, V, Nos. 3–4 (March-April, 1934), 345–48.

The Turkish Delegation—

Efzayis Suat Hanim. Rapport sur l'éducation sexuelle. LB, V, Nos. 1–2 (January-February, 1934), 171–72.

Fazil Ahmed Bey. Rapport sur le rapprochement intellectuel. LB, V, Nos. 1–2 (January-February, 1934), 173–75.

THE MEMORANDA ON ECONOMIC RELATIONS

The Bulgarian Delegation—

Kremenski, G. N. La politique du crédit agricole des pays balkaniques. IV CB, 75–82; LB, V, Nos. 1–2 (January-February, 1934), 113–20.

——— La banque agricole de Bulgarie. IV CB, 83–87; LB, V, Nos. 1–2 (January-February, 1934), 121–25.

Sakazov, Ivan. L'agriculture dans les Balkans en connexité avec le commerce international. IV CB, 88–93; LB, V, Nos. 1–2 (January-February, 1934), 126–31.

Svrakov, G. L'activité coopérative et le besoin d'un service coopératif interbalkanique. IV CB, 94–98; LB, V, Nos. 1–2 (January-February, 1934), 132–35.

Tabakov, Tz. Les modifications nécessaires aux statuts de la C. B. C. I. IV CB, 99–100; LB, V, Nos. 1–2 (January-February, 1934), 136–38.

The Greek Delegation—

Alivisatos, Babis. Le crédit agricole interbalkanique. IV CB, 101–29; LB, IV, Nos. 12–13 (September-October, 1933), 753–80.

Evelpidi, C. La coopération dans le domaine du crédit agricole. IV CB, 130–44; LB, IV, Nos. 12–13 (September-October, 1933), 732–46.

Hallunga, Al. Considérations sur le projet d'union douanière partielle. IV CB, 258–60; LB, IV, Nos. 12–13 (September-October, 1933), 852–54.

Philippacopoulos, Ph. Les assurances interbalkaniques. IV CB, 145–53; LB, IV, Nos. 12–13 (September-October, 1933), 836–44.

Santis, D. C. La solidarité économique et financière. IV CB, 154–59; LB, IV, Nos. 12–13 (September-October, 1933), 747–52.

Sideris, A. D. L'agriculture des pays balkaniques et le commerce international. IV CB, 160–62; LB, IV, Nos. 12–13 (September-October, 1933), 721–23.

Simonides, B. Projet d'accord préliminaire. IV CB, 214–17; LB, IV, Nos. 12–13 (September-October, 1933), 732–35.

——— La première étape vers l'Union douanière. IV CB, 163–213; LB, IV, Nos. 12–13 (September-October, 1933), 781–831.

——— Rapport sur l'Union douanière. LB, V, Nos. 1–2 (January-February, 1934), 176–78.

Tzortzakis, Th. La collaboration des coopératives balkaniques. IV CB, 218–25; LB, IV, Nos. 12–13 (September-October, 1933), 724–31.

Voilas, S. N. L'exploitation des forces hydro-électriques. LB, IV, Nos. 12–13 (September-October, 1933), 706–10.

The Jugoslav Delegation—

Marodich, S. Coopération économique des pays balkaniques. LB, V, Nos. 1–2 (January-February, 1934), 192–95.

Mihailovich, D. P. L'agriculture des pays balkaniques et le commerce international. LB, V, Nos. 1–2 (January-February, 1934), 179–84.

Novakovich, A. Le crédit agricole. LB, V, Nos. 1–2 (January-February, 1934), 185–91.

Popovich, St. L'Office interbalkanique du travail. LB, V, Nos. 1–2 (January-February, 1934), 196–98.

The Rumanian Delegation—

Codrescu, Florin. Considérations sur les échanges économiques interbalkaniques. IV CB, 226–57; LB, IV, Nos. 12–13 (September-October, 1933), 857–888.

Codrescu, Florin, and Manescu, N. Mémoire complémentaire sur l'Union douanière. IV CB, 261–63; LB, IV, Nos. 14–15 (November-December, 1933), 1116–18.

Comité pour l'Union douanière européenne. Rapprochement économique. IV CB, 226–27; LB, IV, Nos. 12–13 (September-October, 1933), 855–56.

THE MEMORANDA ON COMMUNICATIONS

The Greek Delegation—

Agapitos, Sp. Réseau routier interbalkanique. LB, IV, Nos. 12–13 (September-October, 1933), 718–20.

The Jugoslav Delegation—

Josifovich, St. Le réseau routier interbalkanique. LB, V, Nos. 3–4 (March-April, 1934), 320–23.

Krajach, Vuk. Statistiques de la navigation balkanique. LB, IV, Nos. 14–15 (November-December, 1933), 1148–62.

Sirisevich, Sl. Compte-rendu des résolutions précédentes sur les communications. LB, V, Nos. 3–4 (March-April, 1934), 324–35.

Vasskovich, Zdravko. Le réseau ferroviaire des Balkans. LB, V, Nos. 3–4 (March-April, 1934), 313–19.

The Rumanian Delegation—

Codrescu, Florin. L'automobilisme dans les Balkans. LB, IV, Nos. 14–15 (November-December, 1933), 1119–20.

The Turkish Delegation—

Reshid Saffet Bey. Rapport sur les communications. LB, V, Nos. 1–2 (January-February, 1934), 161–62.

———— Rapport au IVᵉ Congrès de la Fédération balkanique de tourisme. LB, V, Nos. 1–2 (January-February, 1934), 163–67.

THE MEMORANDA ON SOCIAL AND HYGIENE PROBLEMS

The Greek Delegation—

Scaramanga, Dr. P. Convention sanitaire interbalkanique. LB, IV, Nos. 12–13 (September-October, 1933), 701–05.

Svolos, A., and Zaccas, A. Exposé des motifs et projet de statuts de l'Office balkanique du travail. LB, IV, Nos. 12–13 (September-October, 1933), 696–700.

Thèodoropoulo, Mme Avra. Le travail des femmes. LB, IV, Nos. 12–13 (September-October, 1933), 691–95.

Vayanos, Dr. D. L'hygiène rurale. LB, IV, Nos. 14–15 (November-December, 1933), 1135–47.

The Jugoslav Delegation—
Atanatskovich, Mlle Milean. La protection du travail de la femme. LB, V, Nos. 3–4 (March-April, 1934), 336–39.

Markovich, Z. B. Les conventions sanitaires des pays balkaniques. LB, V, Nos. 3–4 (March-April, 1934), 340.

The Rumanian Delegation—
Raducanu, I., Mladenatz, G., and Tatos, I. La création d'un Office coopératif des pays balkaniques. LB, IV, Nos. 14–15 (November-December, 1933), 1112–15.

Vladescu-Racoassa, G. L'Office balkanique du travail. LB, V, Nos. 3–4 (March-April, 1934), 369–76.

The Turkish Delegation—
Akil Mukhtar Bey. L'Union Médicale balkanique. LB, V, Nos. 1–2 (January-February, 1934), 168–70.

THE FIFTH BALKAN CONFERENCE

The fifth Balkan Conference has not yet met. The memoranda which have been prepared and published are listed below.

The Greek Delegation—
Kyriazi, Damianos. La coopération industrielle des pays balkaniques. LB, VI, Nos. 10–11 (October-November, 1934), 642–50.

Lachnidakis, J. L'extension de la Convention Postale balkanique. LB, VI, Nos. 8–9 (August-September, 1934), 415.

Lefcoparidis, X. Les résolutions des Conférences balkaniques sur le rapprochement intellectuel. LB, VI, Nos. 8–9 (August-September, 1934), 397–414.

Papanastassiou, A. L'Union balkanique. LB, VI, Nos. 8–9 (August-September, 1934), 369–76.

——— Statuts de la Conférence balkanique. LB, VI, Nos. 8–9 (August-September, 1934), 377–89.

Rhousopoulos, Mme Agnes, and Colocotronis, Constantin. Le trafic des femmes et des enfants. LB, VI, Nos. 8–9 (August-September, 1934), 416–18.

Vayanos, Dr. D. Sur l'hygiène rurale. LB, VI, Nos. 8–9 (August-September, 1934), 397–414.

Voilas, G. N. Travaux publics d'intérêt balkanique. LB, VI, Nos. 10–11 (October-November, 1934), 651–56.

Zakkas, A. Les assurances sociales. LB, VI, Nos. 8–9 (August-September, 1934), 419–20.

The Rumanian Delegation—
Cantacuzène, Mme Alexandrine. La traite des femmes et des enfants. LB, VI, Nos. 10–11 (October-November, 1934), 657–61.

SECONDARY ACCOUNTS OF BALKAN PROBLEMS

SELECTED BOOKS ON BALKAN PROBLEMS

Ancel, Jacques. *Les Balkans face à l'Italie.* Paris, Delagrave, 1928.

Armstrong, Hamilton Fish. *The New Balkans.* New York, Harpers, 1926.

―――― *Where the East Begins.* New York, Harpers, 1929. 139 pp.

Brailsford, Henry N. *Macedonia: Its Races and Their Future.* London, 1909.

The Bulgarian Question and the Balkan States. Sofia, State Printing Office, 1919. 304 pp. Issued by the Ministry of Foreign Affairs.

Chahovich, X. *La minorité "bulgare" en Yougoslavie. Réponse de l'Association yougoslave pour la S. D. N. au mémoire de l'Association bulgare.* Brussels, 1933. 22 pp.

Chandan, K. S. *Les Balkans, la Petite Entente et le Pacte à Quatre.* Paris, 1934. 80 pp.

Codrescu, Florin. *La Petite Entente.* Préface de M. Louis LeFur. Paris, Bossuet, 1932. 2 vols. 343, 323 pp. A comprehensive treatise.

Cosma, Aurel. *La Petite Entente.* Paris, Jouve, 1926. 295 pp. Good summary.

Crane, J. O. *The Little Entente.* London, Macmillan, 1931. 240 pp.

Die Nationalitäten in den Staaten Europas. Ergänzungen 1932. Sammlung von Lageberichten des europäischen Nationalitäten-Kongresses. Vienna, Jasper, 1932. 104 pp.

Ethnopolitischer Almanach. Herausgegeben von O. Junghann und M. H. Boehm. Vienna, W. Braumüller, 1932. 118 pp.

Evelpidi, C. *Les États balkaniques: Étude comparée politique, sociale, économique et financière.* Paris, Rousseau, 1930. 399 pp. An excellent handbook on every phase of Balkan life.

Ghenov, G. P. *Le traité de paix de Neuilly. Au point de vue du droit international public et privé. Conférence faite au IIIᵉ Congrès de juristes bulgares, 6–7 mai, 1926.* Sofia, 1927. 38 pp.

La Grèce actuelle. Éditions de la Direction de la Presse au Ministère des Affaires Étrangères. Athens, 1933. 291 pp.

Howard, Harry N. *The Partition of Turkey: A Diplomatic History, 1913–1923.* Norman, University of Oklahoma Press, 1931. 486 pp.

Iorga, Nicolae. *Le caractère commun des institutions dans le sud-est de l'Europe.* Paris, Gamber, 1929. 138 pp.

Ivanov, J. *La question macédonienne au point de vue historique, ethnographique et statistique.* Paris, Gamber, 1920. 292 pp.

Jászi, Oscar. *The Dissolution of the Habsburg Monarchy.* Chicago, University of Chicago Press, 1929. 488 pp.

Kerner, Robert J. "The Jugoslav Movement." *The Russian Revolution. The Jugoslav Movement.* Cambridge, Harvard Press, 1918.

―――― *The Social Sciences in the Balkans and in Turkey: A Survey of Resources for Study and Research in These Fields of Knowledge.* Berkeley, University of California Press, 1930. 137 pp.

Lefcoparidis, X. *A travers l'Albanie.* Athens, Flamma, 1934. 92 pp.

Machray, Robert. *The Little Entente.* London, Allen and Unwin, 1929. 494 pp.

Matich, Miloslav. *L'Union danubienne d'un point de vue yougoslave.* Paris, Bossuet, 1933. 250 pp.

Petkov, Boris P. *Le traité de Neuilly et la Bulgarie économique. Rapport de l'Association bulgare pour la paix et la Société des Nations présenté à la Conférence de l'Union internationale des associations pour la Société des Nations à Madrid. 20 Mai 1929.* Sofia, 1929. 63 pp.

Puryear, Vernon J. *England, Russia, and the Straits Question, 1844–1856.* Berkeley, University of California Press, 1931. 481 pp.

———— *International Economics and Diplomacy in the Near East, 1834–1853.* Stanford University, California, Stanford University Press, 1935. 264 pp.

Rouček, Joseph S. *Contemporary Roumania and Her Problems: A Study in Modern Nationalism.* Stanford University, California, Stanford University Press, 1932. 422 pp.

Savadjian, Léon. *Dossier économique des Balkans. Albanie, Bulgarie, Grèce, Roumanie, Turquie, Yougoslavie.* Paris, Revue des Balkans, 1932. 77 pp.

Seton-Watson, R. W. *Treaty Revision and the Hungarian Frontiers.* London, School of Slavonic and East European Studies in the University of London, 1934. 75 pp.

———— *A History of the Rumanians from Roman Times to the Completion of Unity.* Cambridge University Press, 1934. 596 pp.

Strupp, Karl. *La situation juridique des Macédoniens en Yougoslavie.* Paris, Les Presses Universitaires de France, n. d. 139 pp.

Tibal, André. *Les communications dans l'Europe danubienne.* Bulletins Nos. 8–9 (1933). La Conciliation Internationale, Paris, Carnegie, 1933. 277 pp.

Union des Associations bulgares pour la paix et la S. D. N. *La situation des minorités en Yougoslavie et en Grèce, en Roumanie, en Turquie.* Sofia, 1932. 92 pp.

Young, George. *Nationalism and War in the East.* New York, Clarendon Press, 1915. Excellent treatment of the Balkan Wars and their results. By a diplomatist.

Winkler, Wilhelm. *Statistisches Handbuch der europäischen Nationalitäten.* Vienna, Wilhelm Braumüller, 1931. 248 pp.

SELECTED BOOKS DEALING ESPECIALLY WITH THE PROBLEM OF
CONFEDERATION AND THE BALKAN CONFERENCES

Averov, E. *Union douanière balkanique.* Préface d'Edouard Herriot. Paris, Sirey, 1933. 275 pp.

Drossos, J. D. *La fondation de l'alliance balkanique.* Athens, Vartsos, 1929. 122 pp. By the director of the Greek Ministry of Foreign Affairs.

Gaziadi, G. *Les rapports des pays balkaniques et l'adoption des mesures les plus appropriées pour le développement économique de ces rapports.* Istanbul, Tevfik, 1932. 76 pp.

Ivanchev, Constantin. *L'Idée des états-unis d'Europe et les projets d'une confédération balkanique.* Paris, Gamber, 1930. 184 pp.

Kiorchev, Dimo. *Balkanski s"iuz ili Iugoslavia?* 2d ed. Sofia, 1926. 56 pp.

Maccas, Léon. *Pour l'Entente balkanique.* Athens, 1929. 18 pp.

Markovsky, D. K. *Iugoslavianska federatsiia.* Sofia, 1924. 13 pp.

260   *Balkan Conferences and Balkan Entente*

Mercouris, George S. *Les Conférences balkaniques et les pactes d'amitié entre les États balkaniques.* Athens, Librairie Elefteroudakis, 1932. 48 pp.
Mishev, D., and Petkov, B. P. *La fédération balkanique: Origine, développement et perspectives actuelles.* Sofia, 1930. 48 pp. This pamphlet represents the Bulgarian case for Balkan confederation.
Padelford, Norman J. *Peace in the Balkans: The Movement towards International Organization in the Balkans.* New York, Oxford University Press, 1935. 209 pp.
Papanastassiou, Alexander. *Vers l'Union balkanique. Les Conférences balkaniques.* Bulletins Nos. 1–3 (1934). La Conciliation Internationale, Paris, Carnegie, 1934. 284 pp. The authoritative statement of the Greek leader in the movement of the Balkan Conferences. Covers the four Balkan Conferences, 1930–34.
Petrov, Cyrille. *La coopération économique des pays balkaniques.* Athens, Flamma, 1934. By the Secretary of the Balkan Chamber of Commerce and Industry.
Petrovich, Stevan. *L'Union et les Conférences balkaniques.* Paris, 1933. 22 pp.
——— *L'Union et la Conférence balkanique.* Paris, Les Presses Universitaires de France, 1934. xxiv + 319 pp. Well-documented Jugoslav study.
Pivec-Stilè, Melitta. *La vie économique des provinces illyriennes, 1809–1813. Suivi d'une bibliographie critique.* Paris, Bossard, 1930. lxvii+359 pp.
Rindov, Constantin H. *Les États-unis des Balkans: Étude critique sur la possibilité d'une entente politico-économique et moyens de réaliser l'union fédérative des États balkaniques.* Paris, Jouve, 1930. 218 pp.
Stoyanov, Tsf. *Federativnaia ideia v b"lgarosr"bskitie otnosheniia priez XIX viek, 1804 do 1870.* Sofia, 1919. 76 pp.
Stragnakovich, Dravoslav. La ligue pour le rapprochement des Serbes et des Bulgares pour l'union de tous les Slaves du sud. *Œuvre du rapprochement et de l'union des Serbes et des Bulgares dans le passé.* Paris, Bossuet, 1930. 32 pp.
Topalovich, Zhivko. *Za balkanski sporazum.* Zagreb, Obnova, 1931. 72 pp.
L'Union balkanique. *Le mouvement pour le rapprochement des peuples balkaniques.* Paris, Revue des Balkans, 1932. 14 pp.
Vaingart, *Slavianskoto Iedinstvo.* Sofia, 1924.
Yeratov, P. *Balkanski s"iuz ili Iugoslaviia.* Sofia, 1919, 58 pp.
Zhigarev, Sergius. *Russkaia Politika v Vostochnom Voprosie* (Moscow, 1896). 2 vols.

SELECTED ARTICLES ON BALKAN PROBLEMS

Armstrong, Hamilton Fish. "After the Assassination of King Alexander," *Foreign Affairs,* XIII, No. 2 (January, 1935), 204–25.
Aulnau, J. "Les essais de confédération et d'entente balkanique," *L'Europe de l'Est et du Sud-Est,* Nos. 1–2 (January-February, 1932), 2–26.
Cassimatis, G. "L'unification du droit privé balkanique," Paris, 1931. Reprinted from *L'Europe du Sud-Est,* No. 1.
Chirkovich, Stevan. "La Conférence préparatoire interbalkanique de juristes et l'unification du droit des pays balkaniques," *Revue de Droit International,* 1932, X (July-August-September), 168 ff.

Coppola, Francesco. "La politique danubienne de l'Italie," *L'Esprit International*, No. 32 (October, 1934), 535–45.

"The Crisis of Democracy and the Slavonic World," *Slavonic Review*, IX, No. 27 (March, 1931), 509–24.

Danev, S. "La politique des grands puissances et les Balkans," *L'Esprit International*, No. 26 (April, 1933), 256–63.

Dascalov, P. N. "La politique extérieure de la Bulgarie," *Les Balkans*, III, Nos. 4–5 (January-February, 1933), 376–78.

Dertilis, P. B. "Le problème de la dette publique des États balkaniques," *Les Balkans*, V–VI, Nos. 8–12 (1934); VII, Nos. 1–7 (1935), and following.

Derzhavin, N. S. "Russkii absoliutizm i iuzhnoe slavianstvo," *Izvestiia Leningradskogo Gosudarstvennogo Universiteta* (Leningrad, 1928), 43–82.

Duranty, Walter. "Europe—War or Peace?" *World Affairs Pamphlets*, No. 7 (1935). 47 pp. The Foreign Policy Association, New York.

Georgevich, Tched. "Le minimum des conditions politiques préalables pour la formation de l'Union balkanique," *Les Balkans*, No. 5 (February, 1931), 1–4.

——— "Autour de la Conférence. I. Réalisation par étapes de l'Union balkanique. II. Action des groupes nationaux et des Conférences balkaniques." *Les Balkans*, No. 7 (April, 1931), 1–6.

——— "L'Union douanière, en tant que solution du problème de l'Union balkanique," *Les Balkans*, No. 8 (May, 1931), 15–18.

——— "Une contribution yougoslave à l'histoire du mouvement balkanique," *Les Balkans*, V, Nos. 3–4 (March-April, 1934), 218–24.

Géraud, André (Pertinax). "France, Russia, and the Pact of Mutual Assistance," *Foreign Affairs*, XIII, No. 2 (January, 1935), 226–35.

Howard, Harry N. "The Re-orientation of Soviet Foreign Policy," *World Unity*, XIV, No. 6 (September, 1934), 348–64.

Hrushevskii, Mikhail. "Sjednocení východního Slovanstva a expansiví plany na Balkaně v letech 1654–55," *Sborník věnovaný Jaroslavu Bidlovi* (Prague, 1928), 340–45.

Jászi, Oscar. "The Economic Crisis in the Danubian States," *Social Research*, II (February, 1935), 98–116.

Jovanovich, Alexander. "Druga balkanska konferencija," *Arhiv za pravne i drushtvene nauke*, 1931, Bk. XL, 378 ff.

Lefcoparidis, X. "Le mouvement vers l'Union balkanique," *Affaires Étrangères* (April 10, 1932), 155–64.

Le Foyer, Lucien. "Un projet de pacte balkanique," *L'Europe de l'Est et du Sud-Est*, Nos. 1–2 (January-February, 1932), 39–40; Nos. 3–4 (March-April, 1932).

Markovich, L. "La Conférence balkanique d'Athènes," *La Revue générale de Droit International Public*, 1931, 228 ff.

Miller, William. "The Balkan Pact," *Contemporary Review*, Vol. 145, No. 821 (May, 1934), 532–39.

Mitrany, David. "The Possibility of a Balkan Locarno," *International Conciliation*, No. 229 (1927), 129–61.

Mousset, Albert. "Les bases d'une collaboration économique entre les États balkaniques," *L'Europe de l'Est et du Sud-Est*, Nos. 1–2 (January-February, 1932), 27–32.

———— "L'Europe danubienne au lendemain des accords de Rome," *L'Esprit International*, No. 31 (July, 1934), 416–32.

Papanastassiou, Alexander. "L'Union balkanique," *Les Balkans*, No. 1 (October, 1930), 2–3.

———— "Vers l'Union balkanique. I. La semaine balkanique. II. Les écueils. III. Le pacte balkanique." *Les Balkans*, No. 8 (May, 1931), 1–15.

———— "La Première Conférence balkanique," *L'Esprit International*, No. 17 (January, 1931), 3–33.

———— "La Deuxième Conférence balkanique," *L'Esprit International*, No. 22 (April, 1932).

———— "De la méthode à suivre," *Les Balkans*, No. 9 (June, 1931), 15–19.

———— "La Conférence et l'Union balkanique," *Les Balkans*, Nos. 13–14 (October-November, 1931), 10–25.

———— "La politique sociale de la Grèce," *Les Balkans*, Nos. 17–18 (February-March, 1932), 258–81.

———— "La Troisième Conférence balkanique," *Les Balkans*, III, Nos. 1–2 (October- November, 1932), 3–9.

———— "La Quatrième Conférence balkanique," *Les Balkans*, IV, Nos. 12–13 (September-October, 1933), 585–91.

———— "La Vᵉ Conférence balkanique," *Les Balkans*, V, Nos. 3–4 (March-April, 1934), 201–13.

Petkov, B. P. "La paix balkanique par la fédération balkanique," *La Revue Mondiale*, CC (October 1, 1930), 233–42.

Petrov, C. "Commerce extérieur des pays balkaniques," *Bulletin de la Chambre de Commerce et d'Industrie Interbalkanique*, Nos. 4–5 (August, 1933), 25–38.

———— "Le commerce extérieur de la Bulgarie en 1933," *Bulletin de CCII*, No. 11 (April, 1934), 35–41.

———— "Le commerce extérieur de la Roumanie durant l'année 1933," *Bulletin de CCII*, No. 12 (May, 1934), 45–47.

———— "Le travail de coopération économique entre les pays balkaniques," *Les Balkans*, V, Nos. 5–6 (May-June, 1934), 430–61.

———— "Le commerce extérieur de la Grèce durant 1933," *Bulletin de CCII*, No. 14 (July, 1934), 57–62.

———— "Le commerce extérieur de la Yougoslavie en 1933," *Bulletin de CCII*, No. 15 (August, 1934), 64–68.

Peyev, Y. "La troisième session du Conseil de la CCII," *Bulletin de CCII*, No. 13 (June, 1934), 51–52. Secretary's report.

P. S. "Les possibilités des pays des Balkans en matière d'échanges interbalkaniques. Exportation-importation." *Bulletin de CCII*, No. 10 (March, 1934), 14–34. Excellent statistical qualitative and quantitative analysis.

"Le premier Congrès annuel de la Chambre de Commerce et d'Industrie interbalkanique," *Bulletin de CCII*, No. 7 (December, 1933), 48–53. Proceedings.

Przhich, Ilija. "Balkanska pravnichka nedelja sastanak medjubalkanske pravnichke komisije," *Arhiv za pravne i drushtvene nauke*, 1932, Bk. XLI, 500 ff.

Revue Internationale des Études Balkaniques. Tomes I–III (1934–35). P. Skok and M. Budimir, Directeurs. Belgrade, Jugoslavia. Published by the *Institut Balkanique.* Authoritative articles on Balkan problems.

Rossi, E. "La seconda conferenza balcanica," *L'Europa Orientale,* XII, Nos. 1–2 (January-February, 1932), 1–28.

Sakazov, J. "Les problèmes de la paix balkanique," *Les Balkans,* No. 4 (January, 1931), 11–14.

Seton-Watson, R. W. "The Problem of Revision and the Slav World," *Slavonic Review,* XII (July, 1933), 24–35.

———— "L'état actuel du problème autrichien," *L'Esprit International,* No. 33 (January, 1935), 34–54.

Smogorzewski, C. "La Pologne entre l'Est et l'Ouest," *L'Esprit International,* No. 31 (July, 1934), 351–76.

Stanciov, Dimitry. "The New Atmosphere in the Balkans," *Contemporary Review,* Vol. 145, No. 819 (March, 1934), 287–95.

Subotich, Ivan B. "Izjednachenje privatnog prava balkanskih drzhava," *Arhiv za pravne i drushtvene nauke,* 1932, Bk. XLI, 308 ff.

Topalovich, Zh. "La Première Conférence balkanique tenue à Athènes du 5 au 12 octobre 1930," *L'Annuaire de l'Association Yougoslave de Droit International,* I (1931), 50 ff.

Vrzalová, V. "Jihoslovanský státní a národní program Iliji Garašanina," *Slovanský Přehled* (Prague, 1932), XXIV, No. 3, pp. 134–43.

Zwitter, F. "Illyrisme et sentiment yougoslave," *Le Monde Slave* (April, May, June, 1933), 39–71, 124–26, 161–85, 232–45.

INDEX

Accad (Babylonia), 8, 9
Adriatic Sea, 34, 37, 56, 163, 169
Advisory Economic Council of Balkan Entente, 166–67. *See also* Balkan Entente
Aegean Sea, 11, 18, 124
Afghanistan, 118, 169
Africa, 5, 10, 11, 164
Agenda: First Balkan Conference, 33; fn. 27, p. 43; Second Balkan Conference, fn. 17, p. 66; Third Balkan Conference, fn. 8, p. 91; Fourth Balkan Conference, fn. 3, p. 114; Fifth Balkan Conference, fn. 30, p. 153
Agricultural conference, 48; coöperatives, 71, 159; credit, 103
Agriculture, Balkan Chamber of, 63, 78–79, 84, 99, 159. *See also* Economics Commission
Air communications, 80. *See also* Communications, Commission on
Akil Mukhtar Bey, 56, 107.
Albania, 3, 12, 18, 23, 25, 34; and Balkan Conferences, 22, 61, 54, 69–70, 74–75; and Balkan Pact, 99–100; and Balkan Entente, 166; and Four-Power Balkan Pact, 125–26, 130, 133, 134, 156–57; and Italy, 34, 52, 162; and Jugoslavia, 138; and Turkey, 161
Albert, King of Belgium, 132
Alexander the Great, 9, 14
Alexander, King of Jugoslavia, 121, 123, 148–49, 162, 163
Alexandrian Empire, 9
Alivisatos, 103
Amphictyonic League, 39
Anatolia, 3
Andrássy, Count, 16
Arabia, 11, 12, 169
Armaments, Conference on Reduction and Limitation of, at Geneva, 51, 69, 97, 118, 140, 141, 147–48
Asia Minor, 9, 15
Association of Hellenic Students, 59
Athens, 14, 56
Australia, 11
Austria, 10, 11, 15, 16, 130–31, 143, 164, 165. *See also* Austria-Hungary; Dual Monarchy; Habsburgs
Austria-Hungary, 11, 161, 162

Baldwin, Stanley, Prime Minister of Great Britain, 146
Balkan Bank, 166–67. *See also* Balkan Entente
Balkan Committee of London, 17
Balkan Conferences: First (Athens), 21–44; Second (Istanbul), 45–67; Third (Bucharest), 68–94; Fourth (Salonica), 95–115; Fifth (not held), 157–58, 168–69
Council, 32, 45–46, 50–51, 54, 69–70, 73–74, 76, 89, 95–97, 98, 102, 134–35
Pact, 33, 34, 38, 49, 50, 51, 52, 53, 63, 64, 69–70, 73–75, 75–77, 80, 82, 84–87, 101, 113, 138, 158. *See also* Political Commission
Statutes, 26–27, 31–32, 43; text, 178–83, Document III
Balkan Entente, 124–25, 126–27, 138, 156–57, 166–67, 168, 169; statutes, 234–35, 236–37, Documents XV and XVI
Balkan Federation, 16, 21, 23, 45–67
Balkan Institute of Intellectual Cooperation, 35
Balkan League, 17, 129
Balkan Locarno, 21
Balkan Pact (of Balkan Conference), 33, 34, 38, 49, 50, 51, 52, 53, 63, 64, 69–70, 73–75, 75–77, 80, 82, 84–87, 101, 113, 117, 138, 158
Balkan Parliamentary and Social Union, 137; statutes, 222–27, Document XI
Balkan region (area and population), 23
Balkan unity, foundations of, 23–25, 75–77, 161, 162
Balkans, 10, 161
Balkans for the Balkan Peoples, 13, 162–69
Baltic Pact, 117, 140, 146. *See also* Esthonia; Latvia; Lithuania
Bank, Balkan, 55, 167–68
Bank, Balkan agricultural, 79
Barthou, Louis, Foreign Minister of France, 138, 140, 145, 148–49, fn. 36, pp. 153–54
Batalov, Constantin, Foreign Minister of Bulgaria, 139, 168
Belgrade, 56, 140